Ye That Are Men Now Serve Him

RELIGION AND AMERICAN CULTURE

Ye That Are Men Now Serve Him

Radical Holiness Theology and Gender in the South

COLIN B. CHAPELL

The University of Alabama Press
Tuscaloosa

The University of Alabama Press
Tuscaloosa, Alabama 35487-0380
uapress.ua.edu

Hardcover edition published 2016.
Paperback edition published 2021.
eBook edition published 2016.

Typeface: Bembo

Cover image: This gathering in 1911 of the Mississippi Conference of the Methodist Episcopal Church, South, reflects the variety of people within the denomination. Urban leaders and rural itinerants, women and men all felt compelled to mark the gravity of the occasion by having their picture taken; courtesy of J. B. Cain Archives of Mississippi Methodism, Millsaps-Wilson Library, Millsaps College
Cover design: Michele Myatt Quinn

Paperback ISBN: 978-0-8173-6039-9

A previous edition of this book has been cataloged by the Library of Congress.
ISBN: 978-0-8173-1922-9 (cloth)
E-ISBN: 978-0-8173-9007-5

For Heather, whose heart, strength,
and love are examples to me every day.

Contents

Figures ix

Acknowledgments xi

Introduction 1

Part I: Establishing the Standards of Evangelical Identity

1. Baptists and Methodists in the New South 15

2. Faithful Baptist Families and Women 21

3. Masterful Manhood in the Southern Baptist Convention 44

4. The Manly Soldiers of Methodism 62

5. Methodist Women as Home Missionaries 79

Part II: Radical Theology and Radical Identity

6. Defining Holiness 99

7. Consecrated Regardless of Sex 112

8. Perfect Masculine Love 130

Conclusion 144

Notes 149

Bibliography 197

Index 215

Figures

Figure 1. A drawing from the Millsaps yearbook, *Bobashela* 7

Figure 2. Baptist men gathered for an Evangelistic Conference 46

Figure 3. Landrum Leavell 51

Figure 4. Women's College of Alabama students supporting women's suffrage 89

Figure 5. Two photographs demonstrating support for and opposition to women's suffrage 90

Figure 6. Men created a stable point around which women could orbit 93

Acknowledgments

This work could not have happened without the help and support of an astonishingly large group of people. As with all historians, my work was enriched through the wonderful help of librarians and archivists. My personal debts stretch across the South; from the McWherter Library at the University of Memphis to the Gorgas Library at the University of Alabama, librarians have offered timely help gathering resources. In addition, the archivists at Millsaps College's J. B. Cain Archives of Mississippi Methodism; Emory University's Manuscript, Archives, and Rare Book Library; Huntington College's Methodist Archives Center; Samford University's Special Collections; and the Southern Baptist Historical Library and Archives all deserve praise for their generosity of spirit and willingness to go the extra mile for young scholars. In addition, the Southern Baptist Historical Library and Archives provided a much-appreciated Lynn E. May Jr. Study Grant that enabled me to work among their collections. Additional financial support for research came through the University of Alabama's Department of History, and the History Department at the University of Memphis has been extremely generous in helping me get to conferences where many of the ideas in this work have been refined.

Many members of the Department of History at the University of Memphis have encouraged my work, and I owe a few particular debts. Janann Sherman and Aram Goudsouzian have set wonderful examples of collegial leadership while Amanda Lee Savage, Chrystal Goudsouzian, and Susan O'Donovan have all provided listening ears at times when I needed to work through issues. Beyond my own department, a number of friends deserve praise for the ways in which they have shaped my thinking, sharpened my analysis, or simply shared their time with me. John Mitcham, Megan Bever, and Becky Bruce all bear special responsibility in this regard.

Numerous people have seen versions of this work, providing comments, criticism, and help with analysis. These include Sarah Potter, Kari Frederickson, Aram Goudsouzian, Lisa Lindquist-Dorr, Robert Yelle, Ted Ownby, and George Rable. John Giggie has been particularly helpful in providing searching questions and in refining ideas. Donna Cox Baker and the editorial team at the University of Alabama Press have been encouraging and understanding. Those who have seen the manuscript have improved it, and any foibles left are my own.

My family, both the one that I was born into and the one that accepted me when I married into it, has provided incredible emotional, financial, spiritual, and every other type of support. Special thanks go particularly to Bryan and Kathy Chapell, my parents, and to Craig and Becky Brown, my in-laws. The one person who has provided more support, more encouragement, and more love than I can ever hope to repay, though, is my wife. Heather, you have enriched my life more than I could have ever thought possible. You have encouraged me when I was down, understood when I had to work late, offered grace and forgiveness, listened when I went on far too long, and kept our lives in perspective by pointing me to Jesus. I can never say it often enough: Thank you. I love you.

Introduction

In 1960, the pastor, editor, and Methodist leader Marion E. Lazenby published a history of Methodism in Alabama and West Florida. Lazenby's account of Methodism, written in a specific mode of denominational and ecclesiastical history, proposed simply that God used the denomination to further his kingdom. Indeed, the volume reads more as an edited collection of conference statistics and eulogies than as an argument-driven historical account. Yet throughout the volume, innumerable sources argued that Methodism promoted manhood.[1]

In one recorded address, called "The Heroes of 1870," the speaker recalled the rugged, martial masculinity of some of the early heroes of Methodism in the area: "V.O. Hawkins, 'a man's man;' M.E. Johnston, called 'Bush-whack Johnston,' a man whose name 'meant to the night riders, outlaws, carpet-baggers, and scalawags of North-East Alabama,' what the name of 'Stonewall Jackson meant to the federals of Virginia; . . . W.C. McCoy, 'a man of wonderful resources and marvelous gifts,' a man 'who followed Quantrell [*sic*] in Missouri, Jackson in Virginia, and Christ in Alabama.'"[2] Certainly no one named "Bush-whack Johnston," or anyone who followed the Confederate guerilla fighter William Quantrill, represented urbane manliness. Such men instead expressed themselves through much more rugged constructions of masculinity. By listing Christ after the guerrilla fighter "Bloody Bill" Quantrill and the Confederate hero Thomas "Stonewall" Jackson, the memorialist for W. C. McCoy suggested that Christianity was a final step in facing the enemy and in fighting perceived evil and oppression.[3] Clearly, the men of the North Alabama Conference of the Methodist Episcopal Church, South, (MECS) wanted others to know that faith enhanced masculinity.

Sometimes Lazenby recorded ideas of manhood in unusual fashion. For example, Lazenby quotes a eulogy for a man named J. E. Collins that called

Collins "a dignified man, with courtly manners rendered doubly charming by a pure heart . . . as calm and gentle as a queenly woman, yet as brave as a knight of old, he met the issues in his work in such a way as to thrill the hearts of those who loved God."[4] Here, Lazenby says the eulogy remembered Collins not only for his refined manhood but also for his exceeding serenity and tenderness, two qualities that the memorialist explicitly denoted as feminine.

Clearly, identity formation was, and is, a complicated process influenced by a multitude of variables. Class, race, region, population density, and generation all modified the ways in which individuals understood themselves and the world around them. Yet during the New South period (roughly the years between 1877 and 1915), religious ideas were some of the most powerful streams of influence on gender identity for many white southerners. This meant that religion was not simply a socially acceptable veneer hiding other motivations, such as economic, class, racial, or ethnic issues. Rather, adherents placed their faith in what they said they believed and attempted to live their theology. This process and experience of lived theology meant that adherents, and particularly church officials, tried to center their lives and identities around what they professed to believe.[5] Thus, for southern church leaders, who felt that religion touched the most intimate part of what it meant to be human, it made sense that faith would have a profound impact on gender identity as "a primary source of individual and social identity."[6]

Exploring how religious leaders used faith to define personal identity begs the question of what religion means. Scholars have spent incredible amounts of time and ink attempting to define religion.[7] While definitions and theories of religion are important, they hold little meaning apart from their connections to adherents' real-world experiences. This is one reason why Thomas Tweed's ideas of religion fit particularly well in this study about the lived experiences of southern evangelicals in the South at the turn of the century. For them, theology defined ideas of gender in ways that pair well with the aquatic metaphors in Tweed's work. (Tweed sees religion as an organic confluence of cultural forces.[8]) Tweed's theory of religion encourages scholars to stop thinking about religion, culture, and human identities as static objects; rather, these entities must be envisioned as constantly moving, shifting, and interacting with each other. Wherever different cultural flows meet, something new emerges. The differences may be subtle, extreme, or somewhere in the middle; but change has happened. Yet even this new thing continues to move. This model has its shortfalls, of course, but is helpful nonetheless, as Tweed's aquatic metaphors remind scholars of the constantly shifting nature of the ideas and paradigms we are trying to pin down.

Tweed's model fits well with the evidence that the more radical the theology, the more divergent the ideas of gender become from the wider culture. Thus, while the theology of the Southern Baptist Convention (SBC) and the Methodist Episcopal Church, South (MECS), had already defined much of culture (and been defined by it in response), the radically transformative flow of the southern Holiness movement's theology created new understandings of gender.

Because church leaders used the language of faith to define human identity, white southern evangelicals had to sort through a number of questions about God and the relationship of humanity to the divine. Some of the relevant questions included: Did God use families or individuals to fulfill divine tasks? Was Jesus the conqueror of sin and death, or was he the tender shepherd who wooed the hearts of his people? How did God intend people to act more like Jesus as they grew in their relationship with the divine? Would God give divine power to believers to enable them to live sinless lives? These were just some of the questions southern evangelical leaders worked through as they tried to develop and disseminate faith that defined identity and gender in particular.

Baptists, Methodists, and adherents of Holiness theology are key groups to explore when studying the influence of theology on personal and gendered identity in the South for several reasons. First, though the influence of Christianity has been a noted feature of the American South for many years, Baptists and Methodists made up the vast majority of self-identified Christians during the New South period (1877–1915).[9] This meant that they had a wider influence on southern culture than many other religious groups. Second, Methodists and Baptists established religious colleges designed to pass down specific theology to the students who attended them. At the same time, these institutions self-consciously taught boys to be men and girls to be women.

The choice of the Holiness movement may seem odd when held against the MECS and the SBC. Holiness groups were part of a highly decentralized movement, were prone to schisms, were dramatically smaller than the other denominations, and had radical theological views.[10] Yet it is exactly because of its transformative theological views that the southern Holiness movement provides such an effective foil to the theological dominance of the SBC and MECS. Holiness proponents focused so overwhelmingly on the doctrine of entire sanctification that they believed that if a person received it, he or she was fully qualified for positions of church leadership—

an outrageous idea in the turn-of-the-century South. Thus, while the SBC and MECS provide a baseline for how faith defined personal and gender identity, the Holiness movement demonstrates how radical theology transformed ideas of gender in the South.

Each New South faith tradition explored in this work had a theological emphasis that changed how denominational leaders conceived of manhood, womanhood, and family life. Adherents believed that they were made in the *Imago Dei*, the image of God, and so their different understandings of the sacred profoundly changed how they constructed gender. To show how theology defined ideas of gender across the American Deep South, this book is organized by the defining faiths of each evangelical denomination.

Part I looks at the standard theology of gender for a large cross section of the white South—the Southern Baptist Convention and the Methodist Episcopal Church, South. Together, these two denominations made up a large majority of white churchgoers in the period. It is thus important to understand the baseline of theologically defined gender identity.

Chapter 1 provides some context for southern culture at the turn of the nineteenth century, and examines how the SBC's tension between individuality and self-sacrifice both altered and reinforced ideas of gender in the South. Chapter 2 looks at how a theology of continual selflessness and sacrifice interacted with conceptions of family life and appropriate expressions of femininity among some of the SBC's leaders. Many white Baptist officials felt that women, in addition to their sacrificial giving of themselves, could be reduced to specific personality traits. This meant that church officials noted which character traits defined the "essential" woman.

Chapter 3 turns to the ways in which Baptist theology defined ideas of manhood. Far from the notions of self-sacrifice that so heavily infused ideas of femininity, individual mastery formed the basis for all other conceptions of manliness among Baptist officials. Certainly other expressions of manhood also made appearances in Baptist writings, and these are mentioned in the chapter. Despite some small dalliances with softer understandings of masculinity, however, Southern Baptist officials defined white Christian manhood through individual mastery.

Not all white Christian men in the New South argued as forcefully for a masterful expression of manliness, though. The idea of conversion—the giving of one's life to Jesus in the belief that His sacrifice was the only way for a sinful, broken person to approach a holy God—and the various interpretations of Jesus's example defined the construction of gender for leaders in the MECS. The need to convert the world to Christianity therefore combined with different understandings of the person of Jesus to open new avenues for expressions of manhood and womanhood.

Chapter 4 examines Methodist manhood and shows how different interpretations of Jesus allowed the adoption of martial imagery into MECS thought. This chapter demonstrates how Methodist leaders appropriated hypermasculine language to define the ideal of the Christian soldier conquering the world for Christ.[11] MECS bishops, itinerant preachers, and even Methodist collegiate officials tried to show how an understanding of Jesus as the conqueror of death and sin meant that Christian men were part of the grand army of God engaged against the forces of evil. While a martial model of masculinity was popular among many in the MECS, other officials in the denomination believed that Jesus wooed the hearts of his people, and so wanted to model their ideas of manliness around affection for their families.

While different interpretations of Jesus's characteristics led to different understandings of manliness, the importance of a saving faith defined Methodist femininity. Chapter 5 shows how MECS officials based their ideas of womanhood on the notion that women needed to nurture the impressionable souls of children and lead them to Jesus by creating Christian homes. Because of this belief, Methodist officials encouraged women to pursue liberal arts educations. This education would combine with the supposedly greater moral authority of women to advance the Kingdom of God in their homes.[12]

While Methodists and Baptists clearly had faiths that for many defined their personal identity, their theology was standard fare among evangelical circles in the New South. To demonstrate how important theology can be for personal and gender identity, then, part 2 explores some of the most radical evangelical theology of the day—the southern Holiness movement. For the preachers, pastors, and evangelists in the Holiness movement, the theology of entire sanctification was the most important marker of personal identity. Attempts to embody and perform the implications of their radical theology transformed the ways in which the sanctified perceived the world and their roles in it. The leadership of the movement believed an identity based in sacred experience superseded even biological sex, a radical idea that led to very hostile opposition from many other groups, both religious and secular, in the New South.

Holiness theology did not just have implications for gender roles and institutional authority; it altered the very ways in which people conceived of and talked about gender. Because of the transformational nature of Holiness theology, this movement provided a clear example of a group whose understandings of personal identity differed dramatically from those of other Protestant groups. Chapter 6 looks briefly at the theology and culture of the Holiness movement. It shows the multiple steps an individual had to go through to be recognized as part of the group. Self-identifying as a part of the Holiness movement was a dangerous undertaking in the South, one that promised derision and social ostracism. The long process that preceded a believer's experience of entire sanctification demonstrated how transformative theology could redefine an individual's identity. Thus, by exploring how different leaders talked about their theological journey and the risks they took to gain this new identity, one gains a sense of the importance of this theology to how Holiness leaders understood themselves and the world around them.

Chapter 7 shows that while Holiness theology defined femininity in ways that encouraged women to take positions of authority within the church, certain sins were still portrayed as unique to women. This tension demonstrated the complex relationship between sacred understandings of gender and the ideas of femininity that adherents learned from the broader culture. Chapter 7 finishes by examining how Holiness theology pointed to marriage as an analogue of the relationship between God and the sanctified believer, transforming both women and men within the movement into the bride of Christ.

Finally, chapter 8 takes as its subject the ways in which leaders believed that Holiness doctrines defined manliness. Preachers and evangelists of Holiness used the theology of entire sanctification, or perfect love, to transform traditional southern ideas of manhood and create space for highly emotive and affectionate expressions of masculinity. Yet Holiness officials did not throw out all contemporary notions of masculinity, and they frequently used martial language to talk about their mission to the world. Owing to their defining faith, Holiness leaders' ideas of gender, while still influenced by the culture in which they lived, looked radically different from the formulations of personal identity among other white evangelicals in the Deep South.

The Deep South states of Mississippi, Alabama, and Georgia are the primary locations for this book and show how theology influenced gender construction during a period of political and social change.[13] The industrialization and urbanization of the New South deeply influenced both Alabama and Georgia, as Birmingham and Atlanta each epitomized the burgeoning industries alive in the region. Even places like Jackson, Mississippi, provided many people from rural communities with their first glimpses

Figure 1. Editors of the Millsaps yearbook thought highly of the school's ability to transform and refine individuals. Courtesy Millsaps College Archives, Millsaps-Wilson Library, Millsaps College, Jackson, Mississippi.

of urban life. These differences were so marked that students at Millsaps College noted in their 1909 yearbook, the *Bobashela*, the changes that supposedly occurred when young women were exposed to the cosmopolitan atmosphere of Jackson (see figure 1).[14] At the same time that increasing numbers of southerners moved to cities, many throughout the rural South struggled against the problems of sharecropping and the crop-lien system.[15]

These states were also important to study for religious reasons. Georgia and Mississippi were important centers for Methodism. Emory College (now Emory University) in Atlanta was home to two of the MECS's best-known bishops, Atticus Haygood and Warren Candler, while Mississippi had its own influential bishop, Charles Galloway. Both states were also centers of the MECS's teachings on entire sanctification and the Holiness movement, though at different times. The Mississippi Conference of the MECS was one of the few places in the South where Holiness teachings had attracted significant numbers in the antebellum period, while the Georgia Holiness Association was one of the first southern Holiness associations to form after the American Civil War.[16] Together, these three states, Georgia,

Mississippi, and Alabama, with their similarities and differences, provide a unique opportunity to see how sacred ideas influenced the construction of gender in the American South.

The years between 1877 and 1915 also constitute a vital period for studying shifts in the construction of personal identity in the South. During these decades, southerners began to reconstruct their identity as a distinct region within the United States after the end of Reconstruction.[17] In effect, they could choose to remember a version of history in which they were no longer a conquered people—and many did just that as the mythology of the Lost Cause continued to develop during this period.[18] In addition, other markers of personal identity underwent severe stress during this period. The political and social upheaval in the region transformed all of these ideas and many more. For example, the period is considered the nadir of race relations. Along with these questions of race were also questions related to gender identity.

By 1915, some of the ideas about what masculinity and femininity meant to white southerners began to coalesce. One of the ways in which this happened was through the founding of the second Ku Klux Klan. The reincarnation of this terrorist organization amplified existing white understandings of gender while providing new avenues for both men and women to express idealized forms of white manhood and womanhood.[19] During the 1910s dramatic migration from the South began to occur. Hundreds of thousands of southerners (both black and white) moved out of the region, bringing with them foodways, racial identities, religious practices, and formulations of gender. In addition, toward the end of the time under study, southerners increasingly interacted with a growing national consumer culture.[20] (The question of whether the nation was growing more southern or the South was losing its distinctiveness is not significant to this study; what is germane is that the unique constructions of theology and gender in the New South started to interact with other ways of understanding personal and religious identity.) Thus, this study examines the period from the removal of federal troops from southern political life to the refounding of the Klan and the out-migration of a significant portion of the South's population. It asserts that theology and religious belief helped many southerners make sense of the puzzle of gender identity during a period of intense political, social, and religious change that deeply affected how men and women understood their own identities and roles in society.

The increasing numbers of religious periodicals established, read, and distributed throughout the region also makes this an influential period.[21] For example, in the Holiness movement alone, the number of daily newspapers published did not merely double but actually quadrupled between 1870 and 1900. Readership also soared, as sales of daily publications increased sixfold during those thirty years.[22] This dissemination of printed materials was vitally important for religious figures who attempted to find as large an audience as possible for their messages during a time of change in the South. This was particularly important for groups like the Holiness movement, whose adherents were a minority that relied on building a community in print.

A brief note on methodology is also important here. I am primarily concerned with the ways in which gender was perceived and constructed during this time. This does not mean that the performative expressions of gender are unimportant but that they largely fall outside of the purview of this study. This work opens up further areas for study by examining how religious authorities articulated and expressed ideas about personal identity and related it to religious belief. The church leaders whose voices appear in this study encouraged their parishioners to change how they thought about manhood and womanhood and argued for conceptions of gender as sacred.

Although a mix of voices appears throughout the book, I show how theology defined gender construction by studying those who could best articulate their own theological beliefs and present these as prescriptive ideas to others. For these reasons, most of the voices in this work come from officials within the SBC, the MECS, and the Holiness movement. Preachers, pastors, evangelists, college and seminary professors, and others in positions of influence left evidence of the ways that their sacred beliefs shaped how they conceptualized gender.

These church officials spoke to, and for, many people throughout the Deep South.[23] When the US Census Bureau released their 1906 report on the numbers of religious bodies in the United States, Mississippi, Alabama, and Georgia each had a large percentage of people who identified themselves as religious—38, 41, and 42 percent, respectively.[24] Even when looking specifically at Baptists and Methodists, these numbers remain large. In Mississippi, which had the fewest people who self-identified as Baptist, just over one-fifth of the population were congregants of that denomination. In Georgia, this number rose to almost one-quarter of the population. Methodist numbers were lower but still held between 12 and 14 percent of the total population in these three states.[25] This does not necessarily mean that they gathered the same numbers from all groups. The Methodist Episcopal Church, South, and the Southern Baptist Convention both drew primarily from the white population of the South.

Although I have focused on the denominations that were, and still are, predominately white, I do investigate the status of African Americans and the idea of black identity when they appear in the writings of SBC, MECS, and Holiness leaders. This investigation includes how the language of mastery excluded African Americans, and how some within the Holiness movement talked about African American believers as an example of how God could lift up the humble. Yet, these same leaders rarely mentioned the ways in which segregation and racial violence went against the ideas of perfect love.[26] Indeed, the white church leaders whose voices appear in my work do not often talk about how race should influence gender, almost certainly because racial categories were an assumed part of their worldview, and most of the religious leaders I studied lived comfortably (and often reflexively) within the white power structures of the time. This meant that many white religious leaders ignored how racial ideologies oppressed people, since they were not among the oppressed. Accordingly, questions of race appeared infrequently in their writings. This study centers on how white Protestant religious leaders talked about faith and personal identity, and the paucity of discussion on the interactions between race and religion reflects the content of my sources.

While many white church leaders did not directly address issues of racial identity, many did use theology to construct exclusively white formulations of gender. Southern Baptist ideas of manhood connected intimately to the idea of mastery—a concept that held overtly racial overtones in the fifty years after emancipation. Similarly, most white southerners would have never allowed the militarized public persona of Methodist masculinity to be applied to African American men. These ideas would have dramatic consequences for ideas of gender in the decades to follow, as whites routinely denied that African Americans could achieve true manhood.[27]

During the New South era, ideas of white masculinity underwent transition, even as old understandings of white manhood did not simply disappear with slavery or the beginnings of the urban South. Understandings of manhood based in honor-driven violence (often used to enhance white manhood at the expense of African Americans) still resonated with many white people in the New South.[28] Even the glorification of the "Southern Lady" had its role in upholding the cult of honor in the South.[29] It is clear that the idea of honor remained a salient feature for many pastors' ideas of proper manliness.

Leaders of each faith tradition in this study worried about how to present the men of their denomination with an honorable, masculine ideal. Leaders of both the Southern Baptist Convention and the Methodist Episcopal Church, South, tried to instill in the men in their congregations the ideal of the gentleman. For Baptists, this meant a promotion of self-mastery, while for Methodists it turned on the rhetoric of building character. Yet the work does not stop with these two models of manliness. They were the dominant modes of manhood in the New South, but the leaders of the southern Holiness movement presented an alternative—a highly emotive, verbally affectionate, insistently pious model of manliness. Thus, while historians of gender have demonstrated the very important role of racism, violence, class ideals, and even honor in constructing both manhood and womanhood, this book will show how church leaders reenvisioned gender.

Similarly, the ideals of femininity prevalent in both the SBC and MECS necessarily excluded huge numbers of African American women in the South. Both Methodist and Baptist understandings of southern womanhood emphasized that femininity flourished in the home—and that only those women who stayed in the domestic world *of their own home* were truly ladies. This automatically excluded the huge numbers of African American women, who labored as laundresses, nannies, general domestic help, and farm hands. Although these African American women clearly did their best to provide loving homes for their families, to many Southern whites, these women did not live up to the racially and theologically circumscribed ideas of femininity.

While many preachers in the MECS and the SBC held to the domestic modes of femininity defined by their faith, adherents of the Holiness movement pushed for sanctified women to take up public preaching roles that conflicted with gendered ideals in the broader culture. This example demonstrates that though the surrounding culture had a significant influence on religious adherents, it did not necessarily hold those adherents captive.[30] The constant interaction between ideas of the sacred and perceptions of individual identity is a significant part of understanding the construction of femininity between 1877 and 1915 in the American South.[31]

My work does not divorce theology from ideologies of personal identity. It looks at how religion in white southern culture worked, how religious leaders tried to persuade laity to realign gendered ideals, and, most significantly, how theology interacted with conceptions of gender. Both SBC and MECS leaders saw a world bifurcated by the saved and the lost and encouraged their congregants to do the same, thus imbuing their everyday lives and activities with eternal significance. This meant that religion could transform mundane tasks into sacred callings and that everyday ephemera, such as newspapers and advertising posters, could have divine importance. Such ideas, even among otherwise prosaic religious groups, had the power to transform individual identities.

While I do not argue that theology created new gender categories, sacred beliefs provided alternate avenues for the conception and perception of what preachers, pastors, and evangelists thought it meant to be a man or woman in the Deep South between 1877 and 1915. Thus, even subtle shifts in theology or interpretations of whom God was could have resounding effects on what church leaders thought it meant to be human. These men and women connected their religious beliefs to gender in new ways and then spread their ideas to parishioners through sermons, speeches, and texts across the region.

Even the hymns that many parishioners sang during worship services could reinforce ideas of faithful manhood and womanhood. One popular hymn of the period was George Duffield's "Stand Up, Stand Up for Jesus." By singing this hymn, the congregation encouraged each other to take courage and hold fast to their beliefs. Moreover, the hymn used martial imagery that many adherents would have recognized as calling for a determined Christian manhood. To make this point clear, the second stanza challenged the male congregants, calling to them, "Ye that are men, now serve Him / Against unnumbered foes; / Let courage rise with danger. / And strength to strength oppose."[32] As they sang, men in the congregation thus saw themselves as part of a military force standing against the encroachment of evil. The lessons of gender construction thus permeated sacred space through congregational singing as well as the voices of church officials.

For the officials whose voices appear in the book, determining what it meant to be a man, woman, or child was not an academic exercise. They believed that they were made in the image of God.[33] They were not simply cogs in a machine whose individual lives held no meaning; they reflected their creator. Thus, different interpretations of who God was and various understandings of an individual's relationship with the divine, and even with other people, were all ways an individual could demonstrate that he or she was an image bearer. It was important for an individual to know what it meant to be a man or a woman. Theology gave church leaders a specific understanding of their identity. Theirs were defining faiths.

I
ESTABLISHING THE STANDARDS OF EVANGELICAL IDENTITY

1

Baptists and Methodists in the New South

The Southern Baptist Convention was founded in 1845, when northern and southern Baptists split over the question of slavery.[1] Just a year earlier, American Methodism had survived a schism over the same issue.[2] These denominational divisions did not dictate disaster for either Baptists or Methodists in the American South. In fact, three decades after these fraternal fights, members of the Southern Baptist Convention and the Methodist Episcopal Church, South, accounted for somewhere between 32 and 39 percent of the entire population across Mississippi, Alabama, and Georgia.[3] In other words, these two denominations, more than any others, constituted a broad evangelical base during the New South period at the turn of the nineteenth century.[4]

For many southerners, the period historians define as the New South, 1877–1915, seemed to be a particularly high point of religious fervency. The historian Ed Ayers suggests that even skeptics were surrounded by religious language and imagery: "It permeated public speech as well as private emotion. For many people, religion provided the measure of politics, the power behind law and reform, the reason to reach out to the poor and exploited, a pressure to cross racial boundaries."[5] Certainly for those who believed, religion influenced every aspect of their lives and could define the very core of their being.

It was thus very troubling for many parishioners who believed that their churches were undergoing a profound shift as the South began to go industrialize and urbanize.[6] Yet even while a growing number of progressive, middle-class denominational officials were located in towns, there was still impressive growth among rural parishioners.[7] The urban/rural split was most pronounced when churches and church officials held to different standards of behavior and discipline, depending on their location in town or country parishes.[8] This trend was even stronger among southern white men, who often viewed the town as a place where sin was tolerated, making market days in county seats across the South a day of drinking, cussing, and fighting.[9]

While occasional violence would break out in town among rural white southern men, perhaps nowhere in New South society was violence as accepted as in the relations between white and black southerners. While there were preachers and pastors who condemned racial violence, there were also, unfortunately, those who believed that racial violence was justified as a means of keeping society functioning. In fact, some parishioners found justification for racial suppression and violence in their Bibles and shouted praises at lynchings.[10]

While white religious southerners split over whether racial violence was justified, many were united in their veneration of the Lost Cause. Scholars have examined how southerners used the myths of the Lost Cause to deal with defeat, reaffirm social norms, and imagine what a good society might look like—effectively creating a civil religion.[11] While there were plenty of laity involved in the celebrations of the Lost Cause, many church officials also participated, and some were afforded almost celebratory status in the American South. Perhaps one of the most revered was Father Abram Ryan, a Roman Catholic priest who wrote a number of well-received poems eulogizing the Confederacy.[12] Another well-known Lost Cause sympathizer was the Methodist bishop Charles Galloway. He was the leader of the Mississippi Conference of the Methodist Episcopal Church, South. His sermons were peppered with references to southern leaders, and one of his most well known addresses was a hagiographic recounting of the life of Jefferson Davis.[13] Many church leaders participated in the veneration of the Confederacy and its leaders, and even children participated in these rituals. Young women, in particular, played important symbolic roles at the unveiling of monuments, as well as at political celebrations.[14]

Yet even as some elements of civil religion seemed to unite most white southerners across denominational lines, many people were fiercely loyal to their specific denomination. Thus, while individuals might attend services wherever there was a preacher on a given Sunday, they retained their denominational identities and were members only of a specific denomination. (In rural communities this might mean that individuals would attend the Baptist church one week and the Methodist the next.) While doctrinal issues were certainly one source of denominational division, different types of church government appealed to different southerners.[15]

Southern Baptists prided themselves on their congregational government, in which each congregation had authority over only itself. Local churches could voluntarily join associations and work together, but they had no authority over one another. These associations could be broken at any point, and the Convention itself had no binding authority over local bodies, except that which each local church had voluntarily given.[16] In this way, each individual church could operate autonomously while freely associating with other local, regional, or national bodies for the purpose of the "prosecution of great Christian work at home and abroad."[17] Perhaps because of this, SBC members hailed from a broad cross section of southern culture, representing "everybody from sharecroppers to school superintendents, lumber camp workers to lawyers, mill workers to mill owners."[18]

The SBC's congregational style of church government meant that theology throughout the denomination could have different emphases, but there were a few points that bound Baptists together. One can point to the doctrine of believer's baptism as an area of agreement for the entire SBC.[19] However, the focus on believer's baptism was a subset of a larger theological emphasis for Baptists across the Deep South. The major stream of theology running throughout this otherwise diverse and dynamic denomination was an emphasis on the individual. While other denominations highlighted the importance of conversion to Christianity, the SBC elevated the importance of the individual to a greater degree than did other groups. Indeed, the SBC's individualistic theology, as demonstrated in the foci of individual responsibility before God, believer's baptism, and congregational church government, wound its way through the worldview of denominational officials and had powerful implications for how church leaders understood the relationship between gender identity and religious belief.[20]

Southern Baptist church leaders felt that individual faith was important, because of their beliefs about who God was and how they understood the relationship between humanity and the divine. They believed that sinful, finite human beings needed to be reconciled to a holy, just God. This understanding was not unique to the SBC; all evangelicals believed that humans needed to be converted to Christianity.

Despite this broad evangelical unity around the central message of Protestantism, many Baptists in the New South believed that they represented the true, unbroken line of Christian worship. Those who so believed earned the sobriquet of "Landmark Baptists" and felt that Baptist churches represented the only true form of Christianity.[21] While there were pockets of Landmarkism throughout the South in the post-Reconstruction era, as well as several significant disputes about these ideas, the biggest controversy concerned the president of the Southern Baptist Theological Seminary in Louisville, Kentucky, William H. Whitsitt. Whitsitt wrote one of the first fully documented histories of Baptists in 1879 and had spent a great deal of time in English archives tracing the denomination's history and practices. In his research, Whitsitt found that he could not trace an unbroken line of Baptist practice any farther back than 1641—suggesting that the Landmark claim of an unbroken succession of Baptists traceable to the first century was tenuous at best.[22] Landmark Baptists excoriated Whitsitt for this article, and heated debate spread across the South. While not immediately schismatic, the controversy reached its height in 1897 and 1898, when a number of Baptist state associations were in danger of splitting apart. It was then in the summer of 1898 that Whitsitt offered his resignation as seminary president.[23]

While at the time outsiders may have been puzzled by the ferocity with which Baptists attacked each other over the question of baptismal succession, historian Wayne Flynt suggests that this controversy, and the anathemas that followed, grew out of widening class divisions within the SBC. As noted earlier, the divisions among rural and urban churches grew during the New South period, and many of the urban churches emphasized Landmark ideas less frequently. In contrast, poor, rural churches sometimes became centers of Landmarkism.[24] While the controversy over these ideas came to a head, and nearly tore apart some churches and associations, Landmarkism gradually lost its place as a hot-button issue for most Baptists after the turn of the century. Yet even within Landmarkism, the stream of individualistic theology could still be found, as one major tenet of most Landmark pastors was the autonomy of the local church in all matters.

While individualistic theology ran through the SBC, Methodists in the American South had different understandings of gender owing to their own theological emphases. Foremost among the theological ideas running throughout the MECS in the New South era was the emphasis on conversion to Christianity. Even the organization of the MECS was designed to highlight the importance of conversion.

The MECS inherited its organizational structure from the Methodist Episcopal Church, having split from the northern branch in 1844.[25] This split, though painful to many in the church, did not negatively affect membership totals, and by the time the American Civil War broke out sixteen years later, the MECS had 749,068 members and attendees—a number that included over 207,000 African Americans—and almost 8,000 additional pastors (both itinerant and settled).[26] In fact, Methodism was "the most pervasive form of Christianity in the United States" in the decades surrounding the Civil War, with almost a million people attending Methodist camp meetings each year.[27]

With such a massive presence around the time of the American Civil War, it is no surprise that at the end of the nineteenth and beginning of the twentieth century, the MECS had a powerful influence throughout the American South. The denomination was highly organized and comprised lay members as well as settled pastors, traveling (or itinerant) ministers, regular preachers, and bishops. Each group of individuals held separate responsibilities within the church.[28]

Despite the incredible organization of the Methodist Episcopal Church, South, the denomination deliberately accommodated a wide breadth of theology at the turn of the century. One writer boldly declared, "There are really no distinctively Methodist doctrines. . . . There is not a single doctrine held by us as a Church that is not held by some other Church."[29] Instead, they believed that the Methodist system of overlapping geographical boundaries and highly organized church government was for the purpose of preaching the message of Jesus and converting people to Christianity. Indeed, each time MECS church officials met together, they were expected to report on the number of new converts and members in their districts.[30] So important to MECS polity and practice was the idea of conversion that Bishop Charles Galloway claimed that the idea "Ye must be born again" was the premier doctrine of the church.[31] Similarly, Alabamian pastor James Madison Crews told his congregants, "The doctrine of regeneration is the most important in all the Scripture. . . . Without it the Bible would be unintelligible."[32] While conversion was an important part of both Baptist and Holiness theology, neither elevated it to the level the Methodist Episcopal Church, South, did.

The focus on conversion to Christianity in the MECS led to a heightened focus on the person of Jesus and his example as the perfect man. This focus on the person of Jesus, for the purpose of conversion, generated specific ideas about gender in the New South. Certainly, other important ideas influenced identity. But for many people within the MECS, the denomination's emphasis on Jesus for the purpose of conversion was the defining stream of theology in their lives.

While Methodism represented a full third of all churchgoers in these Deep South states, the Southern Baptist Convention by the close of the nineteenth century had more members throughout Mississippi, Alabama, and Georgia.[33] Combined, the two denominations comprised between 80 and 90 percent of all churchgoers in the South, and roughly one-third of the total population could be lumped into one of these two theological traditions.[34]

The combined theological dominance of Methodists and Baptists created a broad-based evangelical culture that heavily influenced ideas of gender identity. This theological hegemony meant that ideas of gender flowing from these two denominations, even when watered down, defined the personal identity of hundreds of thousands of people across the New South. These ideas were a significant part of what it meant to be a religious southerner.

Being a religious southerner did not simply equate to being a man, and many women in the post-Reconstruction South chafed against the restrictions of the SBC and the MECS. Indeed, both denominations underwent a period of flux at the end of the nineteenth and the beginning of the twentieth century, when women's auxiliaries and missionary societies became part of the official denominational cultures. In the Southern Baptist Convention, almost a decade of meetings paid off when the Women's Missionary Union (WMU) was founded in 1888. In the same decade, Methodist women launched several missionary organizations within the MECS.[35]

The efforts to establish these organizations, and make them part of denominational culture, were hotly contested among both Baptists and Methodists.[36] The issues at stake ranged from women's roles in the church and home to being a proper southern lady. Even the establishment of the organizations themselves did not answer all of these questions, as there were contrasting ideas even within these groups. For several years after its official affiliation with the denomination, representatives from the WMU were still discouraged from reading the organizational report on the floor of the annual convention and relied on male allies to do so to avoid controversy.[37]

As the fights about women's auxiliaries demonstrated, ideas of gender were highly charged and intimately connected with theology in the New South. The following four chapters outline the ways in which the Baptist and Methodist streams of theology defined gender. Baptist individualism and the Methodist emphasis on Jesus and conversion were serious ideas to many clergy across the South, who used these theological streams as the basis for their ideas of manhood, womanhood, and family life. For many people in the post-Reconstruction South, religion was not something they assented to on Sundays only. Instead, it was a vital part of their lives, giving meaning to the mundane and clarifying the extraordinary.

2

Faithful Baptist Families and Women

Between 1877 and 1915, many white southerners still felt as though they were adjusting to a way of life that did not include the prescriptive ideals of plantation homes.[1] For some southern families this meant leaving farms and moving to cities in hopes of a better tomorrow. Other families dealt with the changes of the period by planting more cotton, buying better farm equipment, and going deeper into debt. Of course, there were also families who chose neither extreme but moved close to county seats while staying on the land.[2] Often as families decided how best to deal with the changes happening in the American South, they turned to their pastors for spiritual guidance and advice. For more than a million southerners, this meant turning to church leaders of the Southern Baptist Convention.[3]

Baptist leaders responded by offering prescriptive ideas on how Baptist theology defined identity. While most officials in the Southern Baptist Convention emphasized the individual in their sermons, this emphasis fell sharply away when Baptist preachers and pastors talked about proper femininity and family life. Rather than encouraging a robust theology of individual mastery as they did with men, most Baptist officials encouraged a model where a large share of the responsibility for the moral integrity of the family fell to women. This does not mean that men were exempt from moral responsibility for rearing their children and families. Rather, Baptist officials believed that both parents shared responsibility for their family's spiritual life.

The Language of Kinship

Utilizing the language of kin and family provided a countercurrent to the denomination's individualistic theology for some SBC officials.[4] Pastors sometimes used the term "sonship" or "divine sonship" to recognize those who had accepted Jesus.[5] While the term had its origin in Scripture, it worked well for Baptists, who emphasized both the familial and the individual natures of Christianity.

Kinship terms could be used for other sacred purposes as well. Many SBC pastors wanted to emphasize God's love for sinners and found the language of the family useful in conveying this idea to their parishioners. T. T. Eaton, a trustee at the Southern Baptist Theological Seminary and editor of one of the denomination's most influential periodicals, was one SBC leader who repeatedly used kinship language in his work. Moreover, Eaton was one of the leading voices that forced Southern Baptist Theological Seminary President William Whitsitt to resign in 1899.[6] Before the Whitsitt controversy revealed Eaton's harder edge, he addressed one sermon to "Babes in Christ,"[7] talking repeatedly about the joy one experienced upon conversion to Christianity and being brought into the "Father's house." Eaton then elaborated the growth that members of Christ's family undertook, from infancy to "full manhood," and the "loving Father who watched and guarded every step" so that Christians might live "as free from worry and anxiety as a happy child in a father's house."[8] Eaton thought that God created a new identity for believers, and used the language of adoption to show how he believed God extended bonds of kinship to new converts, accepted them into his house, and brought them into his family. Eaton made this familial connection clear in the sermon as he talked about the need for a believer's character and actions to change to match that new identity.[9] What Eaton most tried to convey as he preached, though, was a sense of God as a father, ever watchful and able to protect those he loved.

One way that Southern Baptists tried to encourage parents to take charge of their family's well-being was through an active Sunday School program. The Corresponding Secretary for the Education Board was Rufus W. Weaver. In his book *The Religious Development of the Child* (1913), Weaver notes that the greatest "dynamic forces" in that development are the child's parents. The parent's ultimate goal, according to Weaver, was not to encourage the child to gain the high honors that the world has to offer but to get their children to "give their hearts to Jesus Christ."[10] Weaver noted in his book that his own parents and grandparents were very influential in his spiritual formation, remarking that it was under their training that he learned about his own sinfulness before God, about the way of salvation, and about God's power and protection in the midst of the storms of life.[11]

For Weaver, early experiences helped to cement his identity in both a spiritual and earthly family. In his recounting of these events, Weaver noted the ways that both immediate and extended family attempted to get him to join the spiritual family. Although Weaver's place in his earthly family was assured, he was not clear about his place in a spiritual family, and Weaver distinctly remembered listening to the sobbing prayers of his mother as she pleaded with God to give her strength to rear her son.[12] This ideal of a praying mother guiding her children came to fruition as Weaver explained that hearing his mother's prayers for him began a three-year spiritual journey, which eventually ended with his conversion one night as his grandfather preached. Weaver's experience demonstrated how powerful the identification with family and religion could be. Whether it was his memories of the family gathered after a meal to listen to his father read the Bible or of hearing his grandfather read the Psalms amid the roar of southern thunderstorms, religious expression created a sense identity for Weaver—one based around the idea that he belonged not only to an earthly family but also to a heavenly one.[13]

To encourage this identification with a heavenly family, Weaver repeatedly talked about the importance of training children in the way they should go. His own life provided examples of the patriarchs of the family reading Scripture and preaching while the women prayed for family members, and Weaver encouraged similar things in his writing. At one point, he mentioned that children should not be coddled but rather be made to know the realities of the world and sinfulness of their own hearts at an early age.[14] Weaver was careful to note that when teaching children, adults should give each child complete religious autonomy; in other words, each child must be viewed and considered as an individual with a free will. According to Weaver, "Every child coming into the world has the right to the opportunity of realizing personal autonomy. We repudiate the reception of any one, child or adult, into the Church upon any other basis than the personal choice of Jesus Christ as Lord."[15] Thus, though families (and more specifically, parents) were vital to his ideas about how one developed personal religious identity, families were not to coerce their children into belief. Every person's identity was unique, and Weaver expected parents to respect that, even as they taught their children to listen to the voice of God and define their identities through a loving, familial relationship with the divine.

Annie Armstrong, the Corresponding Secretary of the Women's Missionary Union (WMU), believed that teaching children to listen to the voice of God was an important part of a mother's work. In a letter to one of her many correspondents, she opined that the missionary movement of the next generation would depend on how faithfully women taught their children to love missions.[16] One of the ways Armstrong and the WMU tried to encourage a love of missions in young people was establishing a

"Babies' Branch." Mothers would enroll their babies and pay a small due to receive a card, which the child could "treasure . . . until old age as an evidence of a life-long association with mission work."[17] Clearly, Armstrong and the WMU worked to develop creative ways of helping mothers establish a loving relationship with God.

God's love was also the message of William Owen Carver's sermon "The Word Made Flesh." In this address, delivered in 1904, the influential seminary professor, pastor, writer, and founder of the Southern Baptist Historical Society repeated the early-twentieth-century emphasis on the love of God, and told his congregants that Jesus was the highest expression of God's love for the world. Carver informed his audience that Jesus was the Christ and the "love of God bringing the light of life" to the world.[18] Carver also affirmed the idea of the divine sonship to those who believed in Jesus.[19] Once again, an SBC official counseled his congregants to define their identities through the bonds of kinship and love offered by God.

Another influential leader, E. C. Dargan, also emphasized God's love and care for his people. Like Eaton, Dargon was based in Louisville, Kentucky, but his influence was felt throughout the South as he trained students in homiletics, or preaching, at the Southern Baptist Theological Seminary from 1892 to 1907. In *The Doctrines of Our Faith*, Dargan focused an entire chapter on the providence of God and reminded his readers of God's loving, wise, and "tender care" for humans, as for the rest of the universe.[20] Dargan referenced biblical passages that talk about God's care for his people, highlighting for believers the use of fatherly images and kinship references.[21] Dargan also used maternal imagery to show his readers another aspect of God's love. He compared God to a "good mother [who] loves her wayward son, though with all her pure soul she hates his evil ways."[22] Male readers would sense themselves in this passage—they were the sons who continued to hurt their mothers through their actions. Yet this was not where Dargan left his readers; a few chapters later, he explained their new relationship to God by using language of reconciled kinship ties.[23] Throughout this volume on the beliefs of the SBC, Dargan tried to impress upon his readers that their identity should be defined by a familial relationship with an all-powerful God who tenderly cared for them.

Dargan's ideas of the Fatherhood of God dovetailed with those of theologically liberal Christians and Social Gospellers early in the twentieth century. While SBC leaders often derided their theology, Social Gospellers concerned themselves less with theological niceties than with addressing the structural problems of industrialization and urbanization. Thus, despite the differences between Southern Baptists and northern Social Gospellers, their ideas of the Fatherhood of God and the divine's love for believers converged.[24]

While some Southern Baptist officials wanted their parishioners to understand their identities as rooted in the love and bonds of family offered by God through Jesus, other officials stressed the ideal characteristics that individual men and women should exhibit. Some of the ideals that SBC pastors thought that women should embody were a purity of heart, a loving temperament, and an educated mind.

Selfless Baptist Womanhood

At the turn of the century, many people in the South celebrated women as the measure of "moral excellence." These ideas often "reflected an ideology that conflated ideas about femininity with ideas about morality itself."[25] Historians have shown that the paradigm that shaped this idea of women as the arbiters of virtue and morality could prove either a cage or a key for women—all in the guise of pure femininity.[26]

For example, when speaking about feminine purity, one Baptist pastor from Columbus, Mississippi, mentioned the various types of people among his parishioners. Among the "fathers and mothers growing old" and the "young men with hearts . . . strong and true" were young maidens with "thoughts as pure as the milk."[27] The author, John L. Johnson, believed that purity was inherent to young women. Although this could be dismissed as merely a rhetorical set piece, Johnson also essentialized features of other groups. Young men were strong and true of heart; fathers and mothers were growing old in their "simple life and loves," and throughout the countryside, people with "primitive manners" worshiped in "board chapels" and "log meeting houses."[28] In the midst of a rapidly urbanizing New South, Johnson used rhetorical devices to paint an idyllic picture of a rural church; nonetheless, he still attempted to say what he believed to be true, and he distilled each group into its essential characteristics. He believed that innocence and purity defined young women.

While many pastors believed there were key aspects that defined "true Christian womanhood," one of the most spiritually significant was women's ability to give of themselves. Of course, along with this admiration of those women who gave of themselves came a suspicion of those who held something back or seemed overly strong and vocal about their opinions.

William Owen Carver, a student and eventual professor of missions at the Southern Baptist Theological Seminary, worried that some women might have a negative influence on those around them. For example, Carver complained to his diary about his stepmother, saying that his father "married a woman beneath him and with an ungovernable temper."[29] This immediately followed a passage in which his stepmother complained about his father to Carver, and Carver noted that she was a woman who had "nothing to love in character or reputation or finance." He then mused, somewhat disingenuously, "I will not say I am sorry Father married her though I have always wished it otherwise."[30] Carver's complaints about his stepmother stemmed from her temper and colored all of his interactions with her. Even when Carver did not see his stepmother's temper, his interactions with her were colored by the knowledge that her anger was formidable.[31] Although he tried to remain on amiable terms with his stepmother, it was clear that Carver felt she was wrong for his father and a severe drain on the patriarch's energy.[32] Furthermore, this one trait of his stepmother became all-encompassing and definitive of her personality.[33]

When most SBC pastors needed an example of a vile woman, they turned to the biblical Jezebel, the murderous wife of one of the worst kings in biblical history. E. C. Dargan used Jezebel as the ultimate example of evil in his sermon "The Story of a Man Scared by a Woman."[34] The title itself suggests an unsettled situation, as southern white men were not supposed to be afraid of anything, particularly not women. Within the first few sentences, though, Dargan made it clear that Jezebel was no normal woman; rather, she personified evil, and he remarked, "When a woman is bad she is very bad."[35] This SBC official made the assumption that a woman could be classified by an essential trait. When that trait was love or purity, Dargan put women up on a pedestal; but if a woman could be classified by something he considered bad, she became a powerful force for evil. Granted, the biblical character Jezebel was known for her temper, her idolatry, and her murderous ways; yet Dargan used her as merely one example of what happened when women went wrong.[36] He even claimed that the history of the world showed that evil forces were often controlled by the "figure of a strong, bad, vindictive woman."[37] For Dargan, such a figure represented the pinnacle of depravity, as a strong woman led others to their doom.

Rather than focusing on women as powerful figures of evil, though, many Baptist preachers talked about a woman's strength flowing from a uniquely feminine ability to love, particularly in conjunction with motherhood. For example, in 1905, E. C. Dargan noted that he thought mothers could easily love their wayward sons while hating their actions.[38] Dargan described how hard this was; yet mothers willingly sacrificed everything for the ultimate good of their sons.

Landrum Leavell, from Oxford, Mississippi, felt that a uniquely sacrificial religious character and purity defined all women. In 1905, Leavell gave the commencement address at Hillman College, a school for young white women in Mississippi. At the beginning of the twentieth century in the Deep South, many ideas of women's education retained ideologies of class, race, and gender that had their foundations in either the plantation ideals or Lost Cause mythology. Such ideals relegated southern white "ladies" to educations that concentrated on the "domestic arts."[39] Additionally, many male supporters of women's education expected women to "conform to chivalric images of womanhood."[40] Following these, Leavell expected that the women listening to his address in Mississippi would conform to specific ideals of white southern ladies.

The ideals Leavell specified often denoted the women's willing sacrifice of their own desires. For example, Leavell reminded his listeners that "women were among the most heroic of the martyrs" and proceeded to list some of them.[41] One of the words that Leavell used throughout his list of exemplary women was "virgin," marking how some SBC pastors related spiritual purity to sexuality. Leavell listed many other characteristics that he felt defined true womanhood, and gave examples of women who, in their faith and self-sacrifice, personified each trait.[42]

In contrast to many of his examples, though, Levell's description of Queen Elizabeth I valorized her "masculine" traits of energy and ambition rather than her femininity. As a monarch, Leavell suggested, she displayed a "masculine energy and decision that insured to her reign the respect of all surrounding nation [*sic*]." Leavell further noted that this was despite "whatever may have been the vanities and frailties of the feminine side of her character."[43] Thus, even while praising Christian women at a women's college, Leavell decided to describe one of his female heroes according to her *masculine* qualities. He juxtaposed Elizabeth I's energy and decision-making abilities to the "vanities and frailties of the feminine side of her character." Elizabeth I became an androgynous being in Leavell's mind, having all the shortcomings of a woman's character and a few of the supposedly male virtues. According to Leavell, the feminine side of her character that did not deserve admiration, as the "male side" guaranteed the "respect of all surrounding nations." Thus, in Elizabeth I, character traits skewed her gender identity. Rather than praise Elizabeth I for her femininity, as he did most of the other women, Leavell praised her for "masculine" traits *despite* her femininity.

Leavell used the opposite tack when he talked about the Holy Roman Empress Maria Teresa, and declared that in a time of need, it was her "words together with her beauty majesty and sorrow" that gathered Hungarian nobles to her side.[44] Thus, in contrast to Elizabeth I's masculine qualities, it was Maria Teresa's feminine ones, those marked by passivity, that ensured that the loyalist nobles of the Holy Roman Empire would come and fight—thus demonstrating their own chivalry and manhood. It was not Maria Teresa's wise governance or strength of character that Leavell praised. Instead, Leavell believed the qualities she used to awaken Hungarian chivalry were worth imitating. These male nobles responded to her beauty, majesty, and sorrow; thus her passive traits enabled the men around her to prove their own manliness.

Leavell described the Hungarian nobles proving their manhood in ways remarkably similar to how many historians describe white society in the New South period. During that period, many in the white South had a bifurcated view of women. They viewed women as either pure, passive virgins who needed protection from the ravages of the world or as defiled, "low-class" women who could not expect to receive safe haven in white society.[45] Yet the protection offered to paragons of purity did not provide empowerment. Rather, it emphasized a cycle of dependence in which women were passive creatures—just as Leavell described Maria Teresa.[46] Those who did not fit into this framework often fell outside the "protection" of southern white men.

After giving this, inaccurate, picture of a passive monarch, Leavell praised American women, whom he felt were "unequaled in beauty, grace, and varied accomplishments."[47] Although this language appeared to be a tribute to the women of the United States, Leavell still made diminishing claims about women's character. Rather than noting the wisdom, strength, or social contributions of women, he simply remarked that their beauty and grace were unparalleled in the world. Although he remarked that they had "varied accomplishments," by preceding these remarks with demarcations of beauty and grace, he asserted that only aesthetic accomplishments were worthy goals. This became even clearer when Leavell specifically praised the women of the American South, who "achieved triumphs far greater by rendering homes happy by physical comforts, by books, by music, by flowers, and delightful conversation; who diminished sorrow by their sympathy, heightened joy by gayety[,] soothed aching hearts by tenderness, dignified those about them by their intelligence[,] and elevated all by their devotion."[48]

Here, Leavell shifted his discussion slightly, from women's character to the "triumphal" roles of women in the South. These roles centered on the home and its emotional and aesthetic activities. While these were, and are, important things that are essential to healthy families, Leavell assumed that only the women in the family would do these things, and granted few other options for those who did not want to take up such tasks. Those families who were of a lower socioeconomic class and needed to have two incomes just to scrape by, without any comforts or luxuries, were denigrated, as Leavell thought that true womanhood could come only through the lifestyle exemplified by middle- and upper-class white femininity. Even for those of elevated social status, Leavell questioned the femininity of women who did not want to adorn their homes with aesthetic refinement or who were not gifted in the decorative arts.

Certainly, white women learned about domestic affairs in the turn-of-the-century South. Historian Jane Censer notes that domesticity did not always have negative connotations, though. Rather, white "women themselves saw their ability to master the new machinery of housekeeping as a marker of nondependence. To them, their creations, both indoors and outdoors, stood as tangible and worthy achievements."[49] Far from being relegated to a world of domesticity, these women perceived their new roles as demonstrating their mastery over their worlds.[50] Leavell would have approved of this interpretation of his commencement address: one that provided white women, particularly the social elites who would have been attending college, with mastery over their homes.

Although Leavell did not mention race, his ideas of true femininity were bounded by race as well as class. By locating his thoughts about womanhood within the home, he suggested that those who had to work outside of their own house were at a dramatic disadvantage. This instantly excluded most African American women across the South, who worked as domestics or field hands to put food on the table for their families. Yet historians such as Glenda Gilmore and John Giggie have demonstrated that even as whites attempted to deny full femininity to black women in the South at the turn of the century, African Americans highlighted the important roles that women occupied in the home and fully imbibed the idea that the home was a feminine sphere of influence.[51]

Many Southern Baptist officials thought that women best modeled their true femininity by giving of themselves within the home. For example, William J. Holtzclaw, a pastor and author from Georgia, believed that women were, by their natures, best suited to helping others and giving of themselves selflessly. Holtzclaw wrote, "Woman is a born sufferer, and she counts not her life dear to herself if only she can accomplish her purpose."[52] The author created an idealistic model with which he tried to describe all women. Holtzclaw explained to his readers that women were made to suffer and came close to insinuating that it was only in suffering that they attained their true femininity. Holtzclaw's ideas belittled injustices done to women, who were simply "born sufferer[s]." Moreover, he combined this idea of suffering with a type of martyr-like selflessness in which a woman would be willing to lay down her life for any worthy purpose. Although certainly meant as praise, this sacrificial love was not presented as a trait that women might choose but as something essential about all women.[53]

Though Annie Armstrong, the indomitable Corresponding Secretary of the WMU, may have taken exception to Holtzclaw's essentializing tendencies, she also assumed that women would serve others in love. Her own recounting of the history of the Woman's Missionary Union started with the assertion, "Southern Baptist women as the servants of Christ and a part of the working force of the churches, have recognized the beauty and the power of serving others."[54] Of course, Armstrong's description of service differed from Holtzclaw's in its intention. Rather than serving others merely for the sake of service or because women were "born sufferers," Armstrong noted that women served because of the beauty and power to be found in the act of service itself. Thus, while the two may have advocated similar acts of service, Armstrong did so in order to advocate for both the beauty and strength of Southern Baptist women.

Nonetheless, William Holtzclaw praised strong, white, "modern" women who refused "to be any longer regarded as a gentler and saintlier type of humanity, who must be petted, reverenced and protected." He spoke approvingly of the "modern woman, of the advanced type" who faced "men in all branches of business, and in all the professions," calling them "real competitors."[55] Holtzclaw's sentiment was unusual among SBC pastors in the South, as he deliberately eschewed ideas of femininity that put women on a pedestal. Instead, he praised women who competitively engaged men in business professions—a realm frequently thought of as masculine.[56] To become competitive in such an environment, women, Holtzclaw counseled, must get a strong education, in both literature and business.[57]

Holtzclaw's book also included disturbing ideas as to why the modern woman should get an education. Holtzclaw claimed that women of "high culture and broad intelligence" were God's "best gift to man." Lest the reader think that Holtzclaw might be referring to humanity rather than simply the male gender, he clarified, "A well-bred and well-taught woman, who has the additional advantage of good deportment, is in every way capable of filling man's sublimest wish."[58] Here, the author shows that he believed all the advances in women's education, women's rights, and in the state of women more generally were there to benefit men. Women were not simply to benefit men but to fulfill "man's sublimest wish." Though nothing in the text suggested that Holtzclaw alluded to anything erotic, the sexual subtext was impossible to miss. Such language suggested that women's education, the application of that education, the new societal roles a woman might take up, and a woman's good nature were all for the purpose of fulfilling male desires.

While these modern women fulfilled men's desires, the language that Holtzclaw used to describe the women he praised suggested passivity. The women he referred to did not come from healthy families or the "better classes"; instead, they were "well-bred." These women did not apply their mental energies to tasks but were "well-taught." Both phrases suggest that nothing these women had came from within or was of their own doing. They were passive beings whose condition was the result of outside forces working on them. This was strikingly different imagery than that used during this time for white men, which often highlighted independent action.[59]

Passive language commonly appeared in the South at the fin de siècle in white references to white women and African Americans and stood in sharp contrast to the active language of white manhood. In the cases of white women and African Americans generally, white men referred to an entire group of people as passive beings.[60] As if to highlight his belief about the passive nature of women, Holtzclaw concluded that though a woman might have "ornaments and beauty, if she have not good behavior," then she was a fraud.[61] True femininity, he asserted, did not rest in a woman's inner strength, in her ability to care for others, or even in her long-suffering when dealing with a difficult husband; it was simply in "ornaments," "beauty," and "good behavior."

At almost the same time that Holtzclaw made such remarks, J. B. Moody, Dean of the Hall-Moody Institute (an SBC school in Martin, Tennessee), made much broader claims about the roles of women. He stated in one of his books, "God made women to love and to be loved. Man is the head, but the wife is the heart."[62] Moody carefully noted that he fell into a trap that men had been susceptible to from time immemorial—he called the husband by the universal name of the sex, man, while calling the woman by her married title, wife. Moody was progressive enough to realize that in doing so, writers "bind the woman, but leave the man free."[63] Even as he realized (and repented) that he bound women, he nonetheless made claims about their essential nature. He argued that affection was one of the very reasons why women had been created—it was part of their gendered identity.

Using traits such as love and purity to define the essential part of one's being may seem relatively benign. Yet, when these traits were used to put all women on a pedestal, they created a model up to which no woman could fully live. This meant that through the process of essentializing all women based on the traits of a few individuals, these Baptist officials set up a dichotomy in which women were either virgins or whores.[64] There was virtually no middle ground for those who did not live up to expectations; yet this was the message that preachers disseminated to their parishioners. For some Baptist ministers, once this process began it became all too easy for them to believe that certain character traits marked evil and defilement in a woman.

Educating Baptist Women for the Church

To inculcate the good qualities of femininity that were so obviously valued, many SBC officials supported some type of women's education. Many denominational schools believed that women were "educated for families, not for themselves."[65] Practically, this meant that curriculums often focused more on music, expression, art, and foreign languages than on more "masculine" subjects such as business, math, or science.[66] Of course, such curricular choices were not restricted to SBC women's colleges in the turn-of-the-century South, and some Baptists looked for fuller women's educational opportunities.

In a denomination that celebrated its history of congregation rule and the freedom of the individual conscience, there were certainly pastors who felt that a deep and meaningful education for young women could be a spiritual boon. J. B. Gambrell, a pastor from Mississippi, wholeheartedly supported women's education in a sermon he gave before the 1892 meeting of the Southern Baptist Convention.[67] The sermon was ostensibly about the need to convert the entire world to Christianity, and Gambrell firmly believed that women had a large role to play in this process. He rejoiced that there were more women being educated and remarked, "Consecrated womanhood is being turned on the heathendom." He then stated that although SBC men needed to focus on missionary training, what the denomination really needed was more women to "help us save the world."[68]

Gambrell felt that educated Baptist women had a large, eternally significant role to play in the world. He thought education contributed to a divine plan of eternal significance. His statements did not emerge in a vacuum, however. Rather, they came only two years after the Southern Baptist Convention found itself with an auxiliary: the Woman's Missionary Union (WMU).[69] The women of the SBC established the WMU in

1888 as an official auxiliary to the Convention amid controversy and questions about the appropriate role of women in church life.

The fight for an official women's organization within the Southern Baptist Convention began almost two decades earlier, in 1871, when Baptist women in Baltimore began to organize to raise funds for foreign missionaries. Shortly thereafter, women in South Carolina and other states organized for the same purpose. However, it would take years before these various groups would come together under a single organization and even longer before the denomination would recognize the WMU as an official auxiliary of the SBC.[70]

Even before the establishment of the WMU, in 1888, some Baptist leaders felt that properly educated women could make a significant contribution to the church. Mrs. S. A. Chambers, an Alabamian who helped establish the WMU, delivered an address in 1882 in which she forcefully argued that women should work "not only for the good and prosperity of the church of which she is a member, but for also for the advancement of the Redeemer's kingdom in the world."[71] Certainly, this was a more expansive vision of what women might accomplish through church work than the idea that they should just "go to meeting, sing, and make pies for the preachers."[72] While Chambers thought that women should help raise money for their local church, she believed that they should not wait until church buildings had "elegant chandeliers" before sending the "lamp of God's word" throughout the world.[73] This was indeed a larger idea of what women might accomplish—they would help usher in the Kingdom of God. Chambers believed that women should work hard to see that the people throughout the world put their trust in Jesus.

Many women accepted this role and worked very hard to see it through, even if it sometimes meant defying pastors who were not enthused by the idea. Lidd Robertson, a female Sunday School worker from Mobile, Alabama, complained to a friend that her pastor had the "impertinence" to try to get her to stop working so forcefully. In response, Robertson told her pastor, "*I* am an endorsed agent of the Southern Convention. There is no *choice*, but *duty* and I propose to *fulfill* it."[74] Robertson was so angry over her pastor trying to get her to do less that she told her friend, "*We will have* our *mutiny*!"[75] Here was a woman who clearly knew her place in church and believed that someone who should have supported her instead threatened her authority. Robertson responded not merely with anger but with the promise to challenge institutional authority.

Other SBC clergymen also challenged the authority of women and women's organizations within the denomination. Annie Armstrong occasionally noted the opposition she encountered in her correspondence. Sometimes this came in the form of other Baptist organizations that, perhaps, felt that the WMU was intruding on their territory.[76] At other times, though, Armstrong felt personally slighted when male leaders of the denomination refused to endorse the WMU.[77]

While Annie Armstrong dealt with opposition to the WMU as part of her job, Lottie Moon, one of the first unmarried women missionaries to China endorsed by the SBC, frequently sent back letters to the United States asking for more Baptist women to engage in missions work in China. In her letters, she would often appeal to the SBC mission boards to send more women to carry forth missionary work.[78] Moon's requests frequently took on urgent tones; she implored, over the course of a decade, that multiple women should come join her.[79] Indeed, Moon thought the work was so important that she offered to lend one missionary board most of her life savings if they would send women missionaries her way.[80]

William Holtzclaw shared Moon's belief that women's work for the church was vitally important. In *Women of To-day*, Holtzclaw acknowledged that though many women were involved in church work, the type of work they performed was dramatically different depending on the denomination and its interpretation of the Bible. Some groups ordained women to the ministry, others only appointed them missionaries, while still others would allow women to enter theological schools but would not grant them an official place in ministry.[81]

Even within the Woman's Missionary Union of the Southern Baptist Convention individuals had differences of opinions as to the proper role of women in ministry. Annie Armstrong clearly felt that women should have opinions on many areas of denominational polity, and she frequently made her opinions known to her friends, both male and female. However, she heartily opposed the idea of women occupying the same roles as men in the church. In 1896, she wrote to a friend that she regarded it "as the sheerest nonsense for persons to claim that women can do men's work. . . . No, no, no, there are limitations to the work that can be done by women. Our brethren are the God-appointed leaders."[82] Because of Armstrong's belief that women could not do men's work, she resisted the establishment of a Woman's Training School at Southern Baptist Theological Seminary in Louisville, Kentucky. Armstrong's opposition stemmed from her belief that the Bible taught that women should not preach, and yet at the Training School, women could sit in on seminary classes teaching men to preach. She did all she could as Corresponding Secretary of the WMU to oppose the denomination's funding of the Training School, and when that failed, she resigned her position.[83] Her theological position defined women's proper place in the church, and Armstrong would not be convinced otherwise.

William Wilkes, an SBC minister who pastored in Alabama and Texas, grew up in a very different theological atmosphere where the congregation felt strongly that women should not have any active roles in the church. Wilkes recalled how "Ladies' Aids were severely denounced and defied."[84] In his memoir, Wilkes described the Primitive Baptist church his family attended during his boyhood in the 1890s.[85] There, men and women sat on different sides of the sanctuary.[86] Nevertheless, women were a part of the church community and routinely practiced their religious duties—including foot washing. For the men in Wilkes's community, this religious practice enabled them to see "bare feminine feet" at a time when "women were not supposed to protrude shod feet far enough beyond trailing skirts to show well stockinged ankles." Some men and boys were so enraptured that they dispensed with decorum and stood on pews in an attempt to catch a glimpse of skin.[87] Wilkes recognized that times had changed and this practice no longer carried the sexual overtones that it did during his childhood. Yet the men in the congregation made it clear that they thought the ways that women exposed themselves, even if by showing only their ankles, were well worth standing on pews, and all-too-obvious leering occurred.

J. B. Moody of Tennessee would have been appalled at the behavior at Wilkes's home church. In *Women in Churches* (1910), Moody writes in support of women taking greater roles in Baptist churches throughout the world. In fact, Moody was enraged with Baptist preachers who tried to impose restrictions, other than a prohibition against preaching, on women in their congregations.[88] Throughout the volume, Moody argued for an enlarged view of women's roles in the church, because of his interpretation of the Bible. For example, while he thought that women should not become pastors, he had no reservations about individual women becoming missionaries and thought that if a Baptist woman had the opportunity to preach to a foreign man, she should go ahead and take the opportunity regardless of the denominational stance.[89] (Lottie Moon already operated in such a manner and continually asked for more women to join her as missionaries in China.) Moreover, Moody carefully showed Scriptural references of what he believed were instances of women preaching and proclaiming their faith.[90] Moody noted that many Baptist preachers were already encouraging the women in their congregations to engage in enlarging the Kingdom of God. They did so at revivals, where women were exhorted to "go out among sinners, male and female, and persuade them to be reconciled to God."[91] Yet even in this action, women had no official part in revivals, no institutional role; they were merely individuals going out among the crowds in hopes of persuading sinners to believe in Jesus.

Throughout his book, Moody made reference to Scripture as well as to the established Baptist congregational polity.[92] Clearly, Moody did his best to define his conceptions of women's roles in the church, and indeed of women more generally, according to his understanding of the Bible and church policy. Moody, like other SBC officials, then attempted to spread his ideas to the laity through sermons, speeches, and various writings. These Baptist officials tried to envision specific connections between theology and gender and then persuade their parishioners to redefine their identities accordingly.

Baptist Women in Society

Although ministers tried to define appropriate gender roles through theology, the question of what constituted proper womanhood in society remained. In his commencement address to Hillman College, Landrum Leavell talked about the ways that women should influence society. He told his audience that what made the United States so moral and good was the fact that "never was there a country where womans [*sic*] influence was more widely felt than ours."[93] Although Leavell tried to talk positively about the influence of women in society, his habit of essentializing women's traits and characteristics was so ingrained that he talked about women's influence in society as though a single woman were responsible. This single woman was good and moral to be sure, as in his mind she brought "growth in goodness." Nonetheless, Leavell reduced all the women in his audience to one essential person. If any of his listeners did not fit his definitions, Leavell would have disapproved of their influence or may even have denied the idea that they were "ladies," as proper ladies were supposed to have a moralizing influence on the rest of society.[94]

William Holtzclaw similarly believed that women's natural purity helped society. Holtzclaw would have applauded the reform efforts that the women of Galveston, Texas, began after a hurricane destroyed their town, in 1900. Historian Elizabeth Hayes Turner has recorded how, after the storm, the women of the town began to rebuild and reform Galveston society.[95] Texas was not the only southern state to see public reform efforts headed by women however. The historians Lori Ginzburg, Rebecca Montgomery, and Jane Censer all chronicle how white southern women used the ideas of moral authority to institute reform in the South and across the United States at the turn of the nineteenth century.[96] A generation earlier, women would not have been able to engage in public reform efforts.[97]

Holtzclaw thought that each and every woman had a "duty to bring her influence" into every aspect of life and society that needed purification.[98] Indeed, he felt that it would be through a woman's purity that "the whole human race [would be saved] from the corrupt swamps of social and political life."[99] Here Holtzclaw used the feminine singular, thus signaling his attempt to define all women and to condense the complexities, nuances, and uniqueness of the individuals that constituted half of all humanity into a few "essential" traits.

Holtzclaw additionally believed that women could fulfill their purpose through a divinely ordained purpose to rescue society. During this time, when postmillennialism was on the rise and many liberal Protestants looked to the burgeoning Social Gospel movement to bring about the Kingdom of God, Holtzclaw looked to women to redeem secular society. (Postmillennialism is the idea in Christian theology that the world was gradually getting better and that eventually the Kingdom of God would appear on earth.[100]) Despite this, Holtzclaw felt that women should work to help redeem humanity from its downward spiral because women were "better equipped for moral and religious work than men": "They are endowed with natures more tender, emotional and sympathetic than men. They are strong in faith and zeal, and their will-power is far in advance of men."[101] Here, the author showed that he believed that there was something innately religious about women that made them better than men at serving others.

However, the idea that women, defined by their moral and religious nature, were better equipped to rescue and reform society was not unusual during the late nineteenth and the early twentieth centuries. Frequently women themselves used the paradigm of feminine purity or religiosity to implement reform. The idea that feminine moral authority should be used in public reform efforts marked a change in southern culture and opened new roles for women in society between 1877 and 1915. A generation earlier, women were encouraged to use their moral authority, but only within the spheres of their own families—virtually never in public settings and never in political ones.[102] Yet, in the New South period, some Baptist leaders like Landrum Leavell and William Holtzclaw encouraged women to go into the public, even the political, realm and exert their purifying influence. Many white southern women did just that. Whether through their local churches, foreign mission boards, the Woman's Christian Temperance Union, or in the burgeoning women's suffrage movement, southern women tapped into the idea of purity and used it to open new avenues of power and authority in the South.[103]

Holtzclaw tapped into this idea, and throughout his book he suggested that women should receive suffrage because of their moral authority. At one point, Holtzclaw asked his readers: "[Can] any nation fail to be benefited by the franchise of pure and cultured women?"[104] Nonetheless, he worried that some women could lose their character through poor marriages and wanted them to require "purity for purity" and "honor for honor."[105] Clearly, Holtzclaw believed a woman's purity was an essential part of what made her a woman.

The idea of innate purity was not unusual at the time; however, Holtzclaw ended up applying it in some unusual ways. For instance, Holtzclaw worried that women could lose that quality if they married men who had not kept chaste before marriage. Women could purify politics simply by voting, by performing their public duty. However, if a woman performed her "wifely duty" with a husband who was not a virgin when they married, she lost that purity and claim to moral authority.[106] According to Holtzclaw, then, woman's individual purity could be displayed in public and used for the general welfare, but intimate acts of immorality—even those that a woman did not herself commit—could instantly take that purity from her.

Holtzclaw warned women that dancing and the life of the ballroom threatened young women's purity. He believed that the ballroom's "dazzling lights and excited passion" were dangerous to "the soul of a pure woman."[107] Again, though purity might define a woman, she could easily lose it through her actions. A woman's pure character could, according to Holtzclaw, be lost through not only her own actions but also the actions of those she was connected with, whether a husband or the people she interacted with at dances. Fragility and impending doom constantly stalked Holtzclaw's essential woman and her purity.

Despite this, Holtzclaw thought that feminine purity could be a powerful instrument in society if used correctly. For instance, he believed that women should vote because they would help to clean up politics—and whenever Holtzclaw talked about giving women the right to vote, he talked about it in a national context. This was not a popular opinion in 1909, when Holtzclaw published his book. Rather, many southerners lagged a generation behind their northern counterparts in supporting women's suffrage. Those who did support women's suffrage, and there was a sizeable minority who did, often did not support a national movement but instead wanted states to be allowed to write their own women's suffrage amendments. By doing so, each state would be able to decide how it would regulate voting, thus keeping the boundaries of white supremacy firmly fixed.[108] By advocating for women's political rights, including suffrage at the national level, Holtzclaw was thus ahead of many of his readers, even though he based these rights on an idyllic view of feminine moral influence.

Sometimes women made an impact simply through influencing a single person. G. W. Bouldin, an SBC missionary to Japan who grew up in Alabama, recalled his childhood and wrote of the many teachers who influenced him. Bouldin wrote that "'Miss' Ela [Clark] was the only lady teacher in the higher department of the Normal [school] when I was there. But she was a real teacher and the school would not have been the same without her." Although his recollections of the time were most likely colored by the rest of his life experiences (particularly as he related these events in the midst of the Cold War), Bouldin's memories of his childhood reflect a marked difference between the way "Miss Ela" taught and the ways the male faculty did. For example, Bouldin described how Miss Ela brought "life into any public programs" that the school produced.[109] Clearly, Bouldin respected his teacher and enjoyed the way she taught and brought enthusiasm to all that she did. However, it was equally clear that there were differences between the way Bouldin, and presumably most other children, interacted with this female teacher and the way he interacted with the male faculty.

To begin with, the children addressed their female instructor differently from how they talked to the other faculty around them. Mrs. Ela Reed Clark was called "Miss Ela" rather than Mrs. Clark. Those she supervised called her by her given name rather than her surname, as the male faculty were addressed.[110] Moreover, though the title "Miss" was less formal than the married title "Mrs.," the children, and presumably the rest of the faculty, continued to refer to the only woman faculty member by the least formal title. This, combined with the usage of her given name, suggested a lower place of honor or respect in the school's hierarchy. This was something that Bouldin subconsciously acknowledged as he noted that "Miss Ela" was not only the sole female teacher, "*but* . . . a real teacher."[111] The perceived need to describe Miss Ela as a "real teacher" suggests that Bouldin was unsure about female teachers more generally.

Baptist Women at Home

Although not all Baptist officials felt a need to differentiate between male and female faculty, virtually all believed that there were distinctly different roles for men and women in the home. One alumnus of Howard College, in East Lake, Alabama, W. L. Sanford, wrote that each woman was a "flower which only blooms to perfection in the sunny realms of home."[112] Sanford would not approve of Holtzclaw's ideas about women taking a larger role in society, as he was upset even that women had to work with their husbands in the fields to make farms turn a profit.[113] To Sanford, a woman's role in the home was as an ornament of beauty—she was too fragile to labor, and would fade, or even wilt, if the conditions at home were not right, for example, if debt to creditors and liens against the farm piled up so high as to block the sun. This pointed to a contradiction within Sanford's ideology. Clearly, he believed that white women were to make their homes a haven of virtue; yet, to do so, they would have to work hard, often in drudgery, to provide their families with a clean home. One solution to this problem for white women was to supervise women of color doing all the actual labor in their homes.[114] Yet, Sanford worried not only about how women might become ornaments of beauty and provide their families with virtuous homes but also about aspects of society that could choke out a woman's ability to "bloom." Sanford's note came in the midst of a speech on the "Credit System" in 1892. His remarks made it clear that he thought that southern Populists provided the best environment for femininity to flourish.

In the 1890s, Populists argued for an overhaul of the credit system. They argued that white men, particularly small farmers, were being emasculated through the cycles of debt and dependency offered by southern landowners at the end of the nineteenth century. While many Populists were genuinely concerned about the plight of southern farmers, some used such political language for their own benefit. The most famous example of this was North Carolina's "Pitchfork" Ben Tillman.[115] However, neither Ben Tillman nor Howard College alumnus W. L. Sanford were alone in their stands against the sharecropping system. Sanford, in his speech against crop liens, pointed out that the cycles of debt in effect throughout Alabama hurt women and families. Populists often used this refrain and warned that these systems, which helped banks and landowners keep tenant farmers in cycles of debt that were remarkably hard to break out of, injured southern women as well as men. While Populists challenged the white Bourbon Democrats for a time in the Deep South, their inability to rise above racial politics split the Southern Populist movement.[116]

While demagogues across the South used race to break up political coalitions that threatened their power, many people still believed in the idea of a feminine domestic sphere. For example, William Holtzclaw still felt that women needed to attend to their "proper" roles in the home, even though he was a progressive on issues like women's suffrage. He believed that the home was where women could best influence their immediate family, and through them, the nation.[117] This model of femininity proposed that women serve as a purifying influence on their husbands and sons but not get directly involved in the affairs of society, the home being a woman's true place.[118] Holtzclaw thoroughly imbibed the idea that the domestic realm was the proper place for women. This meant that though Holtzclaw and other SBC officials emphasized the primacy of the individual in their theology, this emphasis changed dramatically when applied to women. Rather than fostering a notion of individualism, most Baptist officials encouraged a model in which women were responsible for the moral integrity of their family—including their husbands!

For Holtzclaw, a woman's home was her "workshop, and the wares she turns out demonstrates her skill."[119] Even though he championed the idea that women should be equal in society, Holtzclaw thought the best place for women to exercise their influence was in the home. He chastised women that he thought were neglecting the home for club activities, as Holtzclaw believed that this would degrade families.[120] He even blamed wives for the sins of their husbands, saying, "Some women cook a little and scrub less, and then wonder why husband spends so much of his time at the saloon, and why he so often speaks of the 'good eating' he gets at the saloon counter."[121] Suddenly, the individual emphasis that Holtzclaw had been maintaining, and that so many other SBC officials held to, fell away when it came to women's role in the home. Rather than working for their own good, or doing what they found fulfilling, women were supposed to exercise their "sacred influence" in the home—remaining there lest their husbands became dissatisfied and started to look elsewhere, like the saloon, for comfort at the end of the day. This was a dramatic shift from the theology of individualism. Rather than the idea that "Baptists stand fundamentally on the principle that every man must give acct. of himself [only]," Holtzclaw held women responsible for their husbands' time at the saloon.[122] Because he felt that it was a woman's "duty" to "bring her influence into all these relations where it is needed," if she failed to do so, she was responsible for the transgressions that transpired in her absence.[123]

When considered alongside the fact that Holtzclaw thought women could lose their own purity through the immoral actions of their husbands, this idea—that women were responsible for their husbands lingering in saloons—clarified that Holtzclaw thought women's actions at home were responsible for their moral degradation.[124] Following this logic, if a woman did not provide for her husband's desires at home, then the husband would spend time at the saloon—the woman's fault based on her inattention to the domestic sphere. At the saloon, her husband might not only become a slave to drinking but also commit acts of impropriety—or at the very least engage in conversation with immoral people. Then, his impure thoughts and actions would threaten his wife's purity. Thus, responsibility for the entire scenario—the degradation of manliness and the fallen purity of the wife—lay at the wife's feet, because she did not take proper care of her home or provide her husband with a decent meal. For Holtzclaw, a woman's character and very identity as a pure woman depended on her upholding an understanding of the domestic world as a feminine sphere, and it was her responsibility to uphold her family's moral standing.

Holtzclaw, and others, held women to such a high standard because they believed that a woman's influence in the home, particularly that of a mother, was instrumental in a child's life and faith. Rufus Weaver talked in glowing terms about the mother's place as the first religious teacher in the home.[125] Although he believed that the father should have a prominent place in each child's spiritual formation, Weaver thought that early in life, the mother would create the first spiritual impressions in a child's mind.[126] Annie Armstrong certainly believed the same thing and even voiced her concern that the next generation of missionaries would be woefully unprepared because of how few women and mothers were involved in missions.[127] Both individuals believed that the home was where the earliest religious feelings would make themselves known and where women could best nurture their children's spirituality.

Some SBC officials took a different tack and praised women for their aptitude in the home. A. M. Jackson, a former pastor from Georgia who had to leave the ministry because of his health, wrote about his wife's wonderful ability to manage the house and all the family finances while he recovered in a sanatorium.[128] Similarly, in G. W. Bouldin's memories of his youth, women did a large amount of the daily chores around the house, and Bouldin believed that this was appropriate.[129] J. B. Moody, in his *Women in Churches*, asserted that not only was working around the house appropriate, but the home was also where women belonged: "The wife is, or should be, a help-meet, or helper; she doing the house work in her own way while the man works the fields, and milks the cows."[130] As hinted at here, Moody clearly felt that there was a hierarchy between men and women. The individual emphasis of Baptist theology began to break down, as the author assumed a hierarchy between individuals, the husband assuming headship and the wife becoming the helper. Rather than emphasizing the autonomy of the individual, these Baptist authors encouraged the notion that wives and individual women needed to subordinate their desires for the good of their families.

Officials often obscured a theology of individuality by essentializing femininity and defining it according to a few indispensable traits. Additionally, Baptist leaders talked about the responsibility that individual women had to their families: a woman was the first spiritual teacher of her children, her essential purity was to be used for the good of others, and her education was for the purpose of benefiting those around her. Thus, for many SBC officials, the idea of individuality fell aside as they attempted to instill specific visions of femininity in their congregants.

The same SBC officials had specific ideas about true manhood. While they emphasized selflessness and purity in women, most Southern Baptist preachers and pastors emphasized a version of masculinity firmly rooted in the ideal of individual masterhood. Just what this looked like, and how the idea of being a master worked in various aspects of life, is the subject of the next chapter.

3
Masterful Manhood in the Southern Baptist Convention

In the midst of the rapid urbanization in the New South period, Rev. J. B. Hawthorne worried about a declining masculinity in the pulpit. Howard College, now Samford University, in Birmingham, asked Hawthorne to speak at the fiftieth anniversary of the college, and he used the invitation as an opportunity to combat what he saw as deteriorating masculinity in Baptist pastors. Using the example of John the Baptist, Hawthorne claimed that what defined John was that he was a "man in the noblest sense, before he was a preacher. This is God's order and our disregard of it has let into the pulpit thousands of ecclesiastical parvenus, dudes, and dead-beats."[1] Hawthorne worried that there were too few SBC pastors who fulfilled their roles as men, and he cried out to his audience, "Oh, that there were more muscularity in the manhood of parvenus ministers!"[2] Hawthorne, and other SBC officials, clearly worried about the ways that many southern men expressed their manhood. They felt there needed to be fuller expressions of masculinity to keep Baptist men at the pinnacle of manliness.

Hawthorne's definition of religious masculinity fit well with a movement historians call "Muscular Christianity," which emphasized masculine religion.[3] This movement fought against the notion that religion was an inherently feminine ideal or that being religious somehow emasculated men. However, this movement had different emphases. The northern blend of Muscular Christianity worried obsessively about the male body.[4] In contrast, in the South the language of mastery and the use of hyper-masculine martial imagery defined the push for a more masculine religiosity. Additionally, whereas northern proponents of Muscular Christianity attempted to fit their theology into conceptions of gender, Southern Baptists generally tried to define their ideas of gender through theology. This does not mean that Baptist preachers did not care about gendered constructs; they were simply more concerned about Christian orthodoxy than were many of their northeastern mainline counterparts.[5] Nonetheless, SBC officials worried about the state of manhood in their parishioners and their clerical brethren. Judging from Hawthorne's remarks about "ecclesiastical parvenus, dudes, and dead-beats," he clearly felt that there was something wrong with preachers who were not athletic, reliable men. Hawthorne went so far as to suggest that those who were not physically powerful were not true men.

Popular ideas of white southern manhood intertwined with the idea that white men should be physically powerful and masterful. Indeed, Baptist theology's emphasis on the individual manifested clearly in the notion of masterful Christian men, and these concepts worked as markers of a racially exclusive masculinity.[6] While the concept of mastery did not imply control over slaves after the American Civil War, it did have a highly racialized component. In the New South, mastery could be applied only to whites. This was especially evident when white southern men racialized conceptions of manhood through violent displays of power at the expense of African Americans. Such demonstrations of violence, particularly those evidenced in spectacle lynching, highlighted the mastery of white men over black bodies, over white women (as white men declared themselves the protectors of female purity), and over the communities these men proclaimed themselves to be the righteous arbiters of justice.[7]

The concept of mastery also denoted a level of independence from outside influences. Thus, through various expressions of mastery—racial, personal, domestic, and financial—SBC men could declare their manliness by publicly demonstrating the control they had over the different aspects of their lives.

Baptist Manhood

For writer, pastor, and seminary professor William Owen Carver, seeing another pious and godly man marked an opportunity to praise God in his diary and note that he had prayed that the other man's preaching would be filled with the Holy Spirit.[8] This expression of masculinity in one man did not automatically threaten other men. Baptist manliness was not a contest where everyone competed and only one man won. This change in the conceptions of manhood hailing from the antebellum honor-driven society, so carefully documented by historian Bertram Wyatt-Brown, reflected larger evolutions in the culture of honor in the South.[9] While the South still retained many elements of the honor culture, the supreme emphasis on individual honor was evolving.[10] Southern Baptist officials at the fin de siècle

Figure 2. Southern Baptist leaders gathered in St. Louis for a 1912 conference of Evangelical Field Workers. The back of the photograph reads, "Top Row (Left to Right): Van Ness, Gentry, Hudgins, Joseph Watts. Second Row: Hyman, Rounds, Andrews, L. O. Leavell, C. S. Leavell, F. H. Leavell, L. P. Leavell. Third Row: Strickland, Byrd, Price, Moseley, Middleton, Barnes, Lee, Flake. Bottom Row: Burroughs, Moore, Spilman, Dr. Frost, Foster, Eutzmingen." Courtesy of Landrum Leavell Collection, Southern Baptist Historical Library and Archives, Nashville, Tennessee.

wanted to instill a new idea of manliness in their congregants, one in which an individual's masculinity did not automatically threaten others in the group. Indeed, some Baptist preachers tried to argue that manhood could be a collaborative process in which individual men helped each other. Clay Hudson, a pastor from Decatur, Alabama, wrote about this idea to his friend and mentor, I. J. Van Ness. Hudson remarked that a yearly pastors' conference in Nashville, Tennessee, was of "inestimable value" and helped him become "a better man and a better preacher of the New Testament for having known [those] brethren."[11] Hudson acknowledged the link between becoming a better man and a better pastor, and he believed that both happened because he participated in the meeting. Thus, according to Hudson, manliness, collaboration, and piety bloomed together.

Sometimes men attempted to make physical demonstrations of their piety. Such was the case at a conference of Baptist "Field Workers" who assembled in 1913.[12] In the picture they took together, a sign noting an evangelistic conference in the background signaled their shared belief that Jesus was the only way to be reconciled to God. Yet even as they demonstrated their shared values, many also expressed different aspects of masculinity. In looking at the picture, it is evident that this group of well-dressed men probably did not work with their hands. The condition of their clothes also suggested that they had mastered their financial conditions, even if the varying styles of shirt collars demonstrated a difference in desire to keep up with current clothing fashions. Moreover, almost all the men demonstrated through their body language a sense of ownership over the space around them. With a very few exceptions, most notably the gentlemen third from the right in the front row holding an umbrella, all the men spread themselves out to take up the most space possible on the steps where they were seated. They did not close their legs to make room for each other to take the photograph. Instead, they spread out in an attempt to stake out their own space and declare their mastery over that space with their bodies (see figure 2).

Masterful Manhood

Mastery, whether demonstrated in the body language of a group of pastors or in the explicit claims made in sermons, constituted the defining characteristic of Baptist manhood for many SBC leaders. However, that does not mean that control over other people was the only way most preachers defined mastery. Control over sinful tendencies, strength of character, and the ability to govern or deal with the people around them also gave Baptist men opportunities to demonstrate their mastery.

In one sermon to young men, Kentucky pastor and publisher T. T. Eaton talked about the need to live pure lives so that the men in his audience might have the power of God's righteousness. He compared Christians who lived in sin to a "stunted, misshapen dwarf" who, though pure in God's eyes through Jesus's work, could not accomplish what a "man in the full glory of mature manhood" might.[13] Eaton felt that living a pure life was what young men needed in order to have a strong character, and he encouraged them to "give to God's service the strength and vigor of [their] prime."[14] Throughout this sermon, Eaton assumed that the young men in his audience lived their lives as individuals before God. Yet, unlike many Baptist messages to southern white women, his encouragement to the young men to live pure lives before God did not include an exhortation to purify society, to work together for the betterment of others, or even to go out and evangelize to their neighbors. Men lived for their own benefit. Eaton linked individualistic theology to these young men's strength and power.

Eaton went so far as to tell his parishioners that the use of their strength was essential to manliness. In a separate sermon, he stated, "There can be no manhood without strength and courage."[15] Eaton believed there was an intimate connection between strength and manliness—they were so intertwined that one could not occur without the other. He told his listeners that they must be "strong enough to assert [their] masterhood over [their] passions and evil tendencies . . . to labour with manhood's might for this Saviour who died for you."[16] Yet even as he encouraged young men to use their strength, he recognized that sin had a powerful tug on their hearts and that they would need supernatural help in their battle to remain pure. Eaton's message to young men about living pure lives had sexual connotations. He may have been chiding his male parishioners for their inability to conquer sexual sins and challenging them to look beyond themselves as they battled sexual urges. In fact, Eaton related their ability to master sin to their reliance on Jesus. While unusual in the broader context of the SBC, this was not the only time that Eaton suggested that Baptist men should look outside of their own resources to obtain mastery over the forces of evil.

In a separate sermon first preached in 1883, Eaton turned to martial imagery and exhorted his parishioners to look to the Holy Spirit, who was "ever ready to gird us with his own strength in our battle with our besetting sins" but was disappointed that many people (and he included himself in this) did not turn to the Holy Spirit.[17] This lack of reliance on the Holy Ghost left "many weak and sickly ones in Christ's army where all might be strong and valiant."[18] Again, Eaton made the connection between leading a sinless life and strength, adding that these young men were involved in a spiritual battle against the forces of darkness. The language Eaton used suggested that he worried about the sexual lives of his parishioners. He talked about the "besetting sins" of "weak and sickly ones" in the army of God. During the late nineteenth and the early twentieth centuries, many people believed that each man had only a set amount of energy, and that all sexual experiences, and particularly masturbatory ones, quickly drained that vital energy, sapped a man's strength, and left him sick and weak.[19] The dissipating tendencies of misplaced sexuality was not just a matter of spiritual discipline in Eaton's thought. Rather, it defined part of mastery over sinful tendencies, and thus masculinity.

T. T. Eaton summed up the feelings of many SBC officials when he tried in one sermon to convince his congregants of the importance of mastery:

> There is something grand in manhood, something which bears indeed the image of the Creator. There is no high quality which it does not contain, but chief and greatest and crowning of all is master-

> hood, its regal right of ruling. As God is sovereign in heaven—so he has placed man sovereign upon earth—bound by his allegiance to the King of kings, but under that, supreme ruler. It is a God like power—this masterhood conferred upon man.... It is a duty—this gift of ruling which he is but a coward who endeavours to evade.... Man must master his own passions and appetites or he sinks from his high place as ruler into the vilest of slaves. A king who cannot govern himself is but a mockery of royalty, and a man surrenders his manhood and takes his place among the brutes who does not govern with strong hand his lower nature.... *There is no manhood without masterhood.*[20]

Eaton's parishioners needed no help in recognizing the importance of self-control and mastery for manliness in their pastor's mind. Without mastery, Eaton claimed, it was impossible to define true manliness. Moreover, God gave mastery to males, which meant that men, true men, were closer to being the image of God on earth than were their female counterparts. Eaton believed men should be the supreme rulers of their domain—essentially little gods among their families and dependents. Eaton connected mastery to each man's role as an individual. There could not be two rulers in a relationship, and Eaton made it clear that those who gave up this rule gave up their manhood, becoming mere brutes—a word laced with derogatory racial meaning—instead.

The language of mastery clearly had racial overtones each time Eaton preached this sermon (1876, 1885, 1893, and 1900). Eaton reinforced those ideas when he talked about those who could not master their own "passions and appetites" and sunk from the place of master to the role of the "vilest of slaves." His parishioners would certainly have understood the racial implications. Mastery meant white racial privilege, while slavery, even when mentioned in this spiritual sense, referred to the status of African Americans prior to the American Civil War. Even after the Civil War, many white planters still viewed themselves as masters, though they did not have slaves.[21] Beyond this fact, simply using the term "brutes" could have a double meaning, referring either to animals or to the many African American freedmen whom so many whites still believed made up a lower order of humanity. The double meaning of the term hinted at the idea that many whites believed African Americans had no self-control—particularly on matters of sexuality. In this view, every black man was a potential rapist.

For white people in the Southern Baptist Convention who believed that mastery was an essential part of manliness, the thought that African Americans could not control their own sexuality immediately excluded black men from the ranks of manhood. Unfortunately, the idea that African Americans constituted a lower level of humanity was not limited to the New South. During this period, whites across the nation used such language to talk about people of color.[22] Thus, Eaton's remarks on mastery had racial and gendered implications. He implied that all men who did not practice self-control might lose their racial privilege as well as their manhood. Moreover, because of the distinct racial implications of masterhood, the statement "there is no manhood without masterhood" necessarily excluded black men from true masterful manhood, as Eaton defined it.

The all-important idea of masterful manhood sometimes manifested in the props used in personal photographic portraits. For example, in 1890, Landrum Leavell's parents paid to have a photo made of their son in his first pair of "long trousers"[23] (see figure 3). In the picture, a young Leavell appears awkward and unsure of himself, yet proud nonetheless. He faces the camera with a steady gaze, weight slightly forward as though walking and mastering the space around him; but he also gently leans to the viewer's right on the chair as though he is not sure whether to step forward or stay where he is. The jacket that young Leavell wore was a little too short in the arms and it pinched his shoulders, suggesting that it was either a hand-me-down from an older brother (there were nine brothers in his family) or a coat from his own wardrobe that he was growing out of. The watch fob threaded through his waistcoat suggests a level of sophistication and age that Leavell's childish face decries. It also suggests that Leavell was a master of his time and aware of the requirements of his role as a man. Additionally, it signals Leavell's status as a member of middle- or even upper-class society in Mississippi. Whatever else may be said about the picture, it commemorates the moment a boy received his first pair of long trousers as his introduction to manhood; indeed the very fact that his parents took him to a photographer in 1890 showed how momentous the occasion was.[24] Although he certainly retained elements of boyhood, and some of the things he wore for the picture seem almost silly, they all are part of a carefully planned portrait designed to demonstrate his budding masculinity. Even the fact that this was a solo portrait suggests that the young Leavell was the master of his own space and thus a man.

While Landrum Leavell's parents tried to show that their son in his new long trousers was a lord of time and space, other Southern Baptists hoped merely to bring some larger measure of control into their own lives. For example, in his diary, William Owen Carver resolved at the beginning of the year 1897 to "be a better man" and "gain more control of my life, i.e. to give myself more fully up to the control of God in the Holy

Figure 3. The Leavells paid to have a photographer mark their son's transition from boyhood to manhood. Courtesy of Landrum Leavell Collection, Southern Baptist Historical Library and Archives, Nashville, Tennessee.

Spirit."[25] Carver used his own life to connect the ideas of self-control, or self-mastery, with the hope of becoming a better man. Yet he realized that he could not simply will himself to have more self-control and so hoped that he could give himself more and more to the Holy Spirit, who would enable Carver to gain mastery over his desires. This was an interesting concept—the idea of gaining more self-control by giving up control of oneself to God. Carver believed that by doing so, the divine would further define his life and actions, enabling Carver to be a better man and a stronger leader of his church.

As suggested in his diary entry, Carver felt his self-mastery connected intimately with his religion. He told his parishioners, "One aim and test of our religion is contentment—the balanced view of life and its relations that gives the unperturbed spirit—the life of mastery of which Jesus is the ideal."[26] Again, an individual model defined this ideal of manhood and could be achieved only by an individual. Neither community nor family could produce contentment. Instead, contentment was a state of an individual's heart. Moreover, Jesus provided the ultimate example in Christianity. Even this choice of an example suggested an individualistic manhood. Carver did not say that the Apostles modeled contentment or that

Israel or the early church did; eschewing these different types of communities, he focused on a single person. In Carver's preaching to his congregation, the idea of the individual defined his ideal of masterful manhood.

Along with providing his ultimate example of masterful manhood, Carver talked about the need in the Southern Baptist Convention for men who were filled with the spirits of love, power, and a sober-mind.[27] Here again, Carver laid out very clearly for his parishioners his vision of the connection between individuals and their self-mastery. Carver believed that the SBC needed men who could control their emotions and desires in order to serve the denomination.

Many young, white southern men, bucking ideas of pious self-control, expected to have sexual dalliances before marriage. William Wilkes, in his memoir of growing up in the town of Josie, Alabama, recalled that "every youth was expected to 'sow his wild oats' before being accounted a man" in the 1880s and 1890s.[28] Indeed, throughout the South, ideas that men should have a wild, rough-and-tumble youth held great currency.[29] Wilkes fully imbibed these ideas but did not know how to earn his manhood. He disliked the taste of whiskey, had no idea how to play cards or gamble, and was too afraid of disease to cavort with the local prostitutes, so eventually Wilkes decided that he would attend dances. Wilkes claimed that he was never very good and frequently stepped on his partner's feet. Still, after attending a few, he gleefully exclaimed, "I had finally and fully become a man."[30]

Wilkes's memory of dancing provided just one example of the vast differences between the ideas of masculinity and femininity for many Baptist officials during the turn of the century. While through the sins of their husbands women might lose their claim to purity, effectively ending their identity as "lad[ies]," men, though encouraged to remain chaste by church officials, were half expected to "sow their wild oats." Indeed, the community questioned their manhood until they did so. Men had to lose their purity to be accounted true men, while women could only be ladies by retaining it.

Appropriate Affection

Many SBC preachers also wanted their clerical brethren to know the power of Christian love in the midst of their manly mastery and showed affection for one another in private correspondence, though this virtually always happened between men in unequal relationships. For example, in 1909, when Charles Daniel heard that his old seminary professor, E. C. Dargan, would be moving nearby, Daniel penned a letter in which he professed his feelings for his mentor, saying, "There may be some of the boys who love you more than I, but I do not believe it."[31] It was not unusual for Dargan's former students to sign their letters "Tenderly";[32] they wanted to acknowledge their care and affection for their former professor within the mentor/mentee relationship. These private signs of love and affection between men did not diminish their manhood or masculinity. Nor were such expressions entirely unique to Dargan and his friends. I. J. Van Ness received letters from other pastors signed "Yours with Love" and was even told by one friend, Martin Ball of Mississippi, "I do love you so much for your work's sake, as well as your own personal, lovable character."[33]

These words of love and care for one another recognized the strong homosocial bonds men created.[34] Such admissions of emotion did not threaten but rather strengthened their bonds. Additionally, these New South pastors were not aware of the twentieth- and twenty-first century construct regarding gay, straight, and bisexual divisions of sexual orientation and viewed such homosocial affection as entirely asexual love.[35]

Some pastors even celebrated such manly affection in sermons. E. C. Dargan did so in one address about the biblical figures Elijah and Elisha. Dargan recounted Elijah's role as mentor and that, when the time came for Elijah to be taken to heaven, he appointed Elisha as his successor. Dargan believed that Elisha, "the affectionate yet grieving follower," cried after his "beloved master."[36] Dargan suggested that such expressions were the appropriate results, and expressions, of powerful masculine bonds between a teacher and a beloved student.[37]

Sometimes expressions of affection focused on physical attributes as they related to personal character. For example, when Albert Cummings wrote his friend E. C. Dargan to congratulate him on becoming the head of Mercer's administration, Cummings warned that Dargan was now working in a very large field. Nevertheless Cummings believed that Dargan's "shoulders [were] broad and fully equal to the task."[38] While Cummings relied on this physical analogue, he did not actually mean that Dargan's shoulders had to be broad in order to become the head of Mercer University. Instead, he was referring to Dargan's strength of character and his ability to master any large task set before him—in a word, he affirmed that Dargan's manhood was sufficient to complete the task before him.

The emphasis on mastery and individuality in Cummings's theology led him to believe not that Dargan's identity would be subsumed by those he benefitted but that Dargan's leadership would strengthen his standing as an individual. Thus, his ability to conquer projects as an individual allowed him to set the agenda for the new administration. This important point marked a clear difference in the ways Southern Baptist officials understood individuality for men and for women.

W. J. Bradley wrote E. C. Dargan in 1913 to commend him for his individual command of the meeting of the Southern Baptist Convention in St. Louis. That year, the SBC took the step to form a Social Service Commission. The Social Service Commission was tasked with combating "whiskey traffic," "white slave traffic, and child labor," among other things.[39] Whatever it was that so impressed Bradley, he wrote to Dargan, "I have heard from several [who] say that you have the best control of a large body of people that they have ever witnessed. It certainly lies in brains and not in bulk of body, tho I am just guessing at your physical strength."[40] Bradley admired Dargan's power to command a large group of people merely with the force of his presence. Bradley believed Dargan's mastery of this group of people spoke volumes about his masculinity and how he could use his powerful manly attributes to lead. Bradley's theological understanding of individuality led him to believe that Dargan's ability to control the entire meeting of the Southern Baptist Convention was a powerful sign of manhood.

In addition to the homosocial love mentioned above, pastors demonstrated love for their sweethearts, spouses, and children in a number of different ways. William Carver's diary allows a view into all of these. In 1896, he courted a young woman named Alice and talked about treasuring the letters that he received from her.[41] Eventually, the two were married, and Carver rejoiced when they had a "dear little daughter" named Ruth, whom he loved deeply.[42] While these examples come from Carver's diary, it is clear that such expressions of love and care did not threaten his sense of manliness. Rather, they represented appropriate ways of expressing his manhood as he sought to rear his daughter in Christian faith.

Sometimes men tried so hard to love and get love from their wives and sweethearts that they did things that might otherwise imperil their own masculinity. William Wilkes recorded such a situation in his childhood hometown, Josie, Alabama. He recounted that some of his "earliest memories [were] of beards galore. Every he-man wore one." As Wilkes recalled it, beards demonstrated masculinity during his youth, as every "*he-man* wore one."[43] Indeed, white men throughout the United States wore a wide variety of facial hair throughout the middle and end of the nineteenth century. Despite the fashion of the day, Wilkes believed this expression of masculinity came into conflict with "a growing allergy and consequent resistance of sweethearts and wives to the prickling and tickling sensations experienced in the act of osculation [kissing]."[44] Needless to say, men shaved off their beards and kept on kissing. Thus, though men with unshaved boyish faces may initially have been looked down upon, clean-shaven faces soon won out in Josie, Alabama. Thus, though men may have worried that they were no longer expressing their masculinity, the beard interfered with a much more potent expression of their manhood—their sexuality.

The sexual side of masculinity hinted at other traits that Baptist officials believed expressed manliness—power and strength. These elements made up part of the larger culture's understandings of white southern manhood. Throughout the South at the turn of the century, racialized violence enforced the notion that only white men had the authority to exercise power in society. Indeed, the church leaders studied in this work never explicitly denounced the racial violence in the region that some white southerners used to demonstrate their power over African Americans. Specifically, they never denounced lynching; nor did they suggest, as Ida B. Wells and northern antilynching groups did, that racialized violence was a sign that whites had lost their emotional mastery.[45]

Dignified Manhood

One of the most common ways that many clergy demonstrated their mastery was through their mastery over their own emotions and composure—in other words, their ability to remain dignified at all times. This does not mean that these men remained cold and aloof. Rather, many Baptists felt that there was a specific set of emotions that could be appropriately displayed while retaining one's dignity.

One of the strongest emotional responses that SBC leaders praised as dignified was joy. Author, pastor, and eventual president of Mercer University, Rufus Weaver, wrote about the joy a father would feel whenever his child accepted Christ into her heart and told readers that the entire cosmos rejoiced as well.[46] Elsewhere, T. T. Eaton also mentioned how joy, mixed with love, might be an expression of manly sentiment. In one sermon, he told his congregants to think of the homecoming of a loved one after a long journey: "How demonstrative is our joy in the first meeting—the eyes fill, the voice trembles, the face flushes. We hover around them, we cannot compose ourselves to any occupation, we can only look and talk and rejoice."[47] Eaton believed that joy was an emotion that men might lose themselves to without jeopardizing their manliness. Indeed, this was the one time an SBC pastor seemed to say that it might be manly to lose the mastery over something—here, an expression of joy. However, Eaton's positive remark—that one might not be able to maintain composure, because of emotion—stood in stark contrast to almost every other comment on self-control and mastery that other Baptists, and even Eaton himself, made.

Many SBC pastors were concerned that their parishioners retained an appropriately dignified manhood, not just indiscriminate masculinity. At the baccalaureate of the fiftieth anniversary of Howard College in East Lake, Alabama, Professor D. G. Lyon talked about the differences he perceived between manhood and masculinity. He told the young men about to graduate that their college education should have strengthened their will "so that it may resist all unworthy impulses and stand firm in all that pertains to manliness and nobility of character."[48] Additionally, Lyon advised the young men in his audience that they should leave any profession that relied on strength alone to men "whose only capital is their brawn," and instead choose a career that would enhance character, as a "man's character is all that he really has."[49] He clearly linked the elite ideas of character with manhood in this address. Lyon wanted his audience members to focus on their character as they moved into the fullness of their manhood and left their education behind them.

Lyon's advice suggested that he believed that the careers of the working class might imperil one's character. Certainly, this demonstrated Lyon's own class biases, and though he tried to dismiss this implication by saying that he merely thought that the expensive training one received at Howard could be put to "better account," Lyon clearly wanted his listeners to improve their class status.[50] Nonetheless, Lyon insisted that he did not mean that the use of one's strength might imperil masculinity, but rather that the indiscriminate use of brawn could imperil character and manhood. Thus, Lyon connected character to manhood, not necessarily masculinity. He tried to convince his audience of the ways that manhood (or manliness) intertwined with character and the strength of one's will to "resist all unworthy impulses." Seemingly then, the ability to resist such desires and impulses, to gain mastery over them, marked the transition into manhood.

Sometimes Baptist officials combined self-mastery and the ability to resist shameful desires with dignity and the ability to remain composed; thus failing to maintain one's composure could be inappropriate. William Carver wrote in his diary entry for December 27, 1893, that he attended church services where a friend, Posey Grant, preached the sermon. Carver recorded that even though Grant had "some affection and some embarrassment. The sermon was good."[51] Thus, though the sermon ended well,

Carver seemed to feel that Posey demonstrated too much emotion during the sermon, so much so that there was "some embarrassment." This probably meant that Grant could not master his feelings while preaching. Thus, while some emotion could be viewed as an appropriate expression of manhood, being too emotional could be a detriment in the perception of one's masculinity. The trick was in balancing these two sides. Baptist men were not to be severe stoics, neither rejoicing nor mourning, yet they were always supposed to have mastery over their emotions.

In the American South at the turn of the century, many white southerners believed that displays of emotion undercut the ideals of self-control, dignity, and manhood—except in cases of competition, anger, and violence. Yet, at the 1893 Baptist Congress held in Augusta, Georgia, Rev. John Johnson had no such reservations as he talked about the necessity of emotionalism in religion. Johnson believed that the two theological traditions that had seen the most growth in the South at the turn of the century, the Methodists and the Baptists, had success in converting people because of their appeal to the heart.[52] Moreover, Johnson felt, "There is no religion without Christ; and there is no Christ without emotion."[53] Johnson did not deprecate Methodists or Baptists because of their appeal to emotions; nor did he say that Christ was not manly because he was connected to emotion. Rather, Johnson linked the emotional side of religion with Jesus Christ who was, for many, the ultimate example of manhood. Johnson posited that religion gave men an appropriate way of expressing emotion in a culture that held a stoic ideal of manliness. Johnson's link of emotion with Jesus removed the pejorative idea of religion as a haven for emotional women and clerics so prevalent at the time.[54] Instead, Johnson used the link positively to relate manly emotion to the example of the masculine Jesus. Having a powerful emotional reaction to a sermon about Jesus's death would not have been detrimental to a man's masculinity in Johnson's eyes. As long as there was a connection to Jesus, emotion was perfectly acceptable.[55]

Mississippi minister Fernando McConnell demonstrated this link between emotion and Jesus in his 1902 sermon preached at the meeting of the Southern Baptist Convention. McConnell talked about the necessity that Christ, the only one who was wholly God and wholly man, die to reconcile humanity to God through his willing sacrifice and noted that this was not an easy thing for Jesus to do. It caused Jesus to turn his "face, saddened and tearful . . . towards Calvary."[56] The fact that Jesus willingly gave himself for others made him the ultimate example of manliness for many

SBC pastors; yet McConnell pointed out that even the supreme example of manliness broke down in tears and was "grief stricken."[57] In his mind, grief and sorrow could be entirely appropriate manly emotions.

Independent Manhood

Because Southern Baptist preachers defined manliness through ideas of dignity and mastery, they believed that men needed to be independent actors, living free from the control of others. What worried many pastors, then, were the dangers that they believed threatened this independence. The greatest danger they perceived was the danger of the bottle, and Baptist leaders frequently spoke out against the liquor trade and attempted to bring church discipline against church members who drank or whose businesses sold alcohol.[58] As a warning to his own parishioners, T. T. Eaton described the fate of a pastor whose doctor prescribed a dram of whiskey every day to cure a cough. According to Eaton, the pastor soon fell into the clutches of alcoholism and went to a "drunkard's grave."[59] Similarly, William Holtzclaw warned that the saloon produced fathers who were "slave[s] to the drink habit."[60] Even William Wilkes's otherwise light and playful memoir of growing up in small-town Alabama turned dark when he talked about the men at a local church sneaking off to the woods and staggering back after a few drinks.[61] For all these men, drinking and drunkenness meant that a man lost his mastery. Whether a man simply lost control of his own faculties for a time, or actually lost the ability to control his urges and became a "slave to the drink habit" (thus giving up part of his white racial privilege in making himself a slave in the eyes of those around him), the point was the same—drinking stripped a man of his masterhood. These SBC officials viewed alcoholic beverages not as something that could be enjoyed in moderation but as potential threats to manhood as it threatened self-mastery.[62]

There were also things that could enhance and strengthen an individual's manhood. William Owen Carver told his congregants that there were "Makers of Leaders"; among these, Carver mentioned the Holy Spirit, the denominational seminary, and the Baptist colleges scattered about the South.[63] Some of these schools felt that their role was to train boys into men. *The Fiftieth Anniversary Catalogue of Howard College* made a special point of highlighting the moral training that the young men who attended would receive, adding that anyone who wished to stay at Howard must prove himself both a gentlemen and a scholar.[64] To aid in this endeavor, the college governed its students by a series of rules and regulations designed to "inculcate manly virtue, preserve order, [and] require sobriety and morality."[65] Such rules, along with the requirement that each student join Howard's Cadet Corps, helped students learn to master their bodies, minds, and emotions.

Southern Baptist officials worried about various elements that threatened to undermine mastery and so emphasized the training available at places like Howard College. One speaker at Howard College's Fiftieth Anniversary celebration, W. L. Sanford, believed that the credit and crop-lien system appearing throughout the South took away "independence, ambition, and manhood" by constantly driving farmers deeper into debt.[66] The language of financial independence marked manhood for many Southern men, and so Sanford's warnings were not merely about keeping track of one's financial well-being. Rather, they warned about the all-too-easy ways in which a man could lose his independence and financial self-mastery.[67] Essentially, Sanford believed that if a white man did not master his own money, he became beholden to another and was no longer his own master. He had instead become dependent, and thus emasculated.

The language of manly independence was important during the late nineteenth century.[68] The idea of dependence could be used as a threat that white men, particularly small farmers, were being emasculated. One of the southern politicians who most successfully connected the idea of the independent farmer with white southern manhood was "Pitchfork" Ben Tillman, of North Carolina. Tillman's biographer Stephen Kantrowitz demonstrates time and again how Tillman used the language of independence to his political advantage. He did so by connecting gendered imagery with a version of violent white supremacy that glorified the myth of the white yeoman farmer.[69]

Neither Ben Tillman nor Howard College alumnus W. L. Sanford were alone in connecting the ideas of independence, manhood, and mastery. Sanford's speech against the emasculating lien and sharecropping systems came during the heyday of the Southern Populist movement. The Populist movement, in the early 1890s, attempted to reform the agrarian economic system in the South, in particular the sharecropping and the crop-lien systems. Populists warned that these systems, which helped banks and landowners keep tenant farmers in cycles of debt, emasculated the men who actually worked in the fields by forcing them to depend on other people. This dependence marked a loss of self-mastery and manhood. Ultimately, however, the inability to rise above racial politics split the Southern Populist movement.[70]

Many SBC officials believed that self-mastery epitomized the idea of a powerful masculinity and formed the foundation for their ideas of proper manhood. It mixed the Baptist emphasis on individualism with ideas of race and gender, forming a particular type of masculinity. With amazing consistency, white pastors and preachers in the SBC hoped to convince their congregations of the connections between a theology of mastery and constructions of white manhood.

While the masterful, white, Christian male was in control of his emotions, this did not preclude the use of violence. However, both Baptist clergy and laity could read in their Bibles that Jesus told his followers to turn the other cheek and leave vengeance to God, leaving a gap between Baptist religious teachings and the violent predilections of the culture of the New South, with its enforcement of white supremacy. Many SBC pastors reconciled the muscular warrior image, so popular in the South at the turn of the century, with a self-controlled Christian manhood by talking about battling the forces of evil and conquering the world for Christ.[71] The warrior image and southern Christianity fit together in the image of the conquering church.

The Conquering Baptist Church

Although SBC officials could not look to the American Civil War, still fresh in the mind of many people in the South at the fin de siècle, for examples of a victorious, conquering army, they nonetheless attempted to forge an image of the conquering Christian Church. A. J. Dickinson, an Alabamian pastor, declared furiously, "I belong to the church military, not the church millinery."[72] Clearly, he felt that the idea of a powerful, martial church was something to be proud of.

Throughout numerous addresses and sermons, SBC pastors drew their parishioners' attention to the idea that they fought a spiritual battle. As church leaders, many SBC officials believed that they were not only foot soldiers but, as pastors, officers of Jesus's army.[73] Moreover, as officers in the midst of spiritual warfare, T. T. Eaton felt that it was their duty to "battle against besetting sins" with the strength of the Holy Spirit.[74] Thus, the one who obeyed "all rightful authority [was] the noble man, the true soldier, the earnest Christian."[75] Eaton connected obedience, manliness, and service in Christ's army, and suggested that without one, the other two would not hold together, just as an army would lose a battle if the orders of their commander were not obeyed.

The theme of masculine spiritual warfare echoed in sermons at the annual meetings of the Southern Baptist Convention, where the annual address might focus on the victorious army of Christ, as in J. B. Gambrell's sermon "Call to Universal Conquest of the World." Gambrell told those gathered before him that to "divide and conquer is the doctrine of the New Testament."[76] He warned that without churches dividing themselves and going out into the world to evangelize, "We shall never conquer the world."[77] Other pastors clarified that this division did not mean schism but merely a different order of attack.[78] Sometimes even the title of a preacher's sermon hinted that he thought of the world as a spiritual battleground. Rufus Weaver, for example, preached multiple sermons titled "The Conquest of a World" and "The Conquering Christ."[79]

Many SBC officials also worried about losing a war—one with eternal consequences. Although spiritual in nature, these pastors warned their parishioners that the battles waged were very real indeed. T. T. Eaton warned his congregants that they needed to be ready, as the spiritual foes they battled against were not like little children who could be frightened but were great warriors who must be resisted.[80] Interestingly, this meant that those who overcame their spiritual enemies (rarely personified and often presented as besetting sins) proved their manliness through the defeat of these "great warriors." Spiritual warfare thus offered one way for men who had not taken to the battlefield during the American Civil War to demonstrate true manhood. Additionally, the language that these Southern Baptists used highlighted the individual nature of their spiritual fight. They did not fight the army of the devil. Instead, they fought against great warriors, which in turn implied that they were warriors. Eaton did characterize SBC pastors as officers in Jesus's army, but his emphasis was on the fact that they were officers, not that they were working as a group toward a common goal. Thus, even when the martial language of spiritual warfare was used, the Baptist emphasis on individual manliness shone through.

Whether it was through a focus on femininity or manliness, officials in the Southern Baptist Convention connected in unique ways their theological ideas with the construction of gender. Exactly what individuality meant, and how church leaders applied it, looked vastly different for men and women; yet for these pastors, their theology defined gender. As they preached, they often reduced women's individuality to essential traits to be used in service of their families, in the process all but nullifying their individual identities. In contrast, Baptist leaders told men that they should express their masculinity through power and affection, all the while remaining masters of their faculties and marching forth into the world carrying the message of individual salvation for all.

4
The Manly Soldiers of Methodism

Gentle shepherd or conquering crusader: Many officials in the Methodist Episcopal Church, South relied on these two interpretations of Jesus to define manliness. Many ministers saw Jesus as a warrior battling the forces of Satan and used this model to base their paradigm of masculinity on a Christian soldier conquering the world for Christ. On the one hand, it allowed officials to tell their parishioners about individual Christians who heroically battled sin. On the other, this model provided space for Methodist men to view themselves as part of a larger story of the grand army of the Lord.

Sometimes denominational leaders reinforced this communal image through another interpretation of Jesus's example—that of Jesus as a tender shepherd caring for his followers. Following this model, preachers and pastors tried to persuade Methodist men to demonstrate manly affection in order to woo others to Jesus. For many MECS leaders, this type of manly affection was best displayed within the confines of family life. Scholars note that different types of masculinity prevail in different spaces; sometimes the public/private distinction also denoted differences between sacred and profane interpretations of manhood.[1] However, despite what previous historians have suggested, MECS officials throughout the South consciously connected disparate models of manliness to their religious ideals.

Although officials displayed different types of masculinity in their private and public lives, Methodist leaders based each vision of manhood (Christian soldier or affectionate head of the house) on sacred ideals. Officials in the MECS consistently told their congregants that every aspect of their lives was sacred. Thus, whether preachers courted or conquered hearts, officials infused understandings of manliness with religious meaning.

Onward Methodist Soldiers

Methodist preachers frequently used the analogue of the Christian soldier in their writings. They stressed that godly men led the charge against sin and the devil. Many pastors repeatedly tried to warn their parishioners about the dangerous pitfalls and traps of secular recreation. For example, in 1887, MECS evangelist Sam Jones published a sermon in which he talked about how seemingly innocuous it was to let children play card games in their youth; yet, Jones warned, this seeming innocence would only encourage children to become profligate gamblers later in life.[2] In similar fashion, the 1902 edition of the MECS book of standards, *The Doctrines and Discipline of the Methodist Episcopal Church, South*, continued a decade-long tradition of including an "Address on Worldly Amusements" in its appendix. In this address, the bishops of the denomination argued that pastimes such as theater going, card playing, racetrack attendance, and modern dance corrupted true worship and must be fought because of the "peril which they bring to the souls of men." The bishops worried that these pastimes, in their "multiplied and insidious forms [were] a source of perpetual temptation and damage."[3] As such, these weapons of evil kept people from the church. One pastor told his parishioners that dancing was such a serious threat to the people of God that those who tolerated it would stand before God with their "skirts bloody with the blood of your children and friends" who lost their faith through such amusements.[4] These pastors clearly believed that true followers of Christ needed to gird their loins and fight as soldiers against such insidious threats.

Such martial language also appeared at interdenominational gatherings, such as the 1899 ecumenical International Sunday School Convention. The program schedule for the gathering listed not only the various events of the day but also, at the top of each page, inspiring quotes and relevant passages from Scripture. One of the quotes reminded attendees, "The church is not organized for comfort but for conquest."[5] The quote made clear that participants should remember that Sunday School provided another line of attack from which to conquer the world for Christ.

Although the conference program never attributed the quote, it is entirely possible that it was a reaction against the idea that religion somehow "feminized" adherents, or that Christianity was a religion for women, not active and aggressive men.[6] The timing of the quote may also have added to the perception that the church needed militancy. Only a few months earlier, the US Senate had ratified the treaty ending the Spanish-American

War, and there was still fighting going on in the Philippines.[7] Although the delegates to the International Sunday School Convention probably were not involved in the fighting themselves, they could still appropriate a martial image by encouraging a militant vision of Christianity.

As hinted at by the International Sunday School Convention, the "Church Militant" had long been a term used to signify the spiritual warfare Christians believed they were engaged in. Christian officials used this term several centuries before the founding of the MECS. For instance, in 1662, the Church of England's *Book of Common Prayer* instructed priests to make the sign of the cross over a newly baptized infants and pray that the child would not be afraid to "manfully fight under his Banner, against sin, the world, the devil, continue Christs [*sic*] faithful souldier, and servant unto his lives end."[8] Clearly, spiritual warfare was a serious issue for those believers who felt that even infants should be part of the church's army.

At the turn of the century, the potency of this language only grew in the American South, because of the Confederacy's defeat in the American Civil War. The mixture of Christian theology and Confederate ideology led to a unique understanding of the reasons for the Civil War. For example, some southern religious and political leaders claimed that the reasons for war were not connected to racism and slavery but for the purification of southern society through the shed blood of its soldiers.[9] While the Confederate armies did not win on the field of battle, the use of such religious language provided the South with a more important victory, that of spiritual purity.

Many Methodists would have understood the militarized paradigm of manhood to be an exclusively white ideal. In the turn-of-the-century South, it would have been dangerous for African American men to foster a martial image that could suggest they were out of "place."[10] Across the South, whites had a complicated way of interpreting the image of African Americans in uniform, and they frequently tried to argue that "dressing up" black men in uniform served only as a demonstration of the absurd.[11] Yet donning martial uniforms was one way African American men fought back against the many dehumanizing aspects of white supremacy. Taking on the image of the warrior—by wearing the uniform of the US military or one of the many fraternal orders in the South—was a powerful, and dangerous, way to demonstrate manhood for black men.[12] The danger that accompanied this statement of African American manhood was very real. Only a year after the end of the First World War, the *Chicago Defender* recorded that a group of whites lynched a young black veteran in Blakely, Georgia, because he refused to take off his military uniform.[13] Seeing black men appropriate a militaristic identity frightened some whites so much that they were willing to kill in order to erase that image.

Many MECS officials used violent language to talk metaphorically about spiritual battles. Evangelist Sam Jones used the example of Jesus to demonstrate just how hard Methodist men would have to fight against opposition. He noted, "The Lord Jesus himself never lost a chance to pour hot shot and grape and canister into the Scribes and Pharisees."[14] Such gruesome weapons denoted the type of frontal assault that Jones expected and the ferocity of the spiritual fight he anticipated. His language highlighted weapons that created indiscriminate, gory, mass causalities. Jones's example of Jesus fighting highlighted martial, hyper-masculinity—just what Jones thought was needed among MECS clergy.

In a separate sermon, Jones noted his longing for a masculine clergy willing to follow Jesus's manly example. He cried out, "Good Lord, give us a strong, sinewy, muscular religion! . . . My Lord God, give us a religion with vim and muscle and backbone and power and bravery! A great many people think that Christianity is just a little hot-bed of effeminity. . . . And they don't believe in anything but 'peace.' You pusillanimous wretch, you, you ain't fit to live."[15] Jones minced no words as he boldly pronounced in masculine terms that Methodism needed to be more muscular.

In a tone similar to that of Sam Jones, one of the MECS's most well known bishops, Charles Galloway of Mississippi believed that the MECS had to remember its victorious, conquering mission.[16] In a speech on the progress of the Twentieth Century Fund (a fund-drive for MECS's educational facilities), he described to his audience how "the martial spirit [was] the native air of Methodism." Galloway incorporated martial, hyper-masculine imagery into his vision of the Christian church and told those gathered before him that he envisioned an army of bold Christian men who loved "the notes of the bugle—the intrepid movement of a flying column—the fearless charge upon an entrenched foe." In short, the Mississippi bishop saw the MECS engaged in a war in which an invigorated, masculine clergy led the charge against the powers of evil.[17]

The MECS's episcopal style of church government (i.e., the church was organized by bishops who had authority over pastors and evangelists), as well as its long-running and influential publishing house, would have ensured that Galloway's message reached many readers.[18] Many of his white readers in the New South may also have approved of Galloway's message because the bishop was one of the foremost clerical supporters and propagators of Lost Cause ideology in the first decade of the twentieth century.[19]

Galloway worked hard to spread his vision of Methodism, which connected theology with a distinctly martial ideal of white manliness. According to the bishop, Methodism itself supplied weapons to fight against evil, and he told his listeners that the MECS was "not a museum for mummies, but [was] at once an arsenal for weapons and an army to use them."[20] Even when recounting the history of the Methodists in America, Galloway used powerfully masculine imagery. He recalled that within the borders of the United States, Methodists functioned as a "spiritual cavalry" that moved swiftly over the fields of battle to win souls to Christ.[21] Galloway asserted, "Men of might and majesty believe strongly. Heroes stand for something. Faith is the fibre of a conqueror."[22] In his eyes, Methodism challenged men to become conquerors for Christ and provided the tools for them to do so.[23] The martial imagery that Galloway and other MECS officials presented demonstrated that one mode of white, southern, Protestant masculinity at the turn of the nineteenth century was a soldierly ideal.[24]

The use of martial imagery by Sam Jones, Bishop Galloway, and others allowed interpretations of manhood that could shift focus to either individual or communal masculinity.[25] For example, Galloway's visions of the "flying column" and "spiritual cavalry" evoked a communal manhood in which individual preference became secondary to the needs of the whole. When promoting a communal vision of masculinity, these Methodist men were no longer mere individuals striking out on their own; rather, they became part of Christ's brigade, seeking to win the world for their king. Martial imagery also allowed for the encouragement of individual manhood. Galloway encouraged individual men not to let others take their share of responsibility for fighting evil. Instead, in his 1901 address and article on Christian experience, the bishop encouraged his readers, writing, "Heroes stand for something."[26] Heroes stood apart from or above their community. The ideal Christian soldier marching as to war could then be perceived either as an individual hero or as part of a community. In this way, the Christianized martial masculinity of the MECS allowed for both of these paradigms of manhood to work in conjunction with each other.

Methodist Ideas of Love Divine

While many MECS leaders used a martial understanding of Jesus as conqueror over sin and death to define masculinity, some MECS officials emphasized Jesus as a gentle, loving, affectionate shepherd of his people. They believed that Jesus modeled the freedom fathers and husbands should have to express love for their families. This presentation of domestic affection focused on a communal definition of manhood. In fact, many MECS officials conveyed their love for their wives and children repeatedly in letters and notes. In 1875, James Madison Crews sent his sweetheart a letter in which he talked freely about his love for her:[27] "A man *trembles before the woman he loves* and finds not enough nerve to tell her what is in his heart."[28] Clearly, Crews believed that it was appropriate for a man to "tremble" and that it did not endanger his manliness. Indeed, if this nervousness showed anything, it showed how powerfully a man could love a woman and in that way demonstrate his masculinity even more.

In a letter to the Georgia Methodist pastor John Davis Gray, a pastor who signed his letter C. E. D. also demonstrated the power of manly love. This pastor talked about his newborn baby girl and declared that although she was only a week old, "the little stranger already has a great hold on my affections."[29] In this epistle to a friend, C. E. D. made a statement about his manhood and fatherhood. Rather than paint a picture of the solitary, stoic warrior on the field of battle, this pastor communicated to his friend the power of his feelings for his little girl. As a pastor, C. E. D. would have been familiar with the story of Jesus welcoming the little children to be blessed, and would thus feel comfortable relating his own manly affection. Such pastors presented a strikingly different definition of manhood than the militant masculinity that Bishop Galloway, and others, presented, though there is no record of these two types of manliness causing friction between friends or clergymen within the MECS.

One man who wanted multiple members of his family to know of his love for them was the Mississippian itinerant minister John G. Jones. In 1830, Jones began writing his autobiography "for the perusal of myself and family and relations in the future."[30] Eventually spanning more than fifty-eight years in three volumes of 584 handwritten pages, this narrative of the life of an MECS itinerant minister presented a man who cared deeply for his family, particularly his wife. In describing the year of her death, in 1883, Jones wrote that theirs was "more than an earthly love; it partook largely of sweet foretastes of theavenly [*sic*] union and the communion of the spirits of the just made perfect." Here, Jones evidenced a great love for his wife, one that he believed offered a glimpse of heaven. He further described their pleasant evenings together, when they would talk by the fireside during the winter or converse on the front porch during the warmer months.[31] They loved each other deeply, and as Jones wrote his autobiography, he wanted to convey that love to his children, grandchildren, and anyone who might read his text. He certainly did not believe that these expressions of love, or of his profound grief and sorrow at his wife's death, jeopardized his manhood. Nonetheless, he carefully wept in "secret places" so as not to upset his family.[32] Jones's desire to hide the depths of his sorrow demonstrated that he still retained the ideal of self-control.[33]

Many Methodist leaders thought that educational institutions helped inculcate the self-mastery that denoted upper-class manliness. Yet sometimes these same leaders worried that an upper-class lifestyle could emasculate those who were not careful. College President John Massey warned young men not to pursue money at the expense of their souls, and thus become lured into avarice, and he was equally concerned about people who pursued beauty at all costs and fell into vanity.[34] Although not a stereotypical vice of southern males at the time, Massey's warning about vanity held implications about the masculinity of those men who fell into it.

Issuing blanket warnings against the pursuit of beauty did not fit with Massey's personality, however, and in 1882, he gave a commencement address that sought to explore the "*ultimate ground of beauty*."[35] In the speech, he proposed to his audience that everything beautiful on earth pointed toward an ideal beauty, which found its source in the "King of Beauty himself."[36] It was interesting that in this speech Massey, unlike Bishop Galloway, reveled in the beauty that he found in Jesus Christ. Rather than encouraging his listeners to conquer the world for Christ, he exhorted them to see "the beauty of holiness," and the "loveliness of moral action."[37] Rather than describing Jesus as the victor of a battle, Massey described Jesus as the "King of Beauty," and the college president pled with his audience to "look habitually and reverently upon the face of the All-Beautiful."[38]

This image of Jesus led to a very different construction of manhood. Massey would have been aware of the martial understandings of Jesus prevalent at the end of the nineteenth and the beginning of the twentieth century, but he chose a different interpretation of the divine in 1882. This presentation did not focus on a militant Jesus scourging the temple grounds of moneychangers, or on his victory over sin and death; rather, it focused on his compassionate side, the side that welcomed children to be blessed and that wept at the death of a friend.[39]

A similar message about a tender Jesus also came from pastors who preached about divine care. One pastor from Georgia, James Osgood Andrew Clark, described Jesus as a "tender and gentle shepherd" who lovingly watched over His flock and cared for their needs.[40] Similarly, James Crews, a Methodist preacher from Alabama, described in loving terms the divine mercy of a gentle and affectionate Jesus who gently guided His wayward sheep back into the fold.[41] Rather than a warrior-God leading a "flying column," as Galloway envisioned, these pastors presented a warm, personal God concerned about the welfare of his family of beloved children.

An example of how this type of masculinity played out among the laity can be found in the records of prominent Georgian and Coca-Cola Company founder Asa Griggs Candler. Candler wanted his family to be confident of that fact that he loved them even when he was not in their presence. Although he sometimes wrote stern letters to his family, particularly to his sons when they caused trouble at Emory College, he took care that his children knew he loved them. For example, in 1903, Candler wrote a letter to his son Howard, remarking that there was "nothing that I am more thankful for than that I have two noble sons." Candler then noted that it would be impossible to "be too grateful to my Heavenly Father for them and what they are to me."[42] Similarly, he wrote to his daughter, Lucy, telling her that "papa misses his jewel."[43] Asa Candler obviously thought that expressions of affection were appropriate to his role as family patriarch.

Taking a similar course of action, Mississippian Isaac Borders wrote a number of love letters to his wife while they lived apart for a few months (she was stuck in California selling their house while he took up a ministerial position in Mississippi). During their correspondence in 1912 and 1913, Borders started and ended each letter with an expression of love for his spouse.[44] His true feelings often emerged in the body of the letter. In the first surviving epistle from their five-month geographic separation, the pastor cried, "I yearn so for the little woman" that he loved, and that his "heart hungers so for her."[45] In another letter, Borders wrote that even though they would be apart over Christmas, "Our hearts can be together . . . and so we shall think of each other with unusual tenderness that day."[46]

When Borders learned that his family would be starting on their cross-country move to Mississippi, he wrote them an excited letter, remarking that as their arrival drew closer, he missed them more. Then, in a sentence meant only for his wife's eyes, he noted with a different type of excitement that he was "very, very hungry for" her. In addition, he felt that any long delay in their arrival would be an "insupportable calamity," now that he had "opened up the flood gates of affectionate desire for [her] companionship."[47] In this correspondence, Borders clearly tried to strike a delicate balance between letting his wife know that he desired her and attempting to stay within the boundaries of early-twentieth-century ideas of propriety. Even though these letters were intimate, and meant to be viewed only by husband and wife, Borders did not feel comfortable talking overtly about the sexual desire he felt for his spouse. Yet the fact that he mentioned that he was "very, very hungry" for his wife and that her expected arrival had "opened up the flood gates of affectionate desire" clearly signaled that he loved his wife and desired their physical relationship to commence after a long separation. Borders did not worry that expressions of love and spousal desire imperiled his manhood; rather, his wish to be an affectionate husband and loving father was manifest in his letters.[48] These expressions may have helped him to feel more masculine as he affirmed his sexuality, longing, and deep love for his spouse in the midst of their geographic separation.

As should be clear, most of these expressions of tender, loving care from Methodist officials appeared in private letters and notes they sent to family members. This seemed to present a bifurcation in manhood for many MECS officials. While many encouraged their parishioners to uphold a model of martial, aggressive masculinity tempered with Christian character, Methodist leaders also envisioned that their congregants would be affectionate fathers and husbands. While these two expressions of manliness were separated into the public and familial realms, this did not mean that one was secular and the other sacred. Rather, officials infused both conceptions of manliness with sacred ideas. Bishop Galloway's aggressive Christian soldier was equally as religious as John Jones's affection for his wife. These denominational officials believed that every aspect of life was sacred. Methodist Episcopal Church, South, leaders grounded both expressions of masculinity on the example they believed Jesus had set. Thus, whether they encouraged the members of their congregations to conquer hearts or woo them depended on how each pastor understood the example set by Jesus.

A host of other MECS officials encouraged appropriate character development in male parishioners even as they relied on different interpretations of the person of Jesus to define ideal masculinity. The trope of character allowed middle- and upper-class men to distinguish themselves from those they perceived as lower on the social scale while adding hard-to-define religious elements to a manly ideal. Thus, the language of character was another way theology interacted with class ideals and gender construction in the New South.

Manly Methodist Character

Even though the language of manly character applied primarily to those with middle- and upper-class values, itinerant ministers serving rural circuits (often the lowest within the Methodist hierarchy) sometimes tried to convince their listeners of its importance. James Hamilton Baxter, a pastor who served numerous circuits throughout Georgia over the course of his twenty years in the ministry, worried about the lessons God taught believers and frequently preached about the ways God instilled character. In one sermon, Baxter told his parishioners that the "present life is the schooling period of our existence."[49] Moreover, he believed that "the object of this present life is to develop character" and that all of life's trials had this one great purpose.[50] In another sermon in 1882, Baxter proclaimed that the purpose of the church was to "help men make holy character."[51] Thus, in his mind, while only individuals attained manliness, the community of believers helped refine it.

Many Methodists thought higher education would help rear boys to men while instilling in them a manly character. With this in mind, Atticus G. Haygood, then president of Emory College, in Atlanta, Georgia, addressed the young men (at the time it was still a men's institution and had not yet become a university) on the opening Sunday of the 1884 fall term, telling them that the training they would receive at Emory would serve them for the rest of their lives. However, to achieve proper character, he reminded them that duty was not something that would come to life in the extraordinary events; rather, it was best demonstrated in the daily tasks of life's "regular and honest work."[52] Haygood presented a specific type of masculinity that emphasized duty to the community over individuality. Duty clearly had a communal focus, as it was the job of the entire college faculty to train individuals for "honest work."

Although Haygood believed that work could be the avenue through which men showed their masculinity, he did not believe that manliness simply appeared; rather, the boys who came to Emory needed the proper training to achieve manhood. In another address to his students, from 1883, Haygood spoke about the importance of preparation as he talked about "David and His Sling."[53] The college president told the young men gathered before him that the training that David received watching over his sheep and defending them against predators prepared him to do the work of the Lord in defeating Goliath.[54] Haygood connected this with the students' lives by arguing that the daily tasks of manhood prepared one for the trials of life. The college president then argued that while many men found themselves in positions to do great good as they reached middle age, few achieved their goals because they had not received the training for such things.[55] Haygood told his audience that it was the solemn duty of the students and faculty of Emory to develop characters and minds capable of accomplishing all God had planned for them, thus achieving true manliness.[56]

Many MECS pastors spoke from their pulpits about the proper character of Christian men, a subject that was rare in Baptist congregations. Evangelist Sam Jones sometimes used the example of his own life, and his eventual freedom from long-standing debts, as a model of independent, character-driven manhood.[57] Jones wanted others to follow the example of the apostle Paul, noting, "I admire his character, true, noble, courageous, honest."[58] The emphasis of leaders in the Methodist Episcopal Church, South, at the turn of the century on building character signaled that they leaned heavily toward telling congregants how to live in their communities and the world.

Building character allowed the blending of individual masculinity with communal ideals of manhood through the class-based trope of character. Middle- and upper-class white men frequently used the tropes of character and civilization as markers of true manhood.[59] Using such language enabled them to differentiate themselves from working-class white men, thus claiming a higher level of manhood while affirming a common masculinity. Historian Gail Bederman writes, "Middle-class parents taught their sons to build a strong, manly 'character' as they would build a muscle. . . . By gaining the manly strength to control himself, a man gained the authority, as well as the duty, to protect and direct those less manly than himself—whether his wife, his children, his employees, or his racial 'inferiors.'"[60] Character taught through higher education enabled a balance between the individual aspect of control over one's impulses with the power, prestige, and authority of the community.

As higher education opened new avenues for class mobility, it also enhanced aspects of manliness in the minds of many MECS officials. In Alabama, college president John Massey, of the Alabama Conference Female College in Tuskegee (later Huntington College in Montgomery, Alabama), spoke to the Alabama Education Association in 1895, arguing that the "chief aim in every system of education should be to develop its pupils into the noblest manhood."[61] Massey tried to spread his vision that the way to bring pupils to their noblest manhood was to develop their character, and thus combined the idea of a community that needed to refine manhood with the idea of an individual who needed to work at fulfilling its "noblest" ideals. In a separate commencement speech, Massey encouraged the soon-to-be graduates continually to ask not what they would *do* once they finished their educational pursuits, but "*What will you be*?"[62] With this question in mind, he assured them that the "*formation of right character*" was the greatest thing that they could hope to achieve. He encouraged them to seek after it, since it not only enabled success in this life but also determined their fate after death.[63] Such words showed how MECS leaders defined manliness by connecting religious values with gender and class ideals.

For many MECS leaders who preached on personal character, character was intimately associated with Christian manliness. Charles Galloway made this clear throughout his time in the bishopric. In his speech

"Inflexibility of Purpose," Galloway talked about the moral fiber of the biblical character Daniel. According to Galloway, Daniel came from a pious family and had been reared in "sturdy virtues" that included not only the ability to recognize his holy mission but also an "infinite tact" that enabled him to remain in the court of several dynasties. All the while, Daniel kept his faith steadfast. Galloway posited that in the obstacles and strain of daily life, "steadfastness [is] the highest test of character."[64] Even in a speech ostensibly about Suzanna Wesley, the mother of John and Charles Wesley, the founders of Methodism, Galloway spent almost four of twenty pages telling his audience about the virtues of quiet strength and steadfast faith, as possessed by Suzanna's father.[65] On another occasion, he preached a sermon titled "Stability of Character," remarking that such stability was not only the "surest guarantee of success" but also the best "foundation for happiness."[66] Thus, the bishop from Mississippi argued that men could find success and exhibit their manliness through a steadfast character and through devotion to a righteous cause.

Galloway made it clear that character could define a true man in his 1908 commencement speech, "Jefferson Davis: A Judicial Estimate," delivered at the University of Mississippi.[67] Throughout this hagiographic speech praising Jefferson Davis, Galloway took great pains to point out how his fellow Mississippian embodied the ideal Christian gentleman.[68] The bishop praised Davis for his sense of chivalry and honor and for his affectionate nature toward his family while paying tribute to the man's oratorical skills and statesmanship.[69]

Galloway went even further in his praise of the former president of the Confederate States of America, extolling Davis as the "Greatest of Mississippians, the leader of our armies, the defender of our liberties, the expounder of our political creeds, the authoritative voice of our hopes and fears, the sufferer for our sins, if sins they were, and the willing martyr to our sacred cause."[70] Clearly, Galloway admired Jefferson Davis; but Galloway also helped develop and propagate the ideas of the Lost Cause throughout the Deep South at the beginning of the twentieth century.[71] Thus his spirited defense of Jefferson Davis was not simply an appraisal of someone Galloway thought young men should emulate. Rather, Galloway wanted to believe in a version of history in which Southern men would not lose their masculinity because of defeat on the battlefield, but where "true manhood" could find honor in fighting for a doomed cause. Galloway may have been one of the most well known proponents of the Lost Cause, but this defense of Southern masculinity was very popular during the fin de siècle.[72] Nonetheless, Galloway's interpretation of Jefferson Davis enabled the bishop to portray the former president of the Confederacy as having manly traits that fit perfectly into a Christological model.[73]

While Galloway argued that a messianic Jefferson Davis had martial spirit, the bishop thought Davis did not allow warlike emotions to rule his actions. Galloway told his listeners that even in moments of great emotion, Davis controlled himself with honor.[74] However, by equating Jefferson Davis with Jesus, Galloway made clear some of the characteristics he believed made an ideal man. Galloway's model of ideal masculinity was clearly Jesus—his theology and conception of gender merged entirely on this point—and he posited that Jefferson Davis had virtually attained the goal of perfect manhood. Indeed, Galloway's messianic model of manhood seemed to be the paragon of honor, the epitome of selfless love for others and great leadership in times of need. Thus, Jefferson Davis appeared as a Christ figure who gave his people a system of belief, led them to battle (remember Galloway's insistence that the "martial spirit [was] the air of Methodism"), was wounded for their transgressions, and ultimately gave his life on their behalf. Granting Davis a messianic character allowed Galloway to tell his listeners about the perfect model of manhood that combined Methodist theology with southern cultural ideals.

Although Galloway spent a great amount of time talking about the manly ideals of others, he also talked about his own masculinity. In one speech defending the Bible's place in American society, the bishop argued against the idea that only those who produced something were worthy models of manhood. He told the crowd before him, "I am a non-producer but I believe that when I open the Holy Bible to the people I am doing more for them than any bank president or merchant prince can do."[75] When he talked about being a nonproducer, Galloway tapped into the notion that manhood meant economic independence and a complete lack of reliance on others to supply one's needs.

Across the South at the end of the nineteenth century, Populist politicians like Ben Tillman of North Carolina, Rueben F. Kolb of Alabama, and Tom Watson of Georgia appealed to voters by castigating "non-producers," saying that they preyed on those who actually worked the land. This type of language enhanced the manliness of those who worked the fields at the expense of those who managed from afar or did not work with their hands.[76] By the time Galloway defended his claim to a nonproducing manliness in 1899, the Southern Populists' political strength had faded, but it still resonated in the Mississippi bishop's mind. Galloway acknowledged that the producer was one type of manliness but asserted that there was a separate manhood, one that was greater, that helped others in their spiritual needs.

In another article from 1907, Galloway wrote about his first trip to Cuba, in particular his voyage from Key West to Havana. He believed travelers noticed vast cultural differences as they went "from Protestant progress to Roman effeteness." Thus, Galloway not only talked about his own masculinity but also asserted that Protestantism, in and of itself, created a more manly culture than Roman Catholicism.[77]

In a similar anti-Catholic vein, Josiah Strong's *Our Country: Its Possible Future and Its Present Crisis*, one of the most well known anti-Catholic diatribes of the period, listed "Romanism" as one of the eight major perils facing the United States. Strong ascribed to the idea that Roman Catholics owed their ultimate allegiance to the Vicar of Rome rather than to the country in which they lived, in this case, the United States.[78] Additionally, during the 1890s a number of anti-Catholic secret societies emerged in the United States. Although these groups did not have large membership rosters in the South, the rhetoric that Roman Catholics constituted "disloyal adherents of a foreign potentate" resonated in the mind of the MECS's Bishop Charles Galloway.[79] Galloway believed that while Protestantism promoted progress in the United States, the Catholic Church created a corrupted culture of effete race-mixing in Cuba. These ideas of Catholic effeminacy relied on the notion that men were the only independent entities. Since, according to some Protestant notions of Roman Catholic belief, Catholics depended upon the pope, their perceived dependency feminized Catholic men in the minds of many American Protestants.

While Galloway clearly thought that his manhood superseded that of all the Roman Catholics on Cuba because of their religion, he also thought that his racial identity gave him a higher type of manhood than that of Cuban creoles.[80] Not only did Galloway believe that his own manhood was superior to the manhood of any Cuban he would encounter on the island, the bishop also asserted that his masculinity superseded even that of veteran sailors, as the tumble of the sea failed to diminish his own steady gait. He remarked that the sea trip was often so rough that it "humiliate[d] the sea legs of veteran sailors, but it did not affect the steadiness of my step."[81] The Methodist bishop clearly cared about his masculinity and wanted to prove to his readers (and perhaps himself as well) that he exemplified Christian manhood.

For most people, though, the search for perfected masculinity did not end with Bishop Charles Galloway. Itinerant minister Barney Lewis repeatedly preached a sermon titled "The Search for a Man" during the early years of the twentieth century throughout rural Mississippi.[82] In this sermon, Lewis told his parishioners that God looked for a man who could answer to His "ideal of manly perfection."[83] The minister traced some of the answers he believed defined a "true man." Clothes, money, and physical beauty were all on Lewis's list of false manliness.[84] Instead, Lewis said that "deeds and words reveal the man" and that "the real man is one who seeks to know the truth and do the right," all the while aware of heaven and his future place in it.[85] The minister wanted to convince the laity in his church that true manhood did not come from the adulation of the culture of the world. Instead, Lewis argued, it came from a singular focus on accomplishing the will of God. Thus, manliness could be an individual ideal fulfilled through disciplined character.

Other ministers also had ideas about what it meant to be a true man. James Osgood Andrew Clark, a pastor from Georgia, told his congregants that "delight in the law of the Lord" signified true manhood.[86] While Methodist ministers described the ideal man in their sermons, these pastors did not suggest to their congregations that men would be able to fulfill such high ideals on their own. Many pastors told their congregations that though each individual must make the first step, God would next enable them to do that which they could not—provide the strength to resist temptation. In other words, only through divine help would they overcome the sin in their lives.[87]

While most Methodists did not ascribe to the idea that they could ever be entirely without sin in this lifetime, the language of mastery over sin helped link Christianized masculinity to white southern manhood. During the post-Reconstruction era the idea that spiritual mastery over sin could replace the temporal mastery that white Southern men lost after the demise of chattel slavery became relevant.[88] Methodist leaders thought that spiritual mastery could be achieved only by leaning on the supernatural power of God, the ultimate master of the universe.

Once again, manhood, as defined by Methodist leaders across the South at the turn of the century, could be achieved—but not alone. Instead, the "real man" recognized his limitations and submitted to God's will. Mississippi itinerant minister Lewis explicitly told his congregants that only through submission to God's will would men attain the strength necessary to live as they should, that is, with their attention focused on heaven. Similarly, James Osgood Andrew Clark offered his Georgia congregation the biblical examples of the Israelite captives Shadrach, Meshach, and Abednego as models of spiritually submissive manliness. In the Bible, those captives refused to bow down to the Babylonian King Nebuchadnezzar's idol, though they knew that the consequence was to be thrown into a furnace. The Bible records that though the men were thrown into the fire, they were not harmed.[89] Clark used the story of these young men as examples of faithful men who submitted their lives to honoring God, and God responded by delivering them from being consumed by fire.[90] The example of these three young Israelites demonstrated the limitations of human power while implying that manliness meant being willing to sacrifice one's own life for a cause or belief. Thus, Clark tried to persuade his congregants that true men should acknowledge their limitations and call on a higher power for help in times of need.

Isaac D. Borders frequently acknowledged the limitations of his character in letters to his wife. Borders began his ministry in Mississippi and then moved out to California with his wife and children. Eventually, Borders moved back to Mississippi to take up a new ministerial post. During their time apart, the two corresponded every few days, and while only Isaac's letters survive, they provide a glimpse into the intimate family life of an MECS pastor.

In one of the first letters, penned at the end of November 1912, Borders admitted to his wife that he was unsure of whether to resume the life of an itinerant minister in the Mississippi Conference and desired to have her candid opinion. However, he said that he would take full responsibility for the decision and would never blame her for her opinion either way. He ended his thoughts on the matter by saying that in taking full responsibility, he would "try all the harder to be a man!"[91] Borders was one of the rare MECS officials who hinted at doubts about his own masculinity. Here, he seemed to suggest that he had not yet fully become a man in his own estimation; yet, for Borders, manhood did not emerge in a vacuum. Borders believed that men should take into consideration the opinions of their loved ones in making decisions. However, the man held ultimate responsibility for the outcome of those decisions. Borders's expression of manliness demonstrated his attempts to continue a patriarchal model even while geographically separated from his family. In the next epistle he sent from Mississippi to his wife, Borders admitted that he realized there would be goals and accomplishments he would not achieve in this life—and yet he communicated his desire to be a changed man and reorient his priorities for the sake of his wife.[92] Borders continues to write about his own limitations and, referring to Jesus, cried, "I am so weak—so pitiably weak and helpless, so lonely and so sinful, without Him!"[93] Clearly Borders defined his own manliness by the supernatural.

The longer that Borders and his wife lived apart, however, the more despondent he became, and the more he doubted his call to be a minister in the MECS. At a low point, in February 1913, Borders broke down and wondered why he ever became an itinerant Methodist minister, complaining, "God never made me to be that contemptible, pale-blooded, near-man, a conventional, itinerant Methodist parson." This was one of the few times a pastor recorded that a life of religious duty was less manly than other jobs. Indeed, Borders's statements imply that itinerant Methodist pastors imperiled their own masculinity.

Despite his obvious dislike for his station in life, Borders prayed that he would do his duty in Aberdeen, Mississippi, "fearlessly, firmly, faithfully [and] fully."[94] He clarified his dislike of pastoral duties, telling his wife that before he took up this position, he had "the manhood and the spunk" to pursue God and was once close to the kingdom of heaven. While Borders thought that he had moved away from the Kingdom of God and lost some of the "manhood and spunk" he had earlier in life, he believed that God still had things to teach him; accordingly, he would try to have better character and be a "brave, stout-hearted, dutiful, patient, manly fellow."[95] Although Borders doubted his calling as a pastor and his own manliness, such characteristics still defined manhood. Borders particularly valued strength and bravery; and yet he ascribed to the idea that these were not inherent characteristics. Rather, Borders repeatedly prayed for these in the hope that God would grant them to him.[96] In fact, his theology led him to believe that God could enhance his manliness. Yet Borders did not believe that being part of the clergy equated to having spiritual manhood.

Methodist leaders envisioned spiritual manhood in a number of ways. Some, like Mississippian Charles Galloway, believed Jesus wanted a mighty army of Methodist men to conquer the world. Other members of the MECS clergy had their doubts about this militarized image of Jesus and preferred to see Him as the gentle shepherd who wooed the hearts of his people. However they interpreted the example of Jesus, these clerics attempted to define true masculinity through theology. For these officials, faith defined not only manhood. For while they were concerned about manly Methodists, they also attempted to clarify what faithful femininity entailed.

5
Methodist Women as Home Missionaries

While many officials in the Methodist Episcopal Church, South looked to the example of Jesus to provide models of masculinity at the turn of the nineteenth century, they frequently connected abstract theological ideas to family life and femininity as they attempted to define the ways their congregants understood gender. More specifically, the idea of spiritual rebirth, or conversion (the giving of one's life to Jesus in the belief that His sacrifice was the only way for a sinful, broken person to approach a holy God), had a greater influence on the construction of families, as well as how femininity should be expressed, than other elements of Methodist theology.

The importance of the conversion experience cannot be overlooked in MECS thought. In 1901, Charles Galloway, a bishop from the Mississippi Conference, claimed that the idea "Ye must be born again" was the preeminent doctrine of the church.[1] Other pastors across Mississippi, Alabama, and Georgia made frequent reference to regeneration and the conversion experience in their sermons. The necessity of conversion influenced the organization of the denomination, as well as the ways MECS officials conceptualized gender at the end of the nineteenth and the beginning of the twentieth century.[2]

For church officials in the Methodist Episcopal Church, South, the theological idea of regeneration extended to the entire world.[3] Methodist preachers and pastors viewed every person as a potential convert, and many clergy told their congregants that the home was the first and primary mission field for parents. Even though many MECS officials thought women's "proper" place was at home, tending to the spiritual needs of their children, these pastors believed their female parishioners should receive educations to deal with the complex world.[4] The need for conversion enabled MECS leaders to construct and define different aspects of family life and femininity that they then passed on to their parishioners.

For many MECS officials in the New South era, the conviction that conversion formed the foundation for the church naturally progressed into the idea that the home held the primary mission field for families. Parents thus needed to tend to the souls of their children. The *Pocket Visiting Book*, which James Osgood Andrew Clark used as he visited families in their homes throughout south-central Georgia, made clear in the section on infant baptism the parents' role in their child's spiritual life. According to the *Visiting Book*, the pastor needed to remind parents of their duty to ensure their child would "read the Holy Scriptures, and learn the Lord's Prayer, the Ten Commandments, the Apostle's Creed, the Catechism," and any other things beneficial to a Christian's spiritual health.[5] Clark took this to heart, and in one sermon he told his parishioners that they should practice their beliefs in such a way as to show their children that parents "practice abroad what [was] taught them in the family."[6] Indeed, Clark told his congregants that God commanded parents to teach Scripture to children.[7] Clark believed that the father was instrumental in the spiritual health of all those in the home. He suggested to his congregants that to achieve that spiritual health, the "father and priest of the family" could gather his family around him each night and give them an appropriate lesson from the Bible.[8]

The fact that Clark called him the "priest of the family" had significant theological implications. Throughout the Bible, the priests of Israel were the figures appointed by God to intercede on behalf of others, and it was the priests who offered the sacrifices that atoned for the sins of the people of Israel.[9] The priest occupied an extremely important role in the Bible, one that the Methodists (and all evangelicals) believed Jesus fulfilled when He offered the perfect sacrifice of His own body as the atonement for the sins of all who put their trust in Him.[10] To elevate the role of the father and husband to the priest of the family marked a significant theological statement that required the family to go through the father in order to interact with God.[11] More than a simple teacher, the father's role as intermediary between his family and God made him the most important spiritual figure in his family.

This exalted position of the father-priest did not appear in many other MECS officials' writings in the turn-of-the-century Deep South, but they clearly felt the spiritual formation that took place at home was vitally important in the spiritual health and vitality of the next generation. Indeed, the Methodist emphasis on conversion meant that the home constituted the training ground where parents trained "a child in the way he should go."[12] One bishop from Mississippi, Charles Galloway, in his early-twentieth-century sermon "Inflexibility of Purpose," tried to encourage parents by giving them the example of Daniel, whom he believed was a "son of a pious home" and went on to stand firm in his faith for his entire life, despite persecution.[13]

Being the son of a pious home involved being exposed not only to ideas of the father-priest but also to a devoted mother who nurtured spiritual formation in her children. Methodist Episcopal Church, South, officials often defined home evangelism as the purview of the mother and wife, and they believed that this role was a vitally important one for the spiritual health of the family. For example, John Griffing Jones of Mississippi described how his wife began to lead family prayers soon after receiving entire sanctification. She carefully started family devotions before the children were "overcome with sleep" so as to be the most effective for their souls.[14]

College president John Massey of Alabama would have approved of Mrs. Jones's example and role as a spiritual mother to her own children and a number of adopted ones. Massey told his audiences that a "woman's touch" would influence her children to "lift [their] faith up to God."[15] Massey considered this role so important that he thought a woman who neglected to develop her "moral powers" was "a blot on creation."[16] At the end of the nineteenth century, MECS officials believed that the home was where children might be converted; thus the mother's role in the home was sacred. Massey believed, and attempted to persuade others, that the role of the wife and mother in the home was a place of honor, filled with equal or greater importance to anything that men working outside the home could accomplish.[17] Yet he insisted that those women who spiritually neglected their homes were aberrations. The college president clearly subscribed to an ideology that the proper place for women was in the home, where they could nurture the souls of children and bring them to a saving faith in Jesus.

In one speech, "The Education of our Girls," probably given in the 1890s, Massey lauded the efforts of Frances Willard, Clara Barton, and others who had made strides in showing women's equality in vocations outside their homes. This seemed to contradict his earlier statements about the home being the proper place for women to minister to their families. However, the president of the Alabama Conference Female College quickly shifted his focus and argued that, despite the efforts of Willard, Barton, and others, it remained "true that the *home idea* remains the central idea of this earth."[18] Because of this, he believed that, as a mother and a wife, a "woman is the most potent factor in the development of the [human] race."[19]

Massey's view of women in the home as the "central idea of this earth" ignored those who had to work outside their domestic world to provide for their families. Massey's ideas of femininity had socio-economic implications, and they were also fraught with racial meaning. Many African American women across the South did not have the luxury of staying home during the day and so would not have fit into Massey's circumscribed view of proper southern ladies. This did not mean, however, that these women objected to the idea that the home was the world women were in charge of. Many southern black women accepted and even encouraged the idea that they were in charge of homelife.[20] However, many white Methodist leaders, such as John Massey, could not accept that African American women fit into the model of femininity that highlighted homelife.

Educating Methodist Women for Home Missions

Because of the importance of the home, a number of MECS officials, including John Massey of Alabama, worked to reform and expand women's educational opportunities so that they might be better able to meet the spiritual needs of their future families. (They assumed young women would stay in education only as long as they were single.[21])

While many MECS officials in the New South attempted to connect a theology focused on conversion to a view of the home as a sacred place for rearing children, some did argue that, by its very nature, Christianity promoted the status of women in cultures around the world. In a graduation speech at the Alabama Conference Female College in 1886, Massey talked about the role of women in different civilizations before concluding that the Christian spirit "elevated woman from her minimal place in heathenism to the righthand of honor and love." Massey believed that women should have an elevated place in society—one surrounded by honor and love. Yet even as the college president talked about the ways his faith tradition elevated women, he noted that the women of ancient Rome served as a warning to the world. He believed that these women valued their "*rights* above their *womanly qualities*" and warned that the "result of this emancipation from the laws of God and nature" led to the degradation and eventual fall of the empire.[22] His comments about Roman women demonstrated that Massey's conception of women retained a specific type of femininity, one concerned more with "womanly qualities," such as moral authority, beauty, and purity, than with specific political or social rights. Since the early part of the nineteenth century, similar had ideas circulated; the notion that women should serve as a purifying influence on their husbands and sons, but not get directly involved in political life, was a vibrant part of American culture.[23] Massey certainly would have agreed with this idea, as he wanted the young women graduating in 1886 to concentrate on their "womanly qualities" rather than on their political rights. The college president would not have encouraged his female students to join any type of suffrage movement at the end of the nineteenth century.[24]

Of course, questions about a woman's appropriate role in society caused some people to wonder what was the best way to teach women who attended liberal arts schools. College professor and eventual MECS bishop Atticus Haygood tried to answer this question in a sermon he preached in Atlanta in 1889. In this sermon, Haygood proposed that those who taught women should incorporate the core of womanhood into the "very warp and woof" of his or her teaching.[25] While he did not say exactly what this meant, Haygood carefully articulated that he did not think discussions needed to be any less intellectual when women were engaged. He even warned his audience, "Some fools treat women as if they were too silly for rational intercourse."[26] Thus, Haygood did not think that teaching women required a pandering treatment of the curriculum. Haygood also thought that those who dismissed women as irrational did so to their own detriment. He believed women were fully capable of discussing the pressing topics of the day and should not be treated as mere objects to be seen and not heard.

Later that year, in 1889, Atticus Haygood accepted a position in Sheffield, Alabama, as the head of a proposed school for white women. (This school never opened, and Haygood eventually pulled out when it became clear that the financial backing would not materialize.) Haygood believed that the Deep South needed a better school for white women, and though he acknowledged that it could not be created in a single day, or even a single year, he hoped to "do something worthy [of] the white girls of the South." Haygood believed this enterprise would become one of his "chief joys." Even while Haygood acknowledged the need for a better college for white women, he talked about his desire for it to remain focused on "all womanly industries as truly as all womanly culture."[27] Once again, the (racially circumscribed) message of a full, but uniquely feminine education sounded. Even as Haygood sought to open a school "worthy [of] the white girls of the South," he articulated the twin strands of a braided message focused on Christianity as an uplifting force and on a specifically circumscribed role for women.

The ideas that Christianity elevated women and that women needed to concern themselves less with their rights than with a focus on their moral and spiritual improvement, so that they could help convert others, worked their way into the speeches of John Massey at the turn of the century, as he talked about the importance of a Christian woman's education. In one message before the South Alabama Educational Association, Massey argued that men needed to be trained for science and development in business. Women, he told his audience, should be taught to "deal with the spiritual counterparts of these useful enterprises." This included training to cultivate moral authority, inspire truth and beauty, encourage moral action, remove friction in society, and "attune the chords of domestic life and make them resound with charming melody." More importantly, though, Massey believed that properly educated women could "free the souls of men" by encouraging faith in God.[28]

For such things to happen, Massey wanted a reformation in the curriculum taught to women. He did not think that women should focus on the hard sciences and instead wanted a curriculum that focused on fine arts, literature, and language—certainly a very different focus than at many men's colleges.[29] He believed that this curriculum would enrich women's lives, making them vital members of society. Indeed, Massey told his listeners that the best schools for women worked to educate women "on a more generous scale than in any of the older civilizations"; however, he also warned that women's education should focus on the "sphere in which she will fulfill her highest mission," which was nurturing the souls of her children.[30] Many educators in the early part of the twentieth century would have agreed with the Alabamian college president. These men emphasized the aesthetic elements of the curriculum for women, and parents often did not wish their daughters to receive a "mannish" education.[31] Massey tried to hold together the seeming contradiction that existed between educating women so that they might occupy a greater place in society and asserting that these women should stay in their "proper sphere." This braided message makes sense only when one considers the importance of evangelism to Massey's thought.

The theological necessity of conversion allowed Massey to hold the message that women should receive a high-quality education together with the idea that they needed to remain at home after they acquired this education. The conversion of all people to Christianity was the highest goal in Massey's mind, and since women were "uniquely suited" to nurturing young souls and winning them for Christ, women had a unique responsibility to begin instilling affection for the divine in children. Developing a person's love for Jesus was easiest when that individual was young. To do this better, Massey, and many other educators in the New South period, thought that women should go to college and receive educations that focused on subjects of beauty and language.

An education focused almost exclusively on aesthetic endeavors made it easy for Massey to frequently reference the idea that daughters should be the "polished cornerstones" on which the foundations of society rested.[32] His clear commitment to the ideas of a feminine domestic sphere combined with the notion that the home was the foundation of society.[33] In Massey's mind, this gave women an important role in his view of the world. Women had the responsibility to create, and care for, the foundation of civilization. The idea that women constituted the cornerstone of culture clearly influenced Massey and gave him the impetus to create an college curriculum that would give his students the tools to carry out what he believed was their God-given mission.

Although all Methodist women's colleges considered the education of women to be a high priority, exactly what this education should look like was a contentious issue. In his *Reminiscences*, John Massey talked about how his ideas of his work as a college president at a women's school had changed over the years. As he began his work at the Alabama Conference Female College, Massey heard, among other things, that while it took a man to manage a boy's college, anybody could manage girls. Another friend told Massey that he must step carefully when trying to arrange the women's curriculum, because if he required as much from women as he would from men, he would only discourage the young ladies under his care. However, as Massey got to know his students and encourage their academic work in Alabama in the last decade of the nineteenth century, he found virtually no difference in ability between his former (male) students and his current (female) ones. For Massey, this demonstrated that "the difference in the ability of the sexes is more a difference in taste than in natural talent. Neither is superior nor inferior. They are different. They are counterparts of each other."[34] Thus, though the college president firmly believed that each sex had their proper place in life and should hold complimentary roles, he believed they had equal intellectual capabilities—whether or not they used them in public.

Asa Candler, a high-profile member of the Methodist laity, went further in his support of appropriate levels of teaching and education for women. In 1902, Candler worried that his daughter, Lucy, left school too early to pursue romantic interests, and complained to his son, "She is now fixing to get married. Then she will have tied herself *down* to burdens for which I fear she is poorly equipped."[35] Clearly, Candler felt that his daughter needed to receive more education before she entered married life. Although he did not elaborate on exactly what burdens he worried about, Candler made it clear that he had certain expectations about the role his daughter would soon take.

Pastor Barney Lewis, an itinerant minister from Mississippi, believed that Christianity itself had elevated women throughout the world. In a sermon he delivered in 1902, Lewis argued that every culture "but where the gospel prevails" discriminated against women. In the areas where Christianity had taken hold, Lewis asserted, the good news of salvation through Jesus Christ, without regard to age, gender, or station in life, elevated "the weaker sex and [made] her equal in all its advantages and blessings."[36] While Lewis proclaimed the equality of men and women, the language he used gave a different picture. He still used the term "weaker sex" when referring to women, even though his theology taught that all people must admit spiritual helplessness and depend solely on the saving grace of Jesus.[37] This contradiction in Lewis's thought likely reflected a lingering belief in American theology at the beginning of the twentieth century that though all persons were equal before God, there were temporal differences and stations in life, and so while on earth, everyone must keep his or her "place."[38]

The idea that southern Methodist white women needed to stay in the home was certainly a strong part of official MECS ideas, coming through not only in the statements of individual leaders but also in institutional policies. In the *1904–05 Catalogue of Grenada College* (a college for women that eventually became part of Millsaps College in Jackson, Mississippi), the author proudly declared that from that place had "gone forth numbers of cultivated Christian women to bless the homes, adorn society and further the educational interests of our land."[39] Even though this catalog tried to attract interest in the college, it used only passive verbs that hinted at the proper place for women in the larger culture. Women at the beginning of the twentieth century were intended to "adorn" society, not change or take active roles in anything. If the hints about women's passive roles did not make clear enough the belief that the proper place for women in the New South was in the home, the catalog made it explicit only a few pages later when comparing Grenada College to its brother institution, Millsaps (at that time a men's institution). The catalog asserted, "What Millsaps is doing to build up an effective citizenship, Grenada College is doing to make strong, refined and cultured homes."[40] Grenada College believed that a woman's proper place was in the home, and much of MECS theology supported this idea by emphasizing women's role in nurturing the souls of children. The catalog's assertion that Millsaps built up citizenry lent support to the idea that only men were to participate in politics, while women took care of their families' spiritual needs at home.

The idea of the home as a place for nurturing young souls is also evident in Bishop Charles Galloway's speech on Suzanna Wesley, the mother of Methodist founders John and Charles Wesley. In it, Galloway extolled the motherly virtues of Suzanna Wesley's "*patient, prudent, prayerful*" parenting.[41] The bishop also praised her for praying both with and for each of her nineteen children, for routinely asking them about their private relationships with God, for teaching them about the doctrines of the Christian faith, and for demonstrating what an experiential faith looked like through her own life. Because of Suzanna's faithful witness, Galloway told his listeners, "All the Wesley children became faithful Christians and every one died in the Lord."[42]

Clearly, a major part of young women's education revolved around the idea of the home as a sacred place that was instrumental in developing the spiritual lives of children. John Williams of Galloway Women's College believed that this meant that "women must continue to make and keep the home, and the home must be made and kept with far greater sacredness than we generally find to-day."[43] Williams intertwined his hope of helping women become economically independent with the idea of the home as a sacred place for the nurturing of children's spiritual needs.

Williams's pamphlet took a different tone from many others, though; while advocating the home as the sacred place for women, it argued that the world had entered a new age in which women would be regarded as the equals of men. Williams urged, "[The] Methodist Episcopal Church, South, shall make it known that now and henceforth women shall stand equal with men in privileges, gifts, and opportunities; [and that] their education shall be given just consideration by our Church and such ideals and standards shall be set for them as are worthy the equal partners of our lives."[44] Many of Williams's most well-defined statements of equality of the sexes dealt with the education of women—an education he believed must be serious, challenging, and enriching to women's lives and intellects. Nonetheless, Williams's remark about equal opportunities would not have extended to equal roles in institutional church leadership. Nothing in the rest of his pamphlet suggested this, and it was probable that he referred strictly to educational and financial opportunities. Such an interpretation made sense as Williams reminded his readers that, though he wanted to make it possible for women to be economically independent, he still wanted them to remain at home.[45]

Many white southern progressives agreed with the tension in Williams's statement. The idea that women needed to learn "suitable" trades and have the ability to become economically independent in the event of her (future) husband's untimely death, all while learning to carry oneself as a proper "lady," was important in many industrial and normal schools aimed at working-class and lower-middle-class constituencies at the end of the nineteenth century. For those in middle- and upper-class homes, however, "college was a place to shelter young women . . . not a place to encourage intellectual development. Most students did not stay at college long enough to earn a degree."[46] Instead, music, art, deportment, and expression served as the major elements of the curriculum for many young women who went to school for the purpose of making their homes more aesthetically pleasing. Many MECS schools for women across Mississippi, Alabama, and Georgia also offered courses on religion and ethics so that the young women attending could better meet the spiritual needs of their families.[47]

While many of the faculty at such institutions felt it was their duty to train young women to take up their role as proper ladies, undergraduate students sometimes had other ideas. Students sometimes mocked "proper" ideas of gender, even at the most highly connected religious institutions, such as Whitworth Female College, in Brookhaven, Mississippi. In 1911, the young women there held a gender-bending mock wedding.[48] This unique mock wedding involved no men. While some historians have examined the cultural phenomenon of the "Womanless Wedding" in the South, Whitworth Female College turned this around and held a "Matrimony without Men" ceremony.[49] Many of the young women at the event cross-dressed, posing in tuxedos, waistcoats, and bowties—not just *acting* as men but going to the trouble of finding men's costumes and dressing the part as well. On the same page that the picture of the "Matrimony without Men" appeared, the school's yearbook, the *LeFost,* featured a portrait of a young woman fashionably dressed with multiple strings of pearls and captioned "Portia," while another picture listed the "Faculty Burlesque." These images supplied the only context for the wedding image and suggested that it was part of a series of tongue-in-cheek theatrical performances. Nonetheless, the performance of a matrimony without men reified appropriate roles of women and models of femininity in 1911, even as it made light of the inversion of gender roles.[50]

In a more pointed fashion, the male editors for the 1913 *Bobashela* (the Millsaps College annual) listed the motto for the satirical "'Votes for Women' Club" as "Wanted, a medical preparation for growing a mustache."[51] While no insulting pictures accompanied the club's satirical page, most likely the

Figure 4. The young women at the Women's College of Alabama posed in support of women's suffrage in this 1915 photograph. Courtesy of the Methodist Archives Center, Huntington College Library, Huntington College, Montgomery, Alabama.

editors for the yearbook believed, because Millsaps was at the time a male institution, that voting was a male activity and that women who wished to vote were as absurd as women who wished to grow mustaches.

Not all college women were content to watch society pass them by, though. According to the 1915 issue of the Woman's College of Alabama yearbook, *Belles and Pomegranates*, one of the extracurricular groups with the most members was the Equal Suffrage Club.[52] The club listed fifty-eight members, and its picture suggested its seriousness (see figure 4). The serious nature of the club, unlike the satirical nature of many groups listed in student annuals, may have been enhanced by the fact that this was a women's college and not a coeducational institution.

In contrast to the seeming respect given to the Equal Suffrage Club at the Women's College of Alabama, another Alabama school, Southern University, took a different approach in their student yearbook, *The Southron*. In 1914, they also ran a picture of a Suffragette Club, but immediately above a picture of the Antisuffragette League.[53] Looking closely at the pictures from *The Southron*, it becomes clear that some women ap-

Figure 5. These photographs appeared on the same page of the 1914 *Southron*. The sign in the top image reads "Suffragette Club," while the bottom denotes "Anti-Suffrage League." From the *Southron*, courtesy of Birmingham-Southern College Archives.

peared in both pictures, though they dressed dramatically differently for each shot. In the depiction of the Suffragette Club, the women put on plain clothes, picked up frying pans and rolling pins, and appeared to move menacingly toward the camera.[54] In the picture of the Antisuffragette League, the young women dressed in their finest clothing and stood serenely gazing peacefully forward (see figure 5). The yearbook editors' denunciation of women's suffrage as merely a group of angry, aggressive women came through clearly—as did the message that women should stay out of politics and concentrate on their role in the home.

MECS Women's Ministry

One woman who exemplified the ideal of a Christian woman in James Osgood Andrew Clark's mind was the First Lady, Lucy Webb Hayes. In 1878, the Georgia pastor went to visit Washington, DC, and the First Lady received him at the White House. Clark wrote to his wife in glowing terms about Mrs. Hayes, remarking that she was a "true and perfect Christian woman." In her, the pastor from Georgia felt, visitors met a woman "in whom there [was] no guile, and in whom the gentlest and noblest Christian graces [were] happily blended in associated beauty." Thus, guests felt that they met "a true wife and mother, as well as with a lady of exalted rank and dignity."[55] Clark felt that her mere presence and purity of heart kept her husband on the straight and narrow as he remarked, "Her influence and example alone must keep Mr. Hayes from doing many naughty things, even if he were so disposed." Thus, through her influence on the president, Mrs. Hayes fulfilled the ideal of those who saw Christian women as the polished cornerstones of society, and through her wifely influence on the president of the United States, she set a civil tone in Washington politics.

Mrs. Hayes's purifying influence on her husband and her care for her family (as "a true wife and mother") blended the qualities Clark believed women should exhibit and retained them in their appropriate place in society. According to Clark's letter, Mrs. Hayes did not bother with affairs outside the home (to reach this conclusion, he must have ignored her staunch support for temperance reform) nor did she directly mention her views on particular political matters to her husband. Rather, her "influence and example *alone* [emphasis added]" kept the president acting in an appropriate manner.[56] Such arguments held sway at the end of the Victorian period, and Clark fully imbibed these notions while blending them with his ideas of the sacred.[57] In other words, the proper place for women was in the home, where their moral authority and example might influence their husbands and children, thus gently purifying their hearts and leading them to Christ through their example of Christian femininity.

Rev. John Griffing Jones greatly valued his wife's ability to convert others to Christianity and in his memoirs wrote highly of her abilities. The itinerant minister from Mississippi would often attend camp meetings with his wife, where the two would work hard to convert others to Christianity. Jones recorded in his autobiography that his wife was "gifted in song and extemporaneous prayer, and for an old lady had a large share of endurance." In fact, she had so much energy that she often stayed up much later than her husband with those near conversion. Her husband eventually asked what she talked about with the penitents at these camp meetings because she was so successful at getting people to convert. She replied simply that the Lord directed the appropriate portions of Scripture, songs, or life-stories to her mind as she talked to each person.[58] Jones's obvious admiration for his wife and her skill at leading others to Christ demonstrated his conviction that a Christian woman's role was to evangelize as much as any Christian man did. Jones not only valued his wife's help in ministry but also acknowledged that she did evangelistic work on her own, even after he had to leave the extended meeting and go to bed. Jones connected his ideas of what was appropriate for his wife to do at camp meetings with the purpose of the meeting itself—to convert others to Christianity.

In her role of offering spiritual succor to the penitent, Mrs. Jones could well have fit into the role of a church mother. Religious historian Anthea Butler documented the ways in which African American women, particularly those in the Church of God in Christ, used their roles as church mothers as a vehicle "to remake their religious and social worlds within a framework of piety, devotion, and civic life" at the beginning of the twentieth century.[59] Through their religious work, the women that Butler investigated used the ideal of motherhood in order to take active roles in the world around them.[60] The ways in which John Jones described his wife's work—leading their family devotions, caring for orphan children they adopted, and ministering to the spiritual needs of the penitent at camp meetings—demonstrated that she took on the role of a spiritual mother. In fact, her great success at camp meetings caused her husband to marvel at her spirituality and physical stamina.

By the New South period, though, camp meetings had become less frequent for many in the MECS, particularly those in burgeoning New South cities. In fact, in many urban settings, Sunday Schools became a major focus of churches. In 1904, the young but wealthy Wesley Memorial Church, in Atlanta, celebrated the one-year anniversary of their Sunday School program by publishing a short history called "The First Mile Post."[61] The Sunday School had male officers only, with the exception of two unmarried assistant secretaries. These two female assistants were not listed with the other assistant secretary, a man, but instead came after both the librarian and the treasurer (both male). In contrast to the officers, all the teachers listed were women, with the exceptions of the pastor of the church and one other man, S. C. Aiken.[62] When the time came to present a picture of the Sunday School teachers, Mr. Aiken's picture ended up being surrounded by those of all the women, seeming to give stability to the faces of the female teachers orbiting the man (see figure 6).[63] Taken together, these pictures and lists of Sunday School officials suggested that Methodist leaders expected women to remain in the background, working in supportive rather that executive roles at the start of the twentieth century. Indeed, the only woman in an executive role was Mrs. Roger Williams, the superintendent

Figure 6. Although the only man in this group had the same job and authority as the women, the implication was that men were the point around which women could orbit. Starting clockwise from the upper left, the portraits are of Mrs. Lincoln McConnell, Miss Lizzie Lupo, Mrs. M. M. Davies, Mrs. C. A. Manston, Miss Mamie Baker, Mrs. George Purvis, and Mr. S. C. Aiken. Courtesy of Manuscript, Archives, and Rare Book Library, Emory University, Atlanta, Georgia.

of the Primary Department of the Sunday School. Once again, this implied that women should work with children and nurture their souls rather than be in positions of authority over men. Indeed, this role as the head of the Primary Department could be seen as a motherly role, and thus remained within the home ideal, as Mrs. Williams nurtured the young children in her classes.

Not all historians have interpreted the role of the Sunday School teacher as a possible extension of women's nurturing domestic role. Historian Elizabeth Hayes Turner's study of women in Galveston, Texas, demonstrated that the role of the Sunday School teacher could be an empowering one for some women. The Sunday School teachers in Galveston sometimes created new classes in outlying areas, and some of these classes eventually became independent congregations. By Turner's reading, then, these women acted as church planters.[64] I do not dispute her claims about the women in the churches in Galveston, but this was not the pattern for the

Wesley Memorial Church in Atlanta—there, leaders expected women to fulfill their roles in nurturing, domestic ways. The difference highlights the ways the cultures of specific towns and places, even in the New South, could create different opportunities for women.

Mississippi pastor Isaac Borders believed that his wife should expand opportunities in his life and ministry, even as he began his ministry in Mississippi and waited for her to sell their home in California. In one letter to his wife in 1912, Borders mentioned the tremendous mortgage that the church in Aberdeen, Mississippi, had and what a problem it would be to the ministry. However, Borders noted that he was confident that by "working together in mutual love and trust," he and his wife would be able to make a wonderful life and ministry there.[65] Throughout his letters to his wife in the second decade of the twentieth century, it was clear that Borders viewed her as an equal, and as his partner in ministry. Even in the Borders family, though, Mrs. Borders had a spiritual role rather than an official ministerial one. Yet even this role created controversy among other MECS leaders.

Rev. Borders became involved in a controversy with R. A. Meek, the editor of one of the denomination's major newspapers, the *New Orleans Christian Advocate*. The two disputed various questions in the early 1910s but particularly disagreed on the "woman question" and on whether or not theater could be used as a tool of the gospel.[66] Throughout 1913, Borders wrote repeatedly to Meek in hopes of getting his views published in the *Advocate*. In response to one article, Meek stated that he would very much like to publish what he had received but that he felt it would be better if Sister Borders's remarks were excluded.[67] The fact that Borders would include a written portion of his wife's remarks demonstrated the value he placed on their partnership.

Interestingly, aspects of the personal theologies of both John Griffing Jones and Isaac Borders, two of the MECS officials most comfortable with expanded roles of women, did not align with some of the mainline MECS theology. Jones's theology of entire sanctification as a second blessing, while not unheard of within the MECS, stood outside the official denominational statements by the end of the nineteenth century. Jones even noted in his autobiography that Bishop William W. Duncan's idea of perfect love as a lifelong pursuit did not match his own ideas or experiences.[68] Jones's ideas stepped slightly out of bounds of the prevailing notions of sanctification, but Borders was truly heterodox. His personal statement of faith, called "Credo," though containing elements of orthodoxy, nonetheless questioned important elements of historic Christian faith. At one point, Borders declared, "I make my own capacity for heaven; no imputation of another's righteousness can make it for me."[69] This essentially nullified the influence of orthodox Protestantism in Borders's words and vastly reduced the role of Jesus in his view of salvation. He essentially proclaimed that he could achieve heaven on his own, without divine help. For an MECS pastor in Mississippi during the New South, this was dramatically heterodox.

While both Jones and Borders held views at variance with their larger denomination, these two men also had some of the most expansive views of a Christian woman's role in ministry. Heterodoxy (which, to be clear, was very slight in Jones's case) and an expanded view of a Christian woman's role cannot be made to connect neatly, however.

At the turn of the nineteenth century and into the twentieth, MECS theology focused on conversion. Methodist officials conceived of gender, in particular femininity and family life, through an evangelical lens. Many Methodist leaders rooted ideas of womanhood in the notion that women constituted the cornerstone of a Christian home and would nurture the young, impressionable souls of children and lead them to Jesus. For this to happen, many Methodist leaders argued that women needed to receive an education, even if such an education differed substantially from the education men received. Women's education tended to focus on literary achievements and ideas of beauty and stayed away from the hard sciences or business. Methodist leaders believed that a literary education would prepare women for the many trials and travails they would encounter as homemakers and mothers. Furthermore, it would train them in the necessary Christian virtues so that they might better influence their families and encourage godly behavior in their homes. For many Methodist officials, home was where they might find respite from the world, but more importantly, it was where future generations might learn the truths of the Christian religion. Thus, in a denomination focused so heavily on evangelism and mission work, the home formed the first field where others might be brought to Christ.

In fact, theology influenced every idea that MECS officials had about gender, about what it meant to be a man, about how femininity should be thought of and displayed, and about the nature of family life. Of course, this makes one wonder if radical theology could dramatically reinterpret Southern notions of gender. To answer this question, we turn next to how the Holiness movement in the American South constructed gendered ideals.

II
RADICAL THEOLOGY AND RADICAL IDENTITY

6
Defining Holiness

In the early decades of the nineteenth century, John Griffing Jones found solace for his soul in the doctrines of Methodism. As Jones quickly learned, Methodism involved seeking after something variously called full salvation, entire sanctification, Christian perfection, or perfect love. Whatever the name, the meaning stayed the same—the Holy Spirit would enable the believer to say no to all ungodliness. During the early part of the nineteenth century, the doctrine of Christian perfection constituted a significant part of Methodist theology in the South. However, a little over fifty years later, Jones and many others found that the Methodist Episcopal Church, South no longer held to the doctrine of entire sanctification.

The move away from the doctrines of perfect love deemphasized a unique part of Methodist practice and polity and created a general evangelical theological hegemony throughout the South, as Baptists and Methodists constituted the largest denominations in the region.[1] However, the idea that entire sanctification marked mature believers and qualified them for Christian service led the leaders of the Holiness movement to define themselves differently and to understand gender in ways that did not fit into the larger evangelical culture. The implications of Holiness theology and the ways in which leaders developed new understandings of gender helped fuel the Holiness movement's explosive growth.

The Holiness movement was not an aberration in southern religious culture at the turn of the century. Holiness theology had been a part of Methodism since the antebellum decades. After Reconstruction, though, Holiness adherents began to self-identify not as Methodists but as the sanctified.[2] Those who identified with the Holiness movement often faced harsh criticism, derision, and opposition from family and friends. Yet those who claimed entire sanctification often stood up for their beliefs with a striking confidence.

By claiming insider status in a group with a radical theology, the sanctified leaders of the Holiness movement claimed a new identity for themselves, one rooted not in regional or historic allegiances but in the blessings of God on a peculiar people. Additionally, they claimed an identity rooted in a distinct process of sanctification that separated them from, and elevated them above, everyone else. The leadership of the movement claimed that what set their members apart were not the common markers of the day, such as socio-economic class, biological sex, or even racial identity, but a spiritual state. Thus, the movement's leaders explained, those who were sanctified found in their new identities freedom from the restrictions of their culture, and thus the radically alternate flow of Holiness theology became a defining faith.

Holiness Theology and Experiential Religion

The leaders and evangelists of the white Holiness movement in the American South resembled their evangelical cousins in many ways.[3] The Holiness movement affirmed the traditional Protestant doctrine that sinful, broken humans' only hope of reconciliation to a just and holy God came through faith in the redeeming work of Jesus of Nazareth, who, being fully God and fully man, fulfilled the law of God and made restitution for the sins of humanity. Furthermore, they believed that the Protestant version of the Bible was the inspired, authoritative word of God. Thus, the movement's leaders could affirm many of the doctrines that their friends, neighbors, and family members throughout the South believed. However, the leaders of the Holiness movement departed from their coreligionists in the belief that sanctification was "the central idea of Christianity, the crowning doctrine of revelation, the moving force of the church, the qualification for service, and fitness for heaven."[4] This change in theology defined adherents' identity in ways that were not available to other theological groups in the New South.

While other evangelicals across the South between 1877 and 1915 believed in the idea of sanctification, they neither elevated the doctrine to such a position nor defined it in the same way Holiness adherents did. The leaders of the Holiness movement argued that sanctification was an instantaneous blessing of the Holy Spirit that cleansed the believer's heart of the proneness to sin.[5] The sanctified therefore could live free from willful sin.

According to those in the movement, entire sanctification brought the believer into perfect communion with God, where the sanctified could live entirely in accordance with the law of God. Those who did not believe in entire sanctification did not understand how adherents of this theology believed they could keep the mandates of a morally perfect God. Many of the movement's critics charged that adherents either deluded themselves or were actually insane, as they did not understand how adherents could think they could live without committing sins or making mistakes.[6]

Holiness leaders did not actually advocate the idea that they could live entirely without sin or mistakes, however. Instead, they carefully articulated the fact that they still had limitations. Indeed, the noted Holiness evangelist and preacher W. B. Godbey freely admitted that sanctification did not remove "the liability of mistakes, because the mind is not made perfect until this mortal puts on immortality. Therefore, intellect, memory, and judgment will make mistakes. This perfection is simply that of the heart."[7] The leaders of the movement itself argued that sanctification defined the believer's new identity.[8]

Basing personal identity on the specific theological idea of entire sanctification made experiencing personal holiness virtually the sole focus of the southern Holiness movement. Though they often experienced ridicule and slander, the leaders of the southern Holiness movement believed they did God's work. They felt assured that preaching the second blessing followed in the footsteps of generations of saints and martyrs before them. Everywhere they went, Holiness preachers and evangelists told their audiences that to have a new identity as true, mature believers they needed not only to come to a saving knowledge of Jesus Christ but also to experience the instantaneous sanctifying work of the Holy Spirit.

The experience of Christian perfection marked, for many adherents of the Holiness movement, almost a second conversion experience. Each person's experience of holiness had a slightly different version, but, taken together, experiences of sanctification followed a five-step pattern: an initial recognition that something was missing and a preliminary search for holiness; then an inward examination and questioning; the consecration of self and symbolic leaving of "all on the altar"; a sense of an intimate connection with God or baptism of purifying fire; and a need to proclaim the experience of the second blessing. This process allowed new adherents to adopt a new transformative identity defined by faith in entire sanctification.

However, changing one's sense of self, and gaining a new identity, did not come easily. The first step Holiness evangelists talked about in this process of sanctification began with the believer seeking holiness itself. One of the founders of the annual Indian Springs Camp Meeting, W. A. Dodge, had sought the experience of holiness before staying up late into the night praying for the baptism of the Holy Spirit.[9] Similarly, John Lakin Brasher, one of Alabama's Holiness evangelists, spent several days attending the meetings of the Salvation Army and discussing the doctrines of sanctification with them.[10] Even the preeminent evangelist of Holiness in the South, W. B. Godbey, recalled that before his sanctification, he felt that there was something missing from his Christian walk.[11]

While the initial step in receiving Holiness required a seeking after it, for many, the second stage entailed a period of personal examination led by the Holy Spirit. Evangelist Beverly Carradine recalled a series of almost audible questions pointing him toward sanctification.[12] Some adherents experienced this process of self-examination simply as an inward questioning, while others reported repeating to themselves various Scriptures affirming the reality of sanctification.[13]

In the third stage, in which the penitent symbolically "put all on the altar," the seeker deliberately offered her greatest fears or most treasured object to God. If a fear was offered, the person promised to face it; if a valued object, the seeker promised to give it up, if necessary.[14] This was, perhaps, the most important stage in acquiring a new identity, as each individual had to wrestle with his or her deepest fears and personal insecurities in order to gain a new sense of self. Holiness proponents told their listeners that they needed to put aside their old identities and all that went with them. Only after they had done so could a new, sanctified identity emerge. W. A. Dodge, in his "Consecration," offered for God's use "Myself, my body, eyes, tongue, hands, feet, mind and heart. My wife . . . ; my boy . . . , and my little daughter . . . , my books, clothes, money, all I now have. Yes, all my means are, and shall be, Thine. My time, and if there is anything else that appertains to me, that I have not mentioned, I lay it on the altar to stay there forever."[15] Clearly, the idea of putting all "on the altar" was a significant step. The language of the altar referenced the Old Testament, wherein the Israelites placed their offerings on an altar in the temple in order to sacrifice them to God. Thus, when a person who sought sanctification placed items "on the altar," it signified that the individual was symbolically sacrificing those items to God.

In almost every recounting of the experience of the second blessing, a person, once she had placed all "on the altar," soon entered the fourth step, wherein a sense of abiding peace and deep communion with God confirmed the adherent's new identity. It was only this sense of an intimate relationship with God that kept Mary Lee Cagle, one of the South's premier female evangelists, going, despite her family's fierce opposition to her preaching.[16] Similarly, both Minnie and John Lakin Brasher felt a sense of light and peace at the time they identified as their sanctification.[17] Sometimes adherents described this sense of intimacy as a baptism of fire. W. A.

Dodge recalled that the day after he penned his consecration, he "felt that God sent His fire and consumed the offering."[18] Holiness leaders marked this sense of intimacy or baptism of fire as an indication of a higher, greater Christian experience that marked a spiritual maturity in their lives. When Beverly Carradine noted the difference between conversion and sanctification, he told readers that conversion meant being born into the family of God, while sanctification was a baptism by fire. He then reasoned, "*A baptism of fire would hardly be the proper swaddling-clothes for a newborn babe.*"[19] Clearly, Carradine thought that this experience did not merely mark a transition in the adherent's life; it noted the believer's maturity in faith.

After the experience of sanctification, whether the believer felt a sense of intimate communion or a baptism of purifying fire, the newly sanctified believer needed to testify to her new identity.[20] This important final step helped the individual to understand her experience and encouraged her to identify publicly with the larger Holiness movement. Indeed, this final step marked initiation into the larger community. This testimony of Christian perfection and self-identification with the Holiness movement demonstrated a significant change from the previous ways in which some groups taught the doctrine of entire sanctification in the antebellum period. Throughout the early part of the nineteenth century, though the doctrines of Christian perfectionism were part of orthodox Methodist teachings, adherents did not use these doctrines to define their personal or religious identity. Instead, they identified as Methodists; a belief in personal holiness was simply a part of that identity. However, starting in the 1870s and 1880s, belief in the doctrine of the second blessing became the primary religious identification for many in the Holiness movement across the Deep South.

History of the Southern Holiness Movement

This focus on the experience of entire sanctification defined the Holiness movement. The second blessing doctrines and ideas were not a uniquely southern phenomenon. Indeed, many religious historians note how Methodist theology contained the doctrine of entire sanctification from its arrival in the Americas at the beginning of the eighteenth century. Yet most of these scholars argue that it had little impact in the South until after Reconstruction.[21] Even one of the most prominent Holiness evangelists, W. B. Godbey, traced the transition of the movement south over the Ohio River to 1883.[22]

However, some Southern Methodists did hold the ideas of entire sanctification before the Holiness movement of the late nineteenth century. One itinerant Southern Methodist minister, and the eventual historian of the Mississippi Conference of the MECS, John G. Jones, believed that sanctification was an instantaneous work of the Holy Spirit, and though he never self-identified with the Holiness movement, both he and his wife claimed the second blessing.[23] In his handwritten autobiography, Jones recounted both his and his wife's entire sanctification in the 1820s, nearly fifty years before the doctrines of perfect love coalesced into a larger movement in the New South period.[24]

Jones recorded that other Methodists sought after entire sanctification, and he meticulously recounted friends and acquaintances who believed in Christian perfection. In other words, a community of like-minded individuals wished to experience the Holy Spirit's work of perfect love before the Civil War.[25] This community was recognizable enough that a few years later, Jones identified many people around him who claimed the blessing.[26]

In addition to John Griffing Jones's accounts of those he knew who sought entire sanctification, the *Methodist Magazine* featured in their last issue of 1824 and first issue of 1825 two extracts of a letter from William Winans, a presiding elder of the Mississippi District. Winans asserted that the emphasis on this doctrine of entire sanctification helped to "revive the work of God" and noted that preachers within the Mississippi District were "becoming more earnest in urging their hearers to 'go on to perfection.' "[27]

At the 1855 District Conference in Jackson, Louisiana, Jones preached on this topic, an act that did not go unnoticed. Shortly after leaving the church, another pastor confronted Jones on the issue of full salvation.[28] This encounter led to numerous sermons preached by both the second blessing and gradual sanctification sides of the Methodist Conference.[29]

While some controversy surrounded the doctrine of entire sanctification in the 1850s, John Jones clearly expressed, for the thirty years leading up to the American Civil War, his beliefs about the instantaneous work of the Holy Spirit in a believer's life. Yet nothing suggested that he experienced the disapproval of the Methodist bishops and leaders because of his identification with the doctrines of Christian perfection. In fact, in 1872 Jones received the assignment to write the history of the Mississippi Methodists.[30] While significant currents of Holiness theology moved among the Methodist leaders of the Mississippi Conference before the American Civil War, there is no evidence that those who held to instant sanctification identified themselves any differently than other Methodists in the antebellum period.[31] Indeed, though Jones lived well into the 1880s, a time when Holiness adherents began to self-identify and move into separate denominations, Jones retained his Methodist identity and never indicated that he identified himself with the Holiness movement.[32]

During late 1870s and early 1880s the doctrine of entire sanctification gained momentum throughout the region, and the movement of those who identified themselves primarily by Holiness doctrines began. When this theology started to make large inroads in the American South after Reconstruction, many southern Methodist officials did not know how to respond. Part of this confusion came from the fact that many people spreading Holiness doctrines came from the Methodist Episcopal Church—the northern branch of Methodism in the United States. Since 1844, when Methodists split into northern and southern branches, the regional denominations had maintained an icy relationship. For southern Methodists, northerners further strained this relationship when northern clergy came south during Reconstruction. For a time, the federal government gave northern bishops the authority to fill vacant southern church pulpits, a policy that was eventually revoked. Yet even after this, "carpetbag clergy" spread southward and entreated many churches to switch their denominational affiliation.[33]

In the late 1870s and early 1880s, the fear that Holiness constituted a type of northern religious invasion had not yet spread. The Holiness movement's growth, and the eventual opposition to it, within the North Georgia Conference of the Methodist Episcopal Church, South, provides an example of the waves of popularity and persecution that Holiness adherents faced in the South. While Methodist conferences across the South contained scattered adherents of Christian perfection, the North Georgia Conference's internecine conflicts were particularly well documented.

In 1883, when A. J. Jarrell, W. A. Dodge, and other Methodist clergy and lay members founded the Georgia Holiness Association, one of the first and most influential of the movement's associations, the roll listed 140 individuals who had approved the first resolution to spread the doctrines of Christian perfection throughout Georgia.[34] Within the next year and a half, Warren Candler, eventually the bishop of, and already an influential voice in, the North Georgia Conference, invited the Georgia Holiness Association to hold its annual meeting in his church.[35] Over the next year or two, Candler even took exception to the opposition of Atticus Haygood, his mentor, to the Holiness movement.[36]

While Candler seemingly started out allied with Holiness proponents, in the mid-1880s, his position changed and he became convinced that the Holiness movement was a tool of the northern Methodist Episcopal Church. After this point, in the 1890s, Candler became a strident opponent of Holiness theology. Candler's opposition fell in line with a larger movement within the MECS. By the late 1870s and early 1880s, many within the MECS had begun to fight over what exactly Christian perfection and perfect love meant: One side argued that it meant entire sanctification on earth, while the other insisted that perfect love could be found only in heaven. In fact, by the 1890s the MECS (and the Southern Baptist Convention) fiercely opposed the doctrines of the Holiness movement and often derided the group's activities and theology.

Although by the 1890s Candler was using his influence to quiet ministers who espoused Holiness views, Atticus Haygood was, perhaps, the most determined foe of Holiness theology within southern Methodism.[37] Haygood, no great promoter of orthodoxy himself, felt that second blessing theology hid a political play for power—especially within the North Georgia Conference—and used his own considerable political clout to disrupt the Holiness movement. Haygood's opposition became especially clear after his election as bishop and subsequent demotions of prominent members of the Holiness movement.[38]

Haygood's episcopal authority extended to the North Georgia Conference of the Methodist Episcopal Church, South, and his displeasure with members of the Holiness movement was most keenly felt there. Haygood's treatment of two pastors whom he had known for decades, A. J. Jarrell and W. A. Dodge, provides the clearest example of his use of the bishopric to silence Holiness ministers.[39] In 1883, both Jarrell and Dodge occupied prominent positions in the North Georgia Conference of the MECS, but by 1895 Dodge had been removed from preaching responsibilities and worked in a junior position he had held twenty years earlier. Similarly, Jarrell received a transfer to the South Georgia Conference, finally being "given permission" to transfer to Missouri (both he and his wife claimed that he had never requested the second transfer and he tried unsuccessfully to reverse it).[40]

Despite the opposition of Haygood, Candler, and others, Dodge, Jarrell, and many other members of the North Georgia Conference remained within the MECS. They chose to stick with the denomination, even in the midst of internecine persecution. However, in the mid-1890s, across the South, many of those committed to the doctrines of entire sanctification left their home denominations and started new ones.[41] These new denominations and associations often worked together to promote the doctrines of Christian perfection, and the southern Holiness movement was a highly decentralized conglomerate of microdenominations. Sometimes these groups defined themselves according to geographic areas, other times by theological sticking points. Despite sometimes fractious differences between these groups, most scholars recognize them as a coherent religious movement focused on the promotion of the idea of instant and entire sanctification—as did the people at the time. Evangelists of Holiness doctrines spoke at revivals, camp meetings, and religious services regardless of which group invited them, and the print culture that sprang up gave adherents the sense that though theirs might be a small denomination, the doctrines of Christian perfection were spreading across the South and the nation.[42]

While the doctrine of entire sanctification did spread across the South, mainline MECS ministers did not welcome it. (Southern Baptist ministers also derided the Holiness movement, but to a slightly lesser extent than those in the MECS. This was due largely to the fact that fewer members of the SBC defected to Holiness groups.) Many members of the MECS viewed Holiness adherents with disdain or as a threat to proper religion. In fact, by 1885, those who testified that the Holy Ghost had baptized them had made such a name for themselves that the *St. Louis Globe-Democrat* had a special correspondent's report on the "Holiness People in Georgia." The article mocked those who believed they were sanctified and portrayed a man named Rev. Miller Willis as an offensive rube who accosted strangers in the street with messages of hell-fire and brimstone.[43] This was a common way that outside groups (both religious and secular) attempted to define the Holiness movement. Opponents often portrayed members of the movement as ignorant, offensive, and uncultured.[44]

The preachers and evangelists of the Holiness movement seemed to revel in this (false) identity, and often railed against those with wealth and power in society. W. B. Godbey, one of the movement's most prominent writers and evangelists, warned against those who gave their children large amounts of money, saying this would be used to "pay their way to Hell!"[45] Beverly Carradine, a leading proponent of Holiness throughout the South at the turn of the century, also worried about the dangers of high society. He told his readers not to get involved with the "stirring, fussy, unspiritual Ladies' Aid Society," which he believed held itself aloof from "the class meeting room where testimonies ring clear, tears drip, and shouts abound."[46]

Carradine's advice demonstrated the type of worship that he thought was most appropriate to those baptized by the Holy Spirit. His was not a structured, staid worship; instead, he wanted emotional displays of the love of God among his parishioners. Other pastors and evangelists within the Holiness movement also welcomed expressive worship.[47] Holiness authors and publishers like M. W. Knapp, who denounced those who thought they were above demonstrative worship, staunchly defended the tears and cries in emotional church services. Similarly, many of the leaders of the Holiness movement cast aspersions on those who eschewed boisterous worship.

In Knapp's mind, the real danger came not from groups that derided emotionalism within the Holiness movement but from the "professional preachers" whose excessive education enervated them, their identities defined by educational attainment rather than by religious experience. Knapp told his readers that the requirement of a college degree rather than a testimony of entire sanctification marked an "alarming symptom of apostasy in the churches."[48] He thought that many churches had it backward, and told his readers, "Many an uncouth, unschooled preacher to-day is winning more souls to God and holiness than a whole city full of learned scholastics."[49] According to Knapp, educated but unsanctified and irreligious preachers proved ineffective and only those who received the second blessing made an eternal difference. Interestingly, Knapp appropriated the idea that those in the Holiness movement were uneducated. Rather than trying to shy from the label, he turned it on its head and made it a badge of honor. He worried about the spiritual damage the upper-class, highly educated pastors were doing, and preferred the teachings of those whose experience of sanctification defined their identity.[50]

Similarly, W. B. Godbey loved to talk about the work that sanctified, illiterate ministers did and compared it to those who spent years at seminaries.[51] He even talked about the ways education had "paralyzed their nerves by long years of assiduous study" and had "worn out their voices."[52] Interestingly, though, Godbey was a highly educated man. He had spent six years in college, three in classes and three working to pay his way, and took pride in his education, particularly his ability to read and write biblical languages.[53] Godbey even told his readers, "You need a classical education to qualify you to successfully study the blessed Bible."[54] Godbey was no backwoods rube, and he expected his hearers and readers to work to better their own education. Yet he wanted his congregants to define their identities through faith rather than the number of initials after their names. Thus, though many evangelists in the Holiness movement, including Godbey, claimed that their experience of holiness made them more highly qualified for Christian ministry than those who simply received a college or seminary education, some of them had college degrees and encouraged others to receive as much education as they could.[55] Holiness theology did not discourage education per se—it discouraged the rooting of personal identity in anything other than the experience of Christian perfection.

By defining identity in entire sanctification, many Holiness advocates fell afoul of MECS leaders. Yet, in a rare attempt by MECS leaders to be conciliatory toward those in the Holiness movement in the 1890s, W. S. Harrison, a correspondent to the New Orleans *Christian Advocate*, attempted to placate readers by arguing that the "apparent differences of opinion on the subject have originated, we think, from the effort to shape all men's attainments in grace by some men's experience." The writer argued against the idea that entire sanctification must be an instantaneous, memorable experience—something that almost all Holiness leaders advocated. Harrison noted that he knew many people who had undoubtedly received "the fullness of grace, but not according to that formula [of the second blessing]," and noted that continual growth was normal.[56] While Harrison clearly tried to keep the peace, the idea of growth in sanctification was one of the things that many in the Holiness movement fought against as they defined their new spiritual identities. Indeed, they thought that it would be impossible to mistake the instantaneous experience of transformative perfect love.

The preachers and evangelists of the southern Holiness movement spread these doctrines of entire sanctification throughout the South. Yet, in contrast to their cousins in the Southern Baptist Convention and the Methodist Episcopal Church, South, many leaders of the Holiness movement did not feel circumscribed by geographic location.[57] Instead, Holiness officials deliberately built a culture spanning state and even regional boundaries in the 1880s and 1890s.

The religious periodicals that helped to spread the doctrines of perfect love throughout the New South constituted a major part of the Holiness movement's multiregional culture that worried white southerners like Warren Candler.[58] These newspapers, tracts, and pamphlets came from places as varied as Virginia, South Carolina, Georgia, Ohio, and even parts of New England.[59] The print culture of the Holiness movement meant that the movement deliberately looked beyond regional boundaries as preachers and evangelists sought to instill an identity defined more by religious experience than by geographic place. The leaders who appear in this study, which focuses on the South, do not all necessarily come from the region. Most came from these states, while others only conducted revival services throughout the region, or had tracts, pamphlets, and other publications spread across the area by sanctified revivalists. The leadership of the Holiness movement tried to develop a subculture that deliberately eschewed southern identity in favor of a sense of self defined by entire sanctification.

What eventually split the Holiness movement, and even made it look conservative in its theology, was the arrival of the Pentecostal movement in the South around 1908–1909. For many early Pentecostals, the Holiness movement seemed the logical place to begin to spread the doctrines of glossolalia, faith healings, and other elements of mystic religiosity. However, with these ideas, many Pentecostals also preached that theology that stopped with the doctrine of entire sanctification was incomplete, perhaps even insincere, as it encouraged well-meaning believers to stop at a midway point between "dead religion" and the "true latter-day rain" of the Holy Spirit.[60]

Of course, this characterization of the Holiness movement as incomplete, perhaps even spiritually dangerous to its adherents, did not go unchallenged. W. B. Godbey, perhaps the most prolific Holiness evangelist in the South, thought of Pentecostal theology as demonic.[61] After visiting the Azusa Street revivals, he declared that those revivalists were "Satan's preachers, jugglers, necromancers, enchanters, magicians, and all sorts of mendicants."[62] Meanwhile, other Holiness preachers denounced the movement that consistently took adherents from Holiness congregations.[63] Thus, within the course of a generation, the southern Holiness movement had been lauded revivalists within denominations, then persecuted denominational outcasts, and finally the conservative detractors of the new theological movement.

The willingness to go through this cycle demonstrated just how much Holiness preachers believed in the transformative power of the second blessing. Such power frequently led those in the Holiness movement to envision gender in different ways than did many other people throughout the South, and the following two chapters explore a few of these dimensions. Chapter 7 investigates the ways Holiness leaders reoriented ideals of both femininity and family life around the experience and responsibilities of the second blessing. This meant sanctified leaders encouraged women to take positions of leadership and authority in the church while maintaining "traditional" roles within the home. Leaders also argued that for families, the centrality of the second blessing and the building of a sanctified community of believers should encourage parents to see their faith as a communal identity to be passed down through the generations as they reared children in the doctrines of Holiness.

Chapter 8 focuses on how the leaders of the southern Holiness movement used the theology of entire sanctification to argue for rearranging some of the ideas of manhood and masculinity current in the Deep South between 1877 and 1915. While the Holiness movement used its own categories for defining "true manhood," they retained elements of the masculinity popular in the broader culture of the time. This occurred by continuing to use martial and hyper-masculine imagery to talk about the sanctified church. At the same time, leaders focused on a believer's perfect love of God to envision a distinct type of manliness wherein men talked freely about their love and affection for one another. This stood in stark contrast to contemporary ideas of masculinity that eschewed displays of affection between men. Together, these chapters demonstrate the unique ways that leaders of the southern Holiness movement tried to connect their beliefs about the sacred with personal and familial identity and to pass these views on to their congregants in the turn-of-the-century Deep South.

7
Consecrated Regardless of Sex

Holiness preachers frequently used the theology of entire sanctification to redefine ideas of gender. Their religious ideals, centered on the second blessing, led white Holiness preachers and evangelists to the conclusion that they had a unique spiritual identity that altered how they defined gender.[1] Prominent Holiness leaders' theology encouraged women to take positions of authority within the church. While Holiness officials worried about how an individual defined her identity, they told adherents that their faith in entire sanctification that could be passed down through generations and therefore turned their attention to sanctified parenting. Proponents of Holiness theology also pointed to marriage as a model of the relationship between God and the sanctified believer, allowing both women and men within the movement to consider themselves the bride of Christ. In other words, Holiness leaders believed that their theology transformed personal identity.

Holiness understandings of identity and gender did not break entirely away from secular constructions of gender in the New South. Theology altered ideas of gender and opened new avenues for expression, but it did not create ex nihilo. It may be helpful to think in terms of the historical and cultural flows of gender construction. Holiness theology, as an incoming stream, altered the currents of gender identity and sometimes even moved it into new streambeds. However, Holiness theology did not do away entirely with the old patterns.[2] Even as Holiness leaders promoted spiritual equality, the culture of the South, which often considered women, particularly white women, to be fragile figures that should remain in the domestic world, still heavily influenced sanctified leaders.[3]

"Preach like Lightning"

The Holiness movement's redefinition of gender meant that many people encouraged women to testify to their experience of sanctification and become preachers. This was a radical departure from the contemporary currents of gender roles in the New South. Despite this countercultural stance, most Holiness leaders proclaimed that the second blessing freed women to preach and take leadership roles within the church.

Evangelist W. B. Godbey proclaimed the idea of women preachers to all who would listen. Godbey loved to talk about women holding positions of authority as preachers and evangelists. He believed that the work and power of the Holy Ghost so overwhelmed and transformed those who received it that they gained a new identity that was more foundational than biological sex. In his pamphlet *Shall the Women Preach?* (1891), Godbey declares, "When we are born of the Spirit into the Kingdom of God, sexual distinction goes into eternal eclipse, forever perpetuated by sanctification and glorification. . . . This enfranchisement of the sisterhood is the crowning glory of the present age."[4] (There is little to suggest that W. B. Godbey either supported or criticized the women's suffrage movement in the Deep South at the turn of the century.[5] He rarely spoke about political issues such as the right to vote, and the phrase "enfranchisement" likely was a call for women to take their religious rather than political rights.) Godbey did not care whether an individual was male or female, as long as he or she had received entire sanctification. He clearly felt that the empowerment of women in the ministry was one of the most important points of the Holiness movement. Indeed, he told his readers that it was the "crowning glory" of what Holiness offered to the world.

Throughout his pamphlet about the crowning glory of women preaching the message of entire sanctification, Godbey poses hypothetical questions. After explaining why sanctified women should preach, Godbey turns to the fact that many denominations opposed female preachers and so would not grant preaching licenses. Approaching the problem with his typically assertive stance, Godbey writes, "Oh, women, quit bothering your dead church about [a] license. Go and preach like lightning till the stars fall."[6] Along with this imperative, Godbey compared women preachers to Jesus and the twelve apostles, pointing out that none of them had a preaching license. Godbey implied that those denominations not granting preaching licenses to women opposed Jesus.

In his 1902 tract *Work of the Holy Spirit*, Godbey declared that the doctrine of women's ministry was one of the "grand truths" that the Holiness movement needed to preach to the "ends of the earth."[7] For Godbey, the idea that women should be preachers and evangelists was not merely a side issue but one of the central ideas of the movement. Throughout the tract, W. B. Godbey used Scripture and theological arguments to prove why sanctified women should preach.

Godbey tried to bolster his arguments by using historical examples to support the idea of women evangelists. Throughout his sermons, speeches, and writings, Godbey told his audiences about different female preachers in history spreading the word of God. According to his reading of the Bible, the first woman preacher was Mary Magdalene, who told the disciples of Jesus about the resurrection.[8] Godbey also pointed to a history of women preachers and evangelists in the early church.[9] Godbey praised the women of the Salvation Army (who also believed in entire sanctification) for their preaching to the urban poor, and he compared them positively with the "many collegiate graduates" who had not yet reached Christian perfection.[10] Godbey did not intend the comparison merely to be between Salvation Army women and college graduates, though. Godbey envisioned that through entire sanctification the lowest in society would have a ministry far more effective than those the world trusted.[11] In other words, he deliberately turned paradigms of class and gender upside down.

Godbey demonstrated his belief that the divine overturned worldly ideas of power by using examples of sanctified African American women in his writings. In *The Return of Jesus*, he mentioned coming across "an old negress at the washtub who did not know her letters who would shout as she did her humble duties, and did not know she had sanctification, i.e., did not know what to call the blessing."[12] Godbey used similar examples of illiterate black women in his writings when he wanted to contrast the education given at seminaries with the qualifications for preaching and evangelism given by the Holy Ghost. While he explicitly used these examples to subvert the gender and class norms of society, he rarely condemned, or even made any mention of, racism in the United States. Although Godbey praised Amanda Berry Smith (an African American Holiness preacher) as "one of the most efficient preachers of the world" who had "preached to myriads in America, Europe, Asia, and Africa," his point was to show not how African Americans could take leadership roles in white Holiness church but how the Holy Ghost could transform those considered lowest in society into efficient evangelists.[13]

Even though Godbey infrequently mentioned race, the few examples he did give were more than many others in the white Holiness movement provided, though some leaders bucked cultural trends in order to work with African Americans. For example, Mrs. S. S. Garbutt, at the encouragement of W. A. Dodge, led at least one meeting for black Holiness adherents in Lovett, Georgia, in the final years of the nineteenth century.[14] Although the leaders of the Holiness movement envisioned that the doctrine of entire sanctification should move many to redefine their ideas of gender, these leaders rarely delivered a similar message about effect of theology on racial identities. Holiness doctrines gave leaders the religious paradigm to begin looking past racial differences. However, the currents of violent racism prevalent across the American South were so deeply entrenched that most leaders could not imagine the same transformation, or speak out with the same conviction, as they did about new streams of gender construction.

Historian Randall Stephens has a different interpretation of the Holiness movement's response to southern racism. In his book recounting the history of the Holiness movement in the South, Stephens maintains that Holiness theology led adherents to confront many aspects of racial prejudice.[15] Holiness theology did encourage many people to look beyond the skin color, a dramatic step in the American South at the fin de siècle. Members of the Holiness movement's leadership also did not attempt to reconcile sectional differences in the United States at the expense of people of color like many other religious groups did.[16] However, adherents found it much easier to look for signs of sanctification across gender boundaries than across racial ones, and incidents when the sanctified reached beyond the limits of contemporary racism were few and far between.

While many of the sanctified did not demonstrate the level of antiracist tendencies that twenty-first-century readers would like, they did attempt to have some measure of gender equality in preaching roles. In his tract titled "Pentecostal Preachers" (1897), Holiness author and publisher M. W. Knapp wrote without reservation that women should preach. (It is important to note that when Knapp authored this pamphlet, there was not a separate Pentecostal movement, and the people he referred to identified with the Holiness movement.[17]) Knapp explained to his readers that the most important marker of personal identity was whether someone had experienced Christian perfection, and he assumed that sanctified women had every right to become preachers and evangelists.[18]

Knapp made it clear that he believed women could be church leaders; indeed, he titled one of the sections in his tract *Women may Be Pentecostal Preachers*. In this section, Knapp used Scripture and experience to declare that any sanctified woman that preached had a divine call and "by her gifts and graces and fruitage . . . [was] recognized among the most effective of Pentecostal preachers."[19] Knapp clearly thought that women made a large contribution to the southern Holiness movement at the turn of the century. Knapp showed how theology defined his views of gender and led him to believe women had important leadership parts to play in the Holiness movement.

Sanctified women often took on leadership roles, including preaching ones, as the movement spread across the South. Charles Jernigan, in *Pioneer Days of the Holiness Movement in the Southwest* (1919), recounted many examples of sanctified women preaching, leading revivals, and expanding the reach of the doctrine of perfect love. Jernigan recorded that the first person to promote the doctrines of Holiness in Texas was Mrs. Martha McWhirter, a Sunday School teacher, who persevered despite heavy opposition from her pastor.[20] In Arkansas, one of the preachers Jernigan gave special consideration to was Amanda Coulson, "whose work laid mostly in northern Arkansas, in the days that holiness and women preachers were scarce, and there was much prejudice against women preachers."[21] Even though Jernigan later wrote about her husband, it was clear he felt that Mrs. Coulson was the preeminent preacher in the family.[22] Beyond the numerous positive examples of female preachers throughout the work, Jernigan dedicated an entire chapter to "Women Preachers."[23] In it, the Holiness author wrote, "Whenever the Holy Ghost comes on a people, God has laid His hands on a few choice women and called them into the work of the ministry."[24] Rather than simply defending female clergy, Jernigan went on the offensive and proclaimed that those who were against women preaching actually acted against the divine.

Holiness evangelist Mary Lee Cagle also believed that men and women had an equal right to preach once the Holy Ghost had consecrated an individual's heart.[25] To Cagle, proper theology and religious experience mattered much more than biological differences. She felt that this point was so important that in her autobiography, Cagle included a sermon titled "A Woman's Right to Preach." In it, she remarked, "God is not looking for a man or woman to do His work, but He is looking for someone wholly consecrated to Him, and when He finds someone like that, He will use him or her, regardless of sex."[26]

Cagle did not ignore all gender differences, though. Only a little after mentioning that sex was irrelevant compared to a sanctified heart in the service of God, she asked her readers why God had given "women such a talent to talk, if not to be used for Him?"[27] Earlier in her sermon, Cagle admitted that men surpassed women "physically and mentally" and may even be better at "sermonizing and preaching," though no man could love better than a woman.[28] Cagle did not simply blur gender distinctions or believe that entire sanctification somehow made believers asexual beings; rather, she used the idea of entire sanctification to redefine the culture's restrictions on the roles that women could fill in the church. Cagle's life mirrored her belief that sanctification mattered more than her biological sex. Almost immediately after she received the second blessing, in the final years of the nineteenth century, Cagle felt a call to become a pastor. She knew that she would face opposition from those outside the Holiness movement owing to her sex, and even members of her own family resisted her desire to preach.[29] Nonetheless, Cagle followed what she believed to be God's call on her life and preached the doctrines of Christian perfection throughout the South.[30]

Cagle's idea that men and women could hold equal positions of authority in the church was a radical revision of women's roles for Protestant groups across the New South. At the same time, Cagle blended her views on women's ability to take institutional authority in the church with popular ideas about the differences between men and women. This exemplified how Holiness altered the currents of gender and identity in ways that contrasted sharply with the views of other denominations but did not do away with the entirety of southern gender identity.

Even those leaders who did not directly refer to female evangelists in their writings often supported them. Similar to what religious scholar Grant Wacker argued for the Pentecostal movement of the early twentieth century, the imperative for women to testify to their religious experience was so clear and self-evident that only a few leaders felt the need to argue for it.[31] Some of the male leaders of the Holiness movement who did not specifically defend women preachers gave them their tacit approval. One such example was A. J. Jarrell, the leader of the influential Georgia Holiness Association. Jarrell demonstrated this tendency to simply take for granted women's role as preachers, as he repeatedly quoted from the work of Phoebe Palmer in his tracts.[32]

Phoebe Palmer lived in New York, and from the late 1830s through the early 1870s, she taught a particular version of sanctification that helped define the American Holiness movement after the American Civil War. Palmer emphasized an instantaneous moment of entire sanctification, the idea of an individual placing their "all on the altar," and popularized the idea that women as well as men should seek a place in religious service.[33] Palmer's contribution to the southern Holiness movement was tangible, and the idea that women should have an authoritative role became one of the central symbols of the second blessing in the South.

While Holiness adherents strongly supported female clergy, many denominations opposed women preachers.[34] Sometimes women found that the staunchest opposition came from their own families. For example, according to Charles Jernigan's account of Amanda Coulson, she faced severe opposition from her father, who, readers were led to believe, severed all ties with his daughter once she started preaching.[35] Similarly, Mary Lee

Cagle's family opposed her preaching and threatened to disown her if she continued.[36] John Lakin Brasher, an Alabamian Holiness preacher, even told a story of a woman who wanted to preach but whose husband physically restrained her from doing so.[37] Sometimes female preachers faced not only familial opposition but also angry crowds that threw eggs or spread rumors that these women were lascivious creatures who had not been content with their husbands and so abandoned them, taking lovers in every city they visited.[38] Despite these rumors, women continued to use sanctification as a sign that they were called to preach. Perhaps part of the reason these rumors started was that women preachers took public stands—and were thus becoming "public women."

Being a public woman, even one who preached about Christianity rather than walked the streets, challenged ideas of white southern womanhood, which elevated the importance of the domestic world for women.[39] Of course, being labeled a public woman also challenged the idea that these female evangelists were pure in any sense. In her memoirs, published early in the twentieth century, Mary Lee Cagle talked about how difficult it was for women in the Holiness movement to have their names, reputations, and purity impugned simply because of their roles as preachers or evangelists.[40]

Vanity and Purity

While many preachers and evangelists in the Holiness movement advanced a degree of gender equality through the roles they believed women might take in the church, many retained the belief that there were specific feminine frailties. In particular, many writers believed that vanity and the love of fashion affected women more than men. More than a simple stereotype, the idea that women had a unique propensity to desire expensive or fashionable clothing dated back at least to the founding of the English colonies in America.[41] Religious and material culture scholars have demonstrated that in the nineteenth century, "clothing was a self-consciously defining and communicative feature for a woman in public."[42] Many Holiness leaders would have agreed, as they told sanctified women that their garments should express experiential piety. They often encouraged women to wear relatively plain, unadorned, white clothing to demonstrate a woman's inner purity, quiet spirit, sanctified heart, and, perhaps more subconsciously, group identity. It is highly likely that the women used their white clothing to signify the purity of their hearts, as well as their desire for entire sanctification.

Additionally, such garments served as a visible witness to a woman's self-identification with the Holiness movement.[43] An entire group of women clothed in white communicated a sense of solidarity and group identity to adherents and curious bystanders alike. Holiness leaders argued that, through relatively plain white dresses, these women hoped to convey ideas of both the holiness of the group and the personal sanctification experienced by its individual members. An additional aspect of plain white clothing, perhaps not fully grasped by the leaders or the adherents, was that it minimized class differences among the sanctified. As leaders of the Holiness movement tried to encourage one another to view the second blessing as the most important marker of personal identity, an important part of their encouraging group cohesion would be minimizing the differences between groups. Even as Holiness leaders seemed encouraged by female adherents wearing clothes that marked the state of their hearts, they reiterated the idea that vanity and love of fashion were distinctly feminine sins.

Author B. S. Taylor warned his turn-of-the-century readers, "Love of display of dress is a snare to women."[44] If that were not enough, Taylor claimed, "Fallen women begin their downward career by selling virtue for fashionable display."[45] Here, Taylor intimately linked sexuality and the love of fashion. He made it clear that anyone who called herself a sanctified Christian must eschew all vanity. By claiming that a supposedly uniquely feminine love of fashion precipitated the path to prostitution, Taylor opened the idea that any woman could be a prostitute-in-the-making. The connection that Taylor made between clothing and deviant female sexuality was impossible to miss. Taylor did not rebuke men's lustful advances toward women, nor did he offer any check on male sexual expression.[46] Instead, Taylor believed clothing and appropriate dress were women's issues, as they revolved around attracting and being attractive to men. This issue thus had dramatic importance for women's spiritual and sexual lives.

Mississippi Holiness preacher and author Beverly Carradine also worried about the clothes of the sanctified. In his 1897 book about living a pure life, he wrote, "To obtain the blessing of sanctification is to regulate at once the dress."[47] Carradine did not state exactly how the sanctified should dress, but he cautioned all of his readers, both women and men, to be neither a "fashionable scare-crow for the devil" nor "a fanatical scare-crow for God." Instead, he urged individuals neither to adorn themselves with worldly goods nor to let their clothes become a hindrance in their attempts to serve God.[48] The prohibition on fancy dress also helped cement group identity and forge ties across class lines as leaders attempted to make clear that the only identifying mark that truly mattered was entire sanctification.

In addition to ideas of appropriate dress, obtaining the second blessing meant the sanctified now lived in purity and perfect accord with the will of God. Far from being an obscure spiritual reference, purity became an important trait for preachers and evangelists in the Holiness movement. Purity marked an individual's spiritual condition. Nonetheless, in the larger culture in the New South period, purity had a very intimate component that carried distinctly sexual overtones, particularly for women. These sexual overtones made preaching to revival services uncomfortable when outsiders questioned the purity of sanctified women.[49]

One woman who clearly wanted to convey purity through her dress and wanted others in the Holiness movement to do the same was Rev. Mary Lee Cagle. Cagle viewed the issues of fashion and appropriate dress as a women's problem. In her memoirs, she recounted that early in her ministry, very few sanctified preachers in the Deep South talked about "how women should adorn themselves, and so very often holiness professors were wearing gold, feathers, and flowers, and worldly dress in general."[50] Eventually, Cagle felt that she needed to preach on the issue of proper dress, and did so with dramatic results. She recalled that as she finished her sermon on appropriate dress, the front of the church filled with the penitent who wanted to rid themselves of their worldly adornments. Cagle talked about the women who cast off gold rings, class pins, and other articles of jewelry in an attempt to demonstrate their holiness, thereby establishing that she thought that vanity was a woman's problem. Cagle noted how quickly these women demonstrated entire sanctification, once they had rid themselves of "worldly goods," which would also have been markers of class rather than spiritual identity.[51] In her memory of this event, Cagle built on a tradition of testimonies both in the Holiness movement and in other faith communities that expensive clothing or worldly dress could hinder spiritual growth.[52]

Cagle's memory of the event showed how she blended progressive and conservative views of gender and class with her theology. She believed that appropriate clothing was a women's issue and recalled how her own dress changed as she sought sanctification. Powdering her face, curling her hair, and even wearing any but the "plainest dress she could find" represented to Cagle a distracted and divided heart. Her desire for holiness and wanting to "get right with God" meant that she needed to lose all distractions of fashion and outward appearance.[53] Such ideas about plain dress would also have been instrumental in keeping class distinctions out of the Holiness movement. By doing their best to keep dress relatively plain, Cagle and other church leaders kept the focus on spiritual identity rather than on the differences in wealth among congregants.[54]

Yet Cagle's emphasis on the value of plain dress showed the dissonance within her construction of femininity. While she imbibed a traditional idea that vanity was primarily a hindrance to women's spirituality, she also espoused the idea that women could be preachers and evangelists. Cagle's theology defined her ideas of gender, and she encouraged those who read her book to allow Holiness theology to similarly change their understandings of womanhood. However, the streams of southern femininity were too strong to be completely dammed up, and Cagle repeated traditional ideas of uniquely feminine spiritual stumbling blocks while affirming unconventional roles for those who had removed those blocks and were running in the light of entire sanctification.[55] Cagle offered a wonderful example of the way in which Holiness leaders used theology to redefine gender identity. Church leaders did not simply create their own ideas of gender; instead, their theology changed the currents of how women should express themselves. Sometimes, as with Cagle, this led to conflicting ideas of what constituted appropriate understandings of femininity. She believed that women should take more authority in the church, which was a radical notion for the time; but she retained the traditional idea that women must be especially careful of the sins of vanity.[56]

Childhood and Family Life in Holiness Thought

While many of the leaders in the Holiness movement thought of Christian perfection as an experience that defined femininity, they did not neglect the implications it had for families, and they talked about the importance of familial identities that highlighted the second blessing. For many people in the New South, the family constituted the bedrock of any community, and Holiness preachers frequently talked about the importance of rearing faithful children who would someday experience Christian perfection for themselves. They repeated the idea to their audiences that through families, future generations would learn about the doctrines of the faith and the unique identity that believers acquired when they received entire sanctification. Officials who sought after, or who had received, the second blessing noted the importance of families in several different ways. They frequently wrote about how faith moved through generations and about the importance of rearing faithful children.

W. B. Godbey was particularly concerned that parents rear their children carefully. He warned parents, even those whose children had already professed their faith, that they needed to guard their little ones carefully against temptation, as it was all too easy for children to backslide.[57] Godbey believed not only that it was in the child's best interest for parents to guard their hearts but also that it was the parents' "imperative duty to do our utmost from the beginning to build around our children the strongest wall we possibly can in order to fortify them against temptation." Godbey told his readers that parents had an absolute duty to protect their children's faith, and explained that this meant educating children in the doctrines of Christianity and perfect love from the time they were born.[58] The evangelist believed that his mother influenced his own ministry in dramatic ways, and he encouraged parents to consecrate their own children for the Lord's work.[59] Godbey clearly internalized this model and used it as his archetype of the way in which religious sentiment passed through generations.

Additionally, Godbey warned his audiences that Christian parents should not give their children all types of worldly comforts and possessions. According to him, many of his schoolmates in college slipped into sin because of the money their parents sent them. Godbey celebrated that his parents were "too poor" to give him money for college and he advised other parents that it was a mistake for "Christian parents to pile up money for their children when they are so likely to use it to pay their way to Hell!"[60] Here, Godbey's class prejudices interacted with his ideas of the duties of Christian parents. As noted previously, those within the Holiness movement keenly felt their social status, particularly the fact that outsiders perceived them as lower class. Although some tried to shed this status, most embraced it, saying that their experience of entire sanctification gave them a status in heaven that would far exceed that of their more worldly brethren.[61] Godbey's advice that parents not pile up money and possessions for their children thus denounced those whose children did not have to work because of their parents' wealth. He believed that not having to labor would let children lose the discipline required for work, and possibly even the discipline required to experience the second blessing. Thus, those in the Holiness movement turned their reputation as lower class on its head and held it as a badge of honor that would (hopefully) encourage the children of the sanctified to form their identities as members of a sanctified community.

Many Holiness authors stressed the important influence that family had on building this sanctified community and on passing faith on to children. Mary Lee Cagle happily recalled that her mother was a Christian and, even though her father was not a believer, "she was wholly protected from the vices . . . was never in a dance hall, and attended only one show."[62] Similarly, W. B. Godbey recalled that "a preaching father, a sainted mother and a Christian home" reared him in such a way that he "wasted no time in the devil's workshop."[63] Even Charles Jernigan noted that his parents' faith was a significant factor in his conversion.[64] Each of these authors was extremely thankful that their respective families had sheltered them as children. Within the Holiness movement, there was no thought that young men should "sow their wild oats" before settling down to a life of faith. Holiness writers wanted their children to be faithful Christians all their lives, not just once they reached adulthood.

Pure and Holy Marriage

The emphasis on the family in Holiness writings often dovetailed with the writers' use of marriage to talk about his or her identity after experiencing perfect love. It was common for those in the Holiness movement to use marital language to talk about their relationship with God. According to those in the Holiness movement, the same traits that created a close, affectionate marriage, such as pursuit and intimacy, defined their relationship with God.

The idea that the sanctified were wedded to their savior transformed Holiness understandings of a believer's relationship with God. Both men and women willingly appropriated feminine traits as they affirmed the idea that they were married to Jesus. Neither the Southern Baptist Convention nor the Methodist Episcopal Church, South, used marriage as the primary metaphor for a believer's relationship with the divine. It was an emphasis virtually exclusive to the Holiness movement in the South. More than a simple analogue, marriage, according to many Holiness writers and evangelists, provided the space where a sanctified couple could live each for the other while providing mutual support and encouragement for service and ministry.

Beverly Carradine talked very specifically about the relationship that Holiness believers would have with Jesus. In his publication *Sanctification* (1891), Carradine told his readers that in the moment when they received perfect love, Jesus was "going to give himself to you in his fullness. Such a gift demands that your heart cry out with burning desires and quenchless longings."[65] Carradine's readers would have recognized the language of marriage and identified Jesus as the groom. Jesus, as the groom, established the relationship and gave himself to his people, not the other way around. The readers would have been amazed at Carradine's description of a transcendent God, who created the universe, establishing a tender, delightful relationship with humans. This relationship was so intimate that

Carradine used the language of the wedding night to portray it—Jesus was going to "give himself . . . in his fullness" to those who achieved holiness. While the language Carradine used to demonstrate the appropriate response had sexual tension, readers would have recognized that their pastor was attempting to show the intimacy and close communion with God that the second blessing enabled and would not have thought that Carradine believed in some type of cosmic intercourse.

Even in these passages, Carradine made it clear that it was the groom's responsibility to take the initiative and establish a relationship with his wife. The sanctified people of God, portrayed as the bride, took a passive role in Carradine's writings. Using this model, Carradine made it clear that married women should respond to their husbands' overtures with grateful, loving, urgent responses full of longing and desire. Both partners in a marriage had a responsibility if they followed the pattern set here by Carradine and what he described about Jesus and the sanctified people of God. It was the husband's role to initiate the relationship and to pursue his wife; he was supposed to give himself fully to his wife, holding nothing back. However, once he had done so, a wife was to respond with love, care, and desire.

Other writers used similar language to communicate their ideas about the appropriate role of wives, even as they identified themselves with the bride. These writers implied that a bride should wait for her husband, let him lead, not question his authority or leadership, and look to him to meet all of her needs. Additionally, the bride should make herself ready for reception by her bridegroom.[66] Marriage thus served at the end of the nineteenth century as a metaphor for the intimacy between the believer and her savior, making it clear that those in the Holiness movement took seriously the idea that sanctification provided incredible intimacy with the creator of the universe.

Sanctified authors across the South also talked about human intimacy and appropriate sexuality.[67] While they noted the ways people abused sexuality, writers in the Holiness movement were not ascetics. They believed that sex, within the confines of marriage, was something wonderful.[68] For example, the author B. S. Taylor counseled his readers to enjoy their spouses in order to keep their sexual desire pure.[69] Taylor castigated those who believed that "Christian purity" meant that married couples should only have intercourse for the purpose of procreation.[70] Sometimes this advice came from the pamphlets and marriage guides offering sexual advice to married couples. Although these early sex manuals were rarely as repressive as popular visions of Victorian culture pretend them to be, a number of them did suggest that husbands and wives abstain from sex for purposes other than procreation, often in order to "preserve" what was considered the husband's finite amount of sexual energy. In sharp contrast, Taylor counseled his readers to enjoy their spouse.

Taylor reminded his readers about their sanctification, writing, "Desire in a pure Christian is pure."[71] Not all Holiness writers celebrated marital intercourse in the detail Taylor did. Charles Jernigan, a preacher and author from Texas, simply noted that only "fanatics" counseled husbands and wives to remain celibate, a position that he thought broke up "many once happy homes."[72] W. B. Godbey did not even acknowledge this; he merely noted the ways in which sex within marriage provided "a most effective breakwater against sin."[73] The marriage bed, then, helped stem the tide of sin in an individual's life. A healthy physical relationship with one's spouse took on eternal significance. Marital intercourse was not only something to be celebrated but also provided a safeguard against the temptations of the devil. Those who had perfect love wanted to honor their savior in every aspect of their lives and in every secret part of their hearts. For them, nothing could be more intimate, more sacred, than the physical relationship between a husband and wife, and so even the way couples made love became a way to honor God.

Holiness writers did not view marriage merely as a way to ward off sin; rather, marriage offered a way to talk about their new identity as part of the bride of Christ. When W. B. Godbey identified sanctified believers with the bride of Christ at the turn of the century, he knowingly took on a feminine role. This transgression of gendered norms was not unknown among Christian writers, as the Bible alluded to the idea that the Christian church operated as the bride of Christ.[74] However, few southern male religious writers outside of the Holiness movement took up the title of bride as readily as did Godbey.[75] His appropriation of this term was not merely superficial. Instead, throughout his numerous writings, Godbey clearly portrayed Jesus as taking the initiative. Jesus performed all the action—not those identified as the bride.

Godbey, in his aptly named *Church—Bride—Kingdom* (1905), urged his readers to put their "all on the altar" so that "the Holy Ghost may solemnize your matrimony and thus wed you eternally to the fairest among ten thousand."[76] Godbey told believers that they were to marry Jesus himself. Although Godbey talked about Jesus as the "fairest among ten thousand," he clearly identified Jesus as the groom and all of his readers, both male and female, as the bride. Making this explicit, Godbey told readers that the Holy Ghost would identify the sanctified as Jesus's bride.[77] Similarly, in *The Return of Jesus*, Godbey wrote that Jesus acted as a young man who came in the middle of the night and stole away his betrothed so that they might elope. Godbey responded, "Oh, I want to be stolen. I am so anxious to be stolen."[78]

Godbey clearly wanted to be with his beloved savior and used the most intimate of relationships to declare his longing for a closer union with Jesus throughout his career as an itinerant preacher in the South. Godbey's language also indicated a deep sense of belonging. No longer would he have to go through life alone or have to face spiritual battles by himself. Instead, he was united to God—united not simply through the ties of friendship, but through the bonds of marriage. Using the analogue of marriage allowed Godbey to speak about the intimacy he felt with his savior. He appropriated the title of "the bride" and talked about how Jesus would take the initiative in the relationship. In fact, Godbey put himself in a passive position. Jesus would come and steal him away. Godbey would not run and meet Jesus; he did not do any of these actions on his own initiative. Instead, Godbey believed that Jesus would take the lead and draw Godbey to himself. This was in striking contrast to the ways in which Godbey described the rest of his life. Throughout his writings, Godbey let his readers know how hard he worked for the cause of Christ, and how actively he pursued holiness.[79] Thus, to describe his relationship with Jesus in passive terms marked how fully he had internalized the idea that he belonged to the "bridehood."

While Godbey made his early-twentieth-century readers aware that they could expect an intimate connection with God through sanctification, he also meant that they would have to give themselves fully to God. Given the context of the analogue of marriage, the idea that sanctified believers must give themselves fully to God also took on sexual overtones. It connected the relationship between believers who experienced perfect love with the intimacy of a physical relationship between husband and wife.

Godbey had used similar language more than a decade earlier when he wrote *Spiritual Gifts and Graces*. In that work, he declared that at the second coming of Jesus, the sanctified would "formally consummate the long-anticipated matrimonial alliance which was spiritually plighted at sanctification."[80] While Godbey did not say that believers would engage in some type of sexual relationship with the divine, he did suggest that the relationship between Jesus and the sanctified believers would be on the same level of intimacy as a bride and groom on their wedding night. However,

Godbey's readers would also recognize that Godbey assigned the position of the bride to all those within the movement—both women and men. In this relationship, God, and more specifically Jesus, was the groom and everything moved at his initiative.[81]

Holy Headship

The analogue of union with the divine also served to present a clear hierarchy within the human marriages of these Holiness leaders. Since the bride of Christ was supposed to be the passive one in the relationship and since Jesus, as the groom, initiated the relationship, the model legitimated the idea that men should be the heads of their households. Thus, while many preachers and evangelists in the Holiness movement talked about the spiritual equality between men and women and took the radical stance that sanctified women could preach just was well as men, they retained many of the functional and relational hierarchies of other New South families.

A clear example of this tension between spiritual equality and familial hierarchy came from the pen of W. B. Godbey. In his autobiography, Godbey talked about his own matrimonial bliss, saying, "It has always seemed to me that God, in His mercy, ransacked creation when He selected a helpmeet for unworthy me."[82] Godbey then talked about how he and his wife endured life by constantly supporting each other.[83] Yet even in these statements, Godbey combined ideas of marriage and gender roles in talking about his spouse.[84] Clearly, Godbey loved his wife, and he talked about his unworthiness for her. While it is clichéd for people to declare their unworthiness of their spouse, it was a revealing statement for a man who had experienced entire sanctification and claimed to live without willful wrongdoing.[85] Thus, an otherwise simple statement of a husband's unworthiness of his wife became, from W. B. Godbey, a charged statement and carried interesting connotations when mixed with the term "helpmeet."

The term "helpmeet" has had many different meanings in Christian history. Some scholars interpret this term as ensuring the subjection of women to male authority.[86] However, others have pointed out that the term "helpmeet" was used only four times throughout the Bible, twice being applied to God's role in relationship with the ancient nation of Israel.[87] The latter group of scholars argues that the term did not denote unbalanced power relationships but often was an empowering term. While both interpretations are intriguing, Godbey's use of the term fell somewhere in between the two.[88] The Holiness evangelist was a strong proponent of women's right to preach and equality before God; however, he clearly held to the ideas current in the New South that the domestic world was primarily a feminine sphere.[89]

The retention of gendered hierarchies within marriage and family life, despite a theology of institutional and spiritual equality, did not mean that Godbey loved his wife any less or looked down on her. As has already been mentioned, Godbey, who fervently proclaimed his own experience of Christian perfection to all who would listen, talked about his own unworthiness of his wife. Indeed, Godbey loved his wife dearly and when he wrote his autobiography in 1909, he looked forward to their fiftieth wedding anniversary.[90] His ideas about power relationships in their marriage, then, were not a hindrance to what he perceived to be a close, companionate, loving, and intimate relationship.

White southern Holiness leaders defined gender through their theology in two ways: through an identity within a sanctified community and through the use of marriage as a model of God's relationship to the sanctified believer. Without completely throwing out the larger culture's constructions of gender, the evangelists of the southern Holiness movement used radical theology to modify the ways they imagined proper womanhood, marriage, and family life.

For sanctified writers and preachers, the experience of the second blessing and their belief that the Holy Spirit had completely cleansed their hearts of all willful sin were life changing. That moment in their lives, and the theology they were steeped in afterward, led them to redefine the conceptions of gender with which they had grown up. They took ideas of gender prevalent in southern society at the time and either infused them with sacred meaning or arranged them differently. Holiness leaders encouraged women to testify publicly about their experience of sanctification, and, if they felt called to do so, to preach with the full authority of the church. Holiness proponents also used theology to encourage believers, both male and female, to think of themselves as the true bride of Christ, thus portraying marriage as the best analogy of the intimate relationship between God and the sanctified believer. The movement's leadership also encouraged parents to think about Christianity as a communal faith that could be passed on through the generations.

The laity of the Holiness movement heard sermons and speeches and read innumerable tracts, pamphlets, or periodicals by preachers and evangelists that all affirmed that the second blessing marked a "peculiar people," purified and set apart for God's special purposes.[91] The proponents of Holiness hoped that their audiences would be persuaded by this theology and so reinterpret their sense of self. Holiness authors and speakers believed that restrictions based on things other than the experience of sanctification were secondary. What mattered was whether or not a person had received perfect love. This view of the world, a binary division along spiritual lines, had dramatic implications for their ideas of personhood. Although they never fully dispensed with the conceptions of gender in the culture around them, Holiness leaders argued that the movement's theology created radically different expressions of personal identity. These ideas contrasted so sharply with those of the MECS and the SBC that Holiness leaders, as well as lay members, often faced sharp criticism. Yet the example suggested by Holiness writers, preachers, and itinerant evangelists provided a dramatic demonstration of how ideas of the sacred defined gender in the American South. The transformative theology of the Holiness movement not only opened new currents of femininity but also opened new streams of sanctified manhood.

8
Perfect Masculine Love

As demonstrated in chapter 7, the leaders of the Holiness movement in the American South believed their faith defined a distinct identity for those who received the second blessing. They argued that this identity altered the ways adherents should perceive and express gender. Their theology, which emphasized the Holy Spirit cleansing a believer from all willful sin, defined how preachers and evangelists envisioned manhood and offered a contrast to the manly ideals of the MECS and the SBC. This did not mean that self-identified leaders of the Holiness movement completely dispensed with the ideals of southern manhood and masculinity centered on an honor-based society that encouraged self-assertiveness, aggression, and competitiveness.[1] Instead, their theology modified these ideals to better fit them into the streambeds of faith that emphasized entire sanctification and perfect love. Although Holiness leaders did express militant faith, other types of masculinity—some of which undercut traditional Southern ideals—were also viewed as manly.

The leaders of the Holiness movement emphasized the Holy Spirit's power, the second blessing of sanctification, emotive worship services, and the ways an individual could live free from all willful sin. By doing so, they defined an alternate form of masculinity throughout the New South. Sanctified manhood uniquely blended expressions of publicly affectionate manliness with the traditional southern ideas of aggressive masculinity. There were many ways that this aggressive nature could be displayed in the New South, but it was often through competition.[2] Sanctified manhood offered truly unique ways for men to express their homosocial love for each other in terms markedly absent from other faith traditions. Baptist officials voiced such expressions of manly affection only in private letters. Methodist pastors, on the other hand, directed such gestures almost exclusively toward family members, not other men. The open expressions of intense affection and love among the male preachers and evangelists in the Holiness movement, as well as the highly emotional worship services and camp meetings, stood in stark contrast to the dominant evangelical culture in the South, and provided one reason why other denominations hated Holiness theology so much—it contradicted the ideals of Southern manhood.

At the same time that Holiness leaders used such expressions of affection and love when talking about other men, they retained elements of manhood and masculinity from the wider culture. They kept the hypermasculine, militant language from the larger culture that encouraged the idea that Holiness adherents were engaged in a spiritual battle. Preachers and evangelists consistently used martial imagery to portray a sanctified manhood standing against the powers of Satan, the world, and Christian apostates. Even in this, Holiness proponents carefully expressed a sense of shared community in their spiritual warfare. This shared sense of identity combined the important idea of community with the theology of perfect love.

Similar to the ways that Holiness clergy used the analogy of intimacy in marriage to describe their intense relationship with the divine through perfect love, Holiness authors wrote about how their pure, undivided hearts desired their beloved savior. These Christians believed that God was the true object of their affections and thus defined their deepest longings. Holiness author W. McDonald made this clear when he noted in 1877 that the best test of Holiness was whether a believer's heart was "emptied of sin, and filled with love, and nothing else; if he loves 'God with all his heart, might, mind and strength,' he has 'perfected holiness in the fear of the Lord.'"[3] McDonald believed that those who experienced perfect love needed to move beyond private experience and publicly claim the experience that defined their identities. Adherents delivered these testimonies at camp meetings and revival services as emotional stories of God's faithfulness and the Holy Spirit's blessing. This public testimony confirmed the believer's new identity as a member of the sanctified.

A. J. Jarrell, one of the founders of the influential Georgia Holiness Association, relished times when converts testified to their experience of sanctification. In the tract *Christian Perfection*, he proudly proclaimed that he was among those who "love God with all our hearts," whose love was unmixed with other motives.[4] Indeed, Jarrell took pride in the strength and purity of his love for God. This contrasted sharply with the dominant notions of southern manhood, which derided sentimentality.[5] The type of emotive religion that Jarrell proclaimed was more in keeping with the religiosity many Southern whites saw in black churches and believed to be unmanly.[6]

Rather than focusing on staid masculinity, the Holiness movement's ideal of affectionate manliness emphasized highly emotive love.

In addition to this emotive masculinity, Jarrell highlighted the connections between the doctrine of entire sanctification and a man's character. In his tract *Faint-Heartedness*, Jarrell told readers that he believed a man's character made an all-important difference in life.[7] Only through the experience of perfect love could men win their battles against sin and the devil.[8] Jarrell united his theology with ideas of manliness, claiming that through Christian perfection alone could men cast off their fears and become brave Christian soldiers. Thus, entire sanctification did not merely enhance manliness; true, sanctified spirituality brought males into their manhood. Without it, Jarrell told his readers, a man could not reach his full potential.

Holiness pastor and pamphleteer Rev. B. S. Taylor also focused on aspects of true spirituality in his tract *The Gibeonites* (1896). (The tract was titled *The Gibeonites* after the biblical nation that willingly surrendered to the Israelites and became their slaves. In Taylor's explanation of the text, the Gibeonites represented the infirmities of mind and body that did not constitute sin but could become hindrances to holiness if not properly addressed or repressed.[9]) In the pamphlet, Taylor mentioned the ways that the Holy Ghost whispered to the hearts of believers using "a quiet, tender, loving voice." The way that Taylor framed his image of the Holy Spirit recalled how lovers spoke, and he referenced the idea that the Holy Ghost would woo believers' hearts away from the devil.[10] Taylor gloried in the idea that God was his beloved. Officials in the Methodist Episcopal Church, South and the Southern Baptist Convention almost never used this type of language to describe their relationship with the divine; yet Taylor loved talking about the God of love who courted the hearts of his people.[11]

The theology of perfect love opened up avenues of emotive, manly affection at odds with most other ideals of southern manhood during the early twentieth century, including expressive platonic affection between men. Those in the Holiness movement would not have understood this love between men in the terms of homosexuality or homoeroticism. There was a lack of sexual tension, because at the end of the nineteenth century in the South, there were not codified gay, straight, or bisexual personal identities.[12] Certainly there were men and women in the South who felt same-sex desires and were in same-sex relationships.[13] However, during this period, sexual orientation did not necessarily define personal identity.[14] White male Holiness leaders thus did not have the twenty-first-century construct regarding sexual orientation in mind. Rather, the language embedded in their theology allowed male leaders the freedom to openly express platonic affection for both sanctified women and men. Proponents of the Holiness movement viewed platonic homosocial love between members of the same biological sex as a natural outpouring of the perfect love in their hearts.[15]

Holiness women recognized that platonic love between two men could demonstrate sanctified masculinity. Mary Lee Cagle, one of the South's premier female evangelists, talked about her first husband's male love. Cagle said that when her first husband, R. L. Harris, lay on his deathbed, in 1894, he had a visit from "Brother Mitchum, a dear good man, as tender-hearted as a woman, [who] came in (His and Brother Harris' was something like the love David and Jonathan had for each other)."[16] Cagle's characterization of Mitchum as "tender-hearted as a woman" was not a slight on Mitchum's manhood. Instead, it noted Mitchum's care for, and love of, Cagle's first husband. Cagle then talked about how Mitchum and Harris loved each other using one of the best-known stories of male love in Judeo-Christian Scripture. In the Bible, the story of David and Jonathan is one of platonic male love so strong that Jonathan, the son of the Israelite King Saul, protected David against the paranoid machinations of his own father, the king.[17] Referencing this story to characterize the love between Mitchum and Harris signaled the power of homosocial love between men in the Holiness movement. The Holiness movement recognized that two men could have powerful love for each other, love seen by all those around them, without endangering their manhood or masculinity. Cagle talked about the power of these two men's love for each other in reverential terms. In her eyes, this love flowed out of their experiences of sanctification. Because both men had experienced perfect love, they could express their mutual affection in such a way that their wives recognized the deep love the men shared.

Perfect love acted as a marker for those who had experienced sanctification and had proved, both to themselves and to their community, that they achieved Christian perfection and received a new sense of identity. This mark transformed perceptions of appropriate gender behavior, especially in regard to the love between men. Once the Holy Ghost had baptized them, men could freely express their homosocial love in intimate terms. Men in other religious traditions generally shied away from such emotive language, as their theology did not emphasize perfect love.[18]

Although many white Southern clergy outside of the Holiness movement would have viewed emotive and sentimental language as decidedly unmanly, new adherents to the Holiness movement did not seem surprised that Holiness clergy applied the concept of purity to both women and men.

Many preachers and evangelists in the Holiness movement used the term "purity" (or heart purity) to denote the state of one's heart before God. They did not use the idea interchangeably with holiness or entire sanctification. Whereas perfect love represented a relationship between a person and God, purity did not rely on a relationship with someone else for its definition. An individual could display signs of purity. Purity meant not only that the person was without willful sin, as holiness implied, but also that the pure person desired to do the will of God. Purity meant that the Holy Spirit had cleansed the most intimate parts of a person's heart.[19]

Additional contrasts between how those inside and outside the Holiness movement used the concept of purity are evident in Holiness proponents' use of purity to describe both women and men. Pastors from other denominations routinely talked about purity solely as part of godly womanhood. For example, in 1893 a Baptist pastor from Mississippi talked about young maidens whose "thoughts [were] as pure as the milk."[20] Similarly, in 1905, Baptist preacher Landrum Pinson Leavell exhorted the young women at Hillman College, in Clinton, Mississippi, to follow the examples of Christian women who had served God wholeheartedly. Leavell then gave examples of such women and consistently highlighted their purity.[21] Baptist minister and author William Holtzclaw also believed that purity was a feminine trait and emphasized the idea that a woman's purity could be undone by marriage to an unfaithful man.[22] Such rhetoric highlighted that those outside the Holiness movement viewed the concept of purity as a distinctly feminine, and sexual, trait.

Holiness author and publisher M. W. Knapp noted the importance of purity as a trait of *all* who had experienced the second blessing in his work "Pentecostal Preachers." (It is important to note that when Knapp wrote this pamphlet, in 1897, there was not a separate Pentecostal movement, and the people he referred to would all have self-identified with the Holiness movement.[23]) In "Pentecostal Preachers," Knapp told of the many characteristics that entirely sanctified preachers and evangelists bore. He noted that true Pentecostal preachers were gentle, plain, humble, and devoted, as well as powerful and convicting.[24] Importantly, they were also pure preachers—or preachers whose delight, not burden, was to do the will of God. Knapp went so far as to say, "Pureness is a mark which all His true ministers bear."[25] Purity, in Knapp's mind, happened once the baptism of the Spirit came upon a person; to have impurities remaining in their life would be just cause to question that person's claim to a new identity founded on holiness and entire sanctification. Moreover, the lack of purity demonstrated that God was not with that particular preacher. Purity was an important mark of sanctification, and a requirement for those who would minister and help other people receive the second blessing. Purity thus applied equally to both men and women in the Holiness movement—an idea radically different from the prevailing notions of southern masculinity. Holiness proponents believed that heart purity changed the relationship between God and sanctified believers. Many Holiness clergy believed that the cares of the world no longer distracted their purified hearts from their true love.

Along with ascribing purity to men, Holiness leaders also wrote about how sanctification moved believers toward greater spiritual maturity. Samuel A. Cowan described this phenomenon in the (New Orleans) *Southwestern Christian Advocate*, one of the major African American religious publications in the New South that supported the theology of Holiness. In his 1899 article "Holiness or Entire Sanctification," Cowan urged his readers to seek holiness: "[The] great trouble with the church of to-day is that there are too many who are satisfied to remain in the initial stage of the Christian life, who fail to reach out the hand of faith for a deeper and more blessed experience of grace—entire sanctification."[26] Cowan felt that the experience of sanctification itself defined spiritual maturity.

In a similar line of thought, Godbey, in *Church—Bride—Kingdom* (1905), warned that unsanctified believers remained in "spiritual minority": "They are not saved from the frivolities, trivialities, hilarities, novelties, curiosities, buncombe, glitter, glare, display, and phantasmagoria incident and attractive to childhood and youth."[27] Godbey believed that sanctified Christians were more mature (and thus more manly) than those who had not achieved Christian perfection; he also believed that those who opposed entire sanctification threatened the health of the church.

Expanding on the theme that sanctification defined spiritual maturity in sanctified men, Godbey also wrote that those who did not experience the second blessing were abnormal in their spiritual development and had stunted growth.[28] Unsanctified men lacked an element of true masculinity given only to those who experienced the second blessing. Furthermore, the idea that entire sanctification defined the normal track of spiritual development allowed Godbey to suggest that spiritual maturity mirrored physical maturity. Godbey wrote that when the adherent experienced the second blessing, he passed "triumphantly from the feeble faith of spiritual infancy to the stalwart, triumphant and perfect trust of manhood."[29] In other words, experiencing perfect love marked a rite of passage for believers, and unsanctified men were stuck in arrested development. Godbey even told his readers that the many pastors in the MECS (his home denomination) who had not been baptized by the Holy Ghost were "spiritual dwarfs, having never progressed out of babyhood."[30] Godbey intimately connected his theology to what he believed about manhood, and so thought it impossible to reach the pinnacle of manliness without receiving the second blessing. He proclaimed in his autobiography that entire sanctification was the means by which believers moved from spiritual infancy into "adultage."[31]

The conflation of Christian perfection with manhood among Holiness writers was profoundly provocative. In stating that only those men who had experienced the second blessing had reached their spiritual manhood, Holiness authors emasculated those who opposed the movement, asserting they were not true men. Godbey went even further, claiming not only that were those who did not have the second blessing not true men but also that they were "pygmies."[32] This added insult to injury, as the idea of white adult men turning into spiritual pygmies had both gendered and racial implications. Godbey effectively called into question the supposed racial superiority of those who had not been sanctified. For Southern men whose sense of identity relied heavily on their claims to racial supremacy, physical power, and mastery over their everyday lives, being called pygmies was an extreme insult. Such a remark called into question their racial identity as well as their stature as mature men.[33] At a time of extreme racial violence throughout the South, such a remark about the racial identity of those not part of the Holiness movement would be enough reason for many people to oppose it.

Sanctified Soldiers

Many people in the New South period, including those in the Holiness movement, viewed the idea of men shrinking from conflict as abhorrent. The thought that true men had the ability to hold their own in a disagreement was a major part of what it meant to be a man during the period.[34] In fact, many men across Mississippi, Alabama, and Georgia frequently talked about the ways conflict enhanced manhood. Similar to many other religious groups, the Holiness movement frequently used martial language that encouraged adherents to view themselves as warriors battling sin, Satan, and the world. By doing so, religious groups offered male adherents who had not fought in the American Civil War an "opportunity to participate in their own holy crusade."[35] The use of such hyper-masculine language provided a counterweight to the many critics from other denominations who charged that overbearing women ran the movement. Holiness groups in the north, like the Salvation Army, also used this type of martial language at the beginning of the twentieth century, and this language was particularly important for men in a movement that offered women expanded roles and authority.[36] However, Holiness groups, in both the North and the South, were not the only religious groups to use martial language. As demonstrated earlier, leaders of the Southern Baptist Convention and the Methodist Episcopal Church, South, at the turn of the century routinely used militant imagery in their sermons and speeches to link their understandings of masculinity with their theology. Baptists often talked about Christians as individual warriors, while Methodists advanced the idea that the church should conquer the world for Christ; both groups talked about the necessity of battling sin and the devil.[37]

Godbey fully participated in the trope of spiritual warfare. He felt that sanctification prepared believing men for the battlefield and proclaimed, "We fight under three flags, all simultaneously floating in the air—the blood-red flag means full redemption, and always under the blood; the snow-white flag proclaims the experience of entire sanctification under the blood, while the raven-black flag means death on the battle-field and no compromise with sin and Satan." The bloodstained banner referenced the belief that Jesus's blood washed away the sins of all those who trusted in him, while the white symbolized the sanctified believer's new identity. Both flags, as well as the promise not to sin, served as rallying points for believers in the Holiness movement. Much as a flag at the front line of an armed conflict serves as a rallying point for troops, these banners helped to focus the efforts of those who spiritually saw them going before them.[38]

The ways male Holiness leaders used martial imagery stood in contrast to how Methodists and Baptists talked about spiritual warfare. Rather than making statements about how all Christians needed to join the fray, the leaders of the Holiness movement emphasized that Christians would be ready to do battle only through entire sanctification. A. J. Jarrell, called "the St. John of the Georgia Conference . . . the apostle of love," warned, in his tract *Faint-Heartedness*, that a reluctance to join the battle, indeed faint-heartedness itself, was "too contagious to be allowed in the armies of God."[39] In this statement alone, Jarrell made it clear that those who had not received the second blessing were susceptible to "faint-heartedness," a mighty charge in the turn-of-the-century South.

Even as Holiness leaders charged that the second blessing defined them as soldiers in the army of Christ, they used martial language to describe their clashes with other theological groups. These clashes were sometimes with their parent denominations, which might have disapproved of the theology of entire sanctification. More often, Holiness preachers warned about fighting battles with denominations that did not believe in sanctification as an instantaneous work of the Holy Ghost. Such language denoted the level of conflict between Holiness groups and the denominations that opposed them. Carradine recognized this heightened state of affairs; in 1897, he said, "The internal war is over. The battle is now on the outside."[40] Thus, Holiness writers intimated that those who openly opposed the second blessing were enemies amid a spiritual war. For example, in one edition of the *Full Salvation Quarterly*, a popular Holiness periodical, M. W. Knapp warned his readers that they would face opposition from all quarters. Yet Knapp's response to persecution was typical of many Holiness leaders. He told his readers that true preachers, baptized by the Holy Spirit, remained loyal to the cause despite opposition. In fact, "though bullets whiz and demons hiss, and dead churchmen scorn, with faces firm as flint, they [the preachers who had received entire sanctification] press forward in the name and strength of God, ready to do or die."[41] Knapp expected opposition to greet those who claimed to have received the second blessing in the New South. The author also made it clear that they would face at least three types of opposition. First, they would face the bullets of the world; non-Christians would attempt to destroy the faithful. Second, the sanctified would come across supernatural, even demonic, opposition as they sought to live out their faith. Third, they would encounter the rebuke and scorn from unsanctified clergy. Knapp questioned whether such churchmen even remained in the Kingdom of God, as he pronounced them "dead."[42] However, Knapp made it equally clear that the true believer who achieved full salvation would "press forward," despite the opposition, to further the Kingdom of God and the teaching of Christian perfection.

Naturally, many leaders of the white Holiness movement took such opposition very personally. W. B. Godbey warned those who opposed him that they stood in a precarious position. In his memoirs, published in 1909, Godbey mentioned cases of Methodist pastors who opposed entire sanctification and a few weeks or months later died.[43] Although Godbey obviously felt that those who opposed holiness within Methodism were wrong and risking their lives, he saved most of his invective for those who followed the teachings of Alexander Campbell. This restorationist movement, known by its detractors as "Campbellites," started the Christian Church (Disciples of Christ), and its numbers made it a powerful religious group in antebellum Kentucky, where Godbey grew up. Throughout his autobiography, Godbey talked about his debates with this group, describing them in martial terms and even comparing one debate to the Trojan War.[44] Although Godbey did not feel that debates helped the people of God, he learned never to shrink from a religious debate, fearing "no alternative but cowardly retreat."[45]

While some Holiness preachers warned against the "dead churchmen" from other theological traditions, they used martial language to talk about their fights primarily with Satan and the forces of evil.[46] In his memoirs, Godbey stated, "In this exterminating war with sin and Satan we have no fight with churches. . . . We love all of the churches with a perfect love, which prepares us for martyrdom."[47] This passage suggested the importance of the Holiness movement's emphasis on supernatural warfare, even within Christendom. The use of martial language within the Holiness movement enabled evangelists of the second blessing to envision themselves as warriors equipped with potent weapons to do battle. Publisher and author M. W. Knapp proudly wrote that those in the Holiness movement were also the officers of God's army. He proclaimed, "Satan hates fire-baptized preachers as no other persons. They are the officers of the army that is conquering him and wresting [the] earth from his traitorous grasp."[48] Knapp made it clear to his readers that they were part of the conquering army of God. The mission would not be easy, however, and he warned that his readers would need a "heaven-forged armory."[49] Godbey reminded his readers that the Holy Spirit would supply "the cannon and the powder, the ball, shot and shell." After all, the Holiness movement would need "sixty-four pounders to smash up the devil's citadel."[50] The preacher told his readers that they would be engaged in close combat, warning, "We need a thousand glittering swords constantly unsheathed to fortify our holiness people."[51] Godbey believed that the Holy Spirit was the "Omnipotent Armor-bearer" and quartermaster who gave His people all they needed to fight evil in the twentieth century.[52]

Godbey did not simply talk about these things in the abstract; he believed that God supplied spiritual weapons for his calling as a Holiness preacher. Godbey thus told his readers, "God gave me a regular gattling [*sic*] gun, loaded to the muzzle with red-hot shot and shell."[53] Godbey believed that this fight was deadly serious, and he talked (metaphorically) about using some of the most advanced weaponry of the day for advancing the Holiness cause. Such artillery was not unleashed on Satan alone, though. Godbey and other evangelists unleashed their spiritual arsenal on nonbelievers in order to convert them. In one account of a revival, Godbey talked about how a friend turned a "fresh volley of red-hot Bible shot" on a self-professed "infidel."[54] Godbey and his contemporaries believed that they fought a pitched battle with the forces of evil for the souls of men and women throughout the world and that the most powerful weapon they had at their disposal was Scripture.

Few women in the Holiness movement used the masculine warrior typology to describe their preaching. In marked contrast to the image of the holy warrior wielding a Gatling gun full of "red-hot Bible shot," Mary Lee Cagle told readers that she used another method of evangelism. Writing in the third person, Cagle explained in her autobiography, "One characteristic of her preaching was her tears, and God has used them from one coast to the other to break hardened hearts."[55] This statement reflects both the shared purpose of Holiness preachers and the vastly different methods they used to convert others to Christianity and Holiness theology. Godbey wanted his readers to think of him as a crusading warrior and used militant, hyper-masculine language to show that he wanted to win the battle for the souls of his audience. His writings were full of battle imagery and weaponized spirituality.

Yet even among the radical theological climate of the Southern Holiness movement, women preachers rarely used such martial language. Instead, female evangelists and preachers, like Cagle, maintained a more feminine use of language. Women preachers did not destroy the barricades that Satan had erected in the hearts of nonbelievers; instead, they worked to soften and then woo their listeners' hearts. The use of hyper-masculine language among male Holiness leaders may have thus provided a counterweight to the many critics from other denominations that charged that effete men and overbearing women ran the movement.[56]

Holy Manhood

Many Holiness writers, preachers, and evangelists talked specifically about the qualities of manliness itself. In their writings on the subject, two themes emerge. The first is that true men were strong and physically commanding. The second is that only men made holy through Christian perfection could be counted as true men. These themes of physical manliness and holy manhood each connected in holiness theology with the idea that the second blessing gave the believer a new identity.

As noted previously, those in the Holiness movement throughout Mississippi, Alabama, and Georgia believed that they fought in a life and death struggle with the forces of evil in the New South. Many of these leaders viewed the ideal man as an excellent physical specimen—a sign not only of God's blessing upon that person but also of his readiness to fight the good fight. Accordingly, some preachers felt compelled to talk about their physical exploits. They may have felt compelled to defend their manhood against those outside the movement who charged that it subverted gender identities.[57]

In 1891, Beverly Carradine encouraged his readers not to pay attention to those who disparaged their masculinity. Instead, Carradine argued that sanctification defined true manliness and that the characteristics of Jesus's apostles on the biblical Day of Pentecost, "courage, fearlessness, devotion, love, compassion, and holiness," were now "the marked features" of his readers' lives.[58] Carradine proposed that the infilling of the Holy Spirit gave the disciples of Jesus these traits, and he promised his readers that the Holy Spirit could do the same for them. Thus, the traits that he mentioned became parts of a vision of holy manhood. Carradine argued for a unique vision of manliness characterized by the intimate intertwining of robust masculinity and religious experience.

In a similar line of thought, Rev. B. S. Taylor, in his work "The Gibeonites," noted how sanctification changed men's daily actions and defined their characters. He wrote that men frequently indulged their sinful natures by using "harsh and cruel words and acts" when angry. Taylor believed men would still get angry but would express their anger in a "kind, tearful, and tender way," writing, the "Lord will sanctify your temper, and keep it sweet." Taylor anticipated that some readers would object to his statements, feeling they would leave a man with a decidedly effeminate identity. Thus Taylor carefully noted, "God does not make you a putty man because you are cleansed."[59]

Taylor wanted his readers to realize that there was a difference between sanctified and unsanctified manhood. For him, this difference did not make men "putty men" and thus emasculated; rather, through tempering anger, these men made their anger constructive rather than destructive. Although these men were angry, their experience of sanctification so changed them that they had concern about the welfare of those who wronged them. Thus sanctified manhood worked for the restoration and reconciliation of relationships and provided a determined counterpoint to the traditional model of honor-driven, violent manhood in the American South still current in the early part of the twentieth century.[60] Nonetheless, Taylor envisioned that no one would simply "push over" sanctified males at the pinnacle of manliness. They were not "putty men" who would bend at the first sign of opposition. Instead, they retained their steely nerves and even their anger, but tempered it in love rather than self-serving wrath.

While Taylor did not name any specific men who he believed demonstrated all of the character traits he mentioned, many people believed that one of the founders of the Georgia Holiness Association, W. A. Dodge, was a prime example of a man whose sanctified faith defined his personal identity. Many wrote stories about him in a memorial book. Georgia pastor and Holiness leader Rev. E. M. Bounds wrote in one vignette that Dodge was a man of prayer who lived his life in a state of constant communion with God. Mornings, particularly, Bounds believed, were a special time of prayer for Dodge. In view of Dodge's example, Bounds editorialized, "It would scarcely be decent, surely not manly, not to be at prayer before going out of the sleeping chamber."[61] Bounds clearly believed that prayer was an important part of masculine life. By saying that it would be unmanly to leave the bedroom in the morning before praying, Bounds reinforced the idea that having a strong relationship with God defined true manhood. Bounds's remark used sanctified religious expression to define manliness. The demonstration of manhood that Bounds talked about was a daily exercise, not just a tent-revival religiosity. A few pages later, Bounds reiterated this message for his readers, telling them, "The prayerful man is ever talking with God, breathing out his soul after God, and ever communing with God."[62] Here, Bounds reinforced the idea that a man best demonstrated his character through the constant expression of religion. Prayer did not indicate weakness or desperation; it was a manly action to be engaged in constantly. Similarly, sharing one's inmost thoughts, emotions, and feelings was not viewed with disgust or considered a feminine activity but was part of the prayerful man's daily interactions with God.

In a similar fashion, one of the premier female evangelists of the New South, Mary Lee Cagle, wrote glowingly in her memoirs about the sanctified faith of her second husband, Rev. H. C. Cagle, and his ministerial help. She recorded that her husband was "strong in body, congenial in spirit, and had a fine case of religion, which was a great asset to her work. She had worked so hard and had borne so much responsibility that she was rapidly going down physically. His broad shoulders and willing heart to help carry the load, were indeed a blessing."[63] Here, even as Mary Lee Cagle talked about herself in the third person, she made it clear to her readers that her husband was physically a strong man as well as very religious. Moreover, she indicated that she could not handle her responsibilities on her own and that she needed help. She hinted that women's physicality did not equal that of the ideal man.[64] Instead, her husband's "broad shoulders" rescued her from the crushing weight of her responsibilities. Certainly this did not refer merely to physical work; as Mary Lee Cagle noted, it was not only physical tasks that she needed help with but spiritual tasks, which taxed her feminine constitution and caused her health to decline. Thus, not only was H. C. Cagle's physical strength a reassurance, but his spiritual strength restored his wife's and rescued her from physical (and possibly spiritual) decline.

The connections between the male body, identity, and power or authority linked up with an influential discourse of race and gender that was current at the beginning of the twentieth century. Although physical attributes were one prominent way for preachers and evangelists in the southern Holiness movement to mark the ideal manhood at the end of the nineteenth century, it was not the only way.[65] In fact, for many leaders of the movement who received entire sanctification, there was a distinct division between worldly masculinity (even that of other denominations) and holy manliness. While some historians have argued that the aggressive, rough-and-tumble masculine culture in the New South was opposed to the quiet, self-controlled ideals of evangelical culture, Holiness leaders did not see this division in the same way. Instead the enthusiastic evangelists of the Holiness movement fused the two models of southern manhood. Linking affectionate devotion, holiness, and compassion with courage and fearlessness, Holiness proponents created a unique masculinity focused on religious experience while retaining ideals of southern masculinity as they argued for a refashioning of religious manliness.[66]

For leaders in the southern Holiness movement, the theology of the second blessing opened up avenues of spiritual identity not available to men in other Southern white denominations. Preachers and evangelists in the Holiness movement did not talk about these new spiritual identities in the abstract; rather, they defined their sense of self through theology. By doing so, Holiness proponents tied together their spiritual and gendered selves and redefined their gendered identities through Holiness theology. The theology of perfect love allowed leading Holiness men to express deep affection for one another in ways that would have been highly suspect in other faith communities in the New South. Similarly, the idea that those who experienced entire sanctification should live in purity promoted the male appropriation of a character trait that many outside the Holiness movement considered a feminine ideal. However, not all expressions of sanctified manhood contradicted the masculine ideals of the larger Southern culture, and male Holiness proponents routinely used marital language to describe themselves. The ways that the Holiness movement wedded theological ideals to gender provided space to reconfigure manly ideals in the New South, demonstrating how transformative theology defined personal identity.

Conclusion

For many people of faith, the idea that belief transforms identity is axiomatic. Devout people of diverse traditions across the globe look to the sacred to understand the world and their place in it. For example, the physical articles of faith that baptized Sikhs carry and wear are constant reminders to the faithful of their beliefs and identity.[1] In a similar fashion, many orders of women religious within Roman Catholicism use specific articles of clothing to demonstrate their religious identity. Before the Second Vatican Council, many of these orders encouraged initiates to take new names along with their vows of poverty, chastity, and obedience—an act that literally changed the individual's identity.[2] While these examples hardly touch the surface of religious belief across the world, it is clear that beliefs about the divine can radically transform individual identity.

Within contemporary American evangelicalism, many believers attempt to define their identity through their faith. Like their historical forebears, modern American Christian responses to faith and identity vary dramatically. In the 1990s, the popular group the Promise Keepers offered one vision of manhood defined by faith.[3] More recently, other evangelical ministries have appealed directly and exclusively to men in attempts to instill a faith-driven identity. These groups include Act Like Men, Mighty Men Conference USA, Stepping Up, Iron Sharpens Iron, National Coalition of Ministries to Men, and Christ in the Rockies.[4]

David Murrow, a successful evangelical author, wrote from a perspective shared by many of the above organizations when, in 2005, he published *Why Men Hate Going to Church*. In his book, Murrow opines, "God made men for adventure, achievement, and challenge, and if they can't find those things in church, they're going to find them somewhere else. But if you allow your church to embark on a great adventure, the men will return."[5] In a similar vein, Seattle's former celebrity pastor Marc Driscoll reportedly told the attendees at a 2013 conference that he drove an SUV because "if you drive a mini-van, you're a mini-man."[6] Taking this hyper-masculine ideal to its extreme, the 2014 documentary "Fight Church" chronicles the story of cage-fighting pastors. These men of God step into the mixed-martial arts octagon asking, according to one pastor in the film, "Can you love your neighbor as yourself, and then at the same time, knee him in the face as hard as you can?"[7]

Questions about faith and identity are not restricted to masculinity, and while it is rare for evangelical women to ask about inflicting violence on the neighbor they love, there are those who appropriate martial imagery in their understandings of faithful femininity. For example, Elizabeth, the original writer for the popular blog *Warrior Wives* featured in the *Atlantic* in 2014, talks about the battle to preserve marriages. She encourages her audience of evangelical women to fight for their marriages saying, "You can fight. You can be a warrior wife."[8]

Clearly, theologically defined gender and identity did not end after the second decade of the twentieth century. One hundred years later, many of the same questions remain for the devout. In the twenty-first century, evangelical leaders published a number of books about what it means to bear the image of God, and how that relates to human gender. *Manhood Restored, Called to Womanhood, The Dude's Guide to Manhood, The Gospel-Centered Woman*, and *What's the Difference?: Manhood and Womanhood Defined According to the Bible* are only a few of the volumes that have touched on the subject, and there is even a peer-reviewed journal devoted to the topic.[9]

Thus far, the most popular book in this century that touches on how faith defines identity promotes the stereotype of an adventurous, gas-guzzling, outdoor and achievement-oriented, Christian he-man. John Eldredge's *Wild at Heart: Discovering the Secret of a Man's Soul* sold more than a million copies in the first three years after its publication, in 2001.[10] Since then, *Wild at Heart* has gone into multiple editions, has workbook versions for group study, and the Eldredges (John and his wife, Stasi) have organized ministry conferences designed around its central themes.[11] And they have not neglected the question of what Christian femininity looks like. The Eldredges have written similar works on what it means to be a Christian woman and mother.[12] While both John and Stasi Eldredge have had significant success getting their message to a mass audience, what they most emphasize is that faith defines a proper understanding of gender.

What the evangelical speakers, authors, and conference attendees above would affirm, along with their forebears in the American South, is that they defined their personal identities through their faith. This meant that the task of discerning what true manhood and womanhood entailed was a theological task; it was not merely an intellectual exercise. Church officials across the South between 1877 and 1915 tried to figure out what it meant to be a man or a woman in the changing world of the New South, thus constructing ideas of manhood and womanhood defined by their faith.

The leaders of the Southern Baptist Convention connected ideas of Christianity to individuals, and this changed how denominational officials defined identity. The intertwining of individualistic theology with gender had very different outcomes for their understandings of masculinity and femininity. While preachers and pastors highlighted the ways in which Baptist men should act as masters over their individual lives, such expressions rarely appeared in connection with women. Rather, officials emphasized the importance of an idealized femininity expressed through essential traits meant to define all women. Moreover, while men could frequently act in ways that were best for their individual good, SBC leaders expected women to maintain a higher standard and consistently sacrifice their individual goals and desires for the good of their children and families.

The tension between faithful Christian manhood and womanhood also appeared among leaders of the Methodist Episcopal Church, South. The main theological thrust of the MECS emphasized the conversion of sinners to Christianity and the person and work of Jesus. Different interpretations of Jesus's character and work led to alternate definitions of masculinity. These alternate interpretations changed the ways that MECS leaders conceptualized and imagined the construction of manhood. Alternately, the emphasis on conversion within Southern Methodism meant that many church officials strongly believed that women should receive a full, challenging, liberal arts education—but not for their own sake. Rather, the fathers of the church thought that education would make women better at nurturing the impressionable souls of the young ones in their homes.

While the SBC and MECS leadership had distinct theologically based visions of both manhood and womanhood, there were similarities in how they viewed gender. Officials in both denominations found it important to define masculinity through their faith. Similarly, the vast majority of officials in these two denominations, which constituted the two largest religious bodies in the South at the time, believed that proper womanhood came through correct belief. Because of the overwhelming dominance of these two denominations in the American South, these constructions of gender became part of the larger culture's formulations of personal identity. Certainly, there were differences and tensions, but many white southerners would have been comfortable with the gendered theology of both the SBC and the MECS.

Not all southern Christians came to such conclusions, however. At the turn of the nineteenth century, some Christians thought that the Holy Ghost had given them unique identities founded in the ability to live sinless lives on earth. Some preachers and evangelists thus believed that the most important mark of personal identity was whether the Holy Ghost had blessed an individual with entire sanctification. The resultant gendered ideals provided a stark contrast to both Baptist and Methodist ideals. Many preachers and writers in the Holiness movement used this radical theology to define personal identities. In other words, Holiness preachers and evangelists argued that for both men and women, the radical theology of entire sanctification and perfect love defined what masculinity and femininity entailed. Their radical theology opened up avenues of institutional authority for sanctified women. Men in the movement found an environment where homosocial expressions of intense affection and love were entirely acceptable because of the shared experience and theology of perfect love.

In the decades after the turn of the century, many southern whites continued to use theology to construct gendered ideals, many of which had their roots in these turn-of-the-century constructs. White southerners used the individualized ideals of masculinity prevalent in both the Southern Baptist ideas of mastery and the Methodist militarized masculinity to deny manliness to African Americans. In a similar fashion, many constructions of womanhood denied African American femininity. These ideas of femininity emphasized that only those women who stayed in their own home to nurture to the spiritual needs of their families were true ladies, a construct that denied true womanhood to the many African American women working outside their homes to provide for their families. Both of these constructs flowed from theological ideas propagated by evangelical leaders.

Across the South, theology defined the ways that church officials understood gender. Whether it was the combination of individualism and mastery, perfect love, or the tensions in the ideas of Jesus as a divine warrior and a tender shepherd, preachers and pastors across the American South altered their conceptions of manhood to match more closely what they believed. Likewise, an idealized womanhood, the need for conversion, and empowering ideas of entire sanctification changed the ways denominational authorities perceived femininity. The fact that understandings of the divine had a profound influence on church leaders' personal identity was easily understood and disseminated through sermons, speeches, and published works. In fact, many denominational authorities in the American

South thought that it was self-evident that their theology changed their understandings of themselves—they would have been confused if it did not. Their theology (whether Baptist, Methodist, or Holiness) provided them with new identities that superseded old understandings of gender. This examination of a few of the ways church leaders talked about religion and identity in the American South makes clear that theirs were defining faiths.

Notes

List of Abbreviations

BWL	Barney Washington Lewis Papers
CBG	Charles B. Galloway Papers
IDB	Isaac D. Borders
JGJ	John G. Jones Papers
AGCP	Asa Griggs Candler Papers
AGH	Atticus G. Haygood Family Papers
BFP	Burge Family Papers
CCJ	Charles Crawford Papers
JHB	James Hamilton Baxter Papers
JOAC	James Osgood Andrew Clark Papers
ACFC	Tuskegee Female College and Alabama Conference Female College
JMPP	Dr. John Massey Personal Papers
CASC	Catherine Allen Sesquicentennial College
SAC	Mrs. S. A. Chambers
BCPC	Baptist Congress Proceedings Collection
ECD	E. C. Dargan Collection
FBP	Frost-Bell Papers
GWB	G. W. Bouldin Collection
IJVN	I. J. Van Ness Papers
LPL	Landrum Pinson Leavell Collection
LBP	Lansing Burrows Papers
RWW	Rufus W. Weaver Collection
SBC	Southern Baptist Convention Sermon Collection
TTE	Thomas Treadwell Eaton Papers
WOC	William Owen Carver Papers

Introduction

1. Marion Elias Lazenby, *History of Methodism in Alabama and West Florida: Being an Account of the Amazing March of Methodism through Alabama and West Florida* (Nashville: Parthenon, 1960).

2. Lazenby, *Methodism*, 375.

3. It is also easy to see here how the Lost Cause becomes a Christian cause as Christ tops the list of Confederate heroes.

4. Lazenby, *Methodism*, 484.

5. Carlos M. N. Eire, *A Very Brief History of Eternity* (Princeton: Princeton University Press, 2010), 18–19. For more on the ideas and concepts of "lived theology," see the University of Virginia's Project on Lived Theology, www.livedtheology.org, as well as the work of some of its scholars. For example, Albert J. Raboteau, "Holy Ordinary: Locating the Sacred in Literature and Life," The Sixth Annual Capps Lecture in Christian Theology at the University of Virginia, (November 4, 2009); and Charles Marsh, "What is Lived Theology?," Unpublished Paper presented at the Conference on Lived Theology and Civil Courage, (June 12–14, 2003).

6. Ursula King, ed., *Religion & Gender* (Oxford: Blackwell Publishers, 1995), 4, 6.

7. Martin Riesebrodt and Thomas Tweed are two scholars who have heavily influenced my understanding of the academic definition of religion. These two scholars' theories of religion are certainly different, but despite these differences, they are compatible. Riesebrodt essentially views religion as the promise of salvation, while Tweed's understands religion as an organic growth of culture. Both scholars view religion as something meant to alleviate suffering and enhance joy. For more, see Martin Riesebrodt, *The Promise of Salvation: A Theory of Religion*, translated by Steven Rendell (Chicago: University of Chicago Press, 2012), xii–xiii, 71–90, 155; and Thomas Tweed, *Crossing and Dwelling: A Theory of Religion* (Cambridge, MA: Harvard University Press, 2006), 54–79.

8. Tweed, *Crossing and Dwelling*, 54–79.

9. See Paul Harvey, *Redeeming the South: Religious Cultures and Racial Identities Among Southern Baptists, 1865–1925* (Chapel Hill: University of North Carolina Press, 1997), 1; and Department of Commerce and Labor, Bureau of the Census, E. Dana Durand, Director, *Bulletin 103 (Second Edition, Revised and Enlarged): Religious Bodies: 1906* (Washington, DC: Government Printing Office, 1910), 42–47.

10. So schismatic were these groups that I do not attempt to delve into the many splits and theological differences. However, it is important to note that I do not attempt to use sources from the Pentecostal movement, which, along with an emphasis on entire sanctification, believed that speaking in tongues was a sign that a believer had been baptized by the Holy Ghost.

11. The historians Ted Ownby and Ann Douglass have argued that at the turn of the century, evangelical culture was, in some sense, opposed to many models of masculinity and viewed as the domain of women. See Ted Ownby, *Subduing Satan: Religion, Recreation, and Manhood in the Rural South, 1865–1920* (Chapel Hill:

University of North Carolina Press, 1990); and Ann Douglass, *The Feminization of American Culture* (New York: Alfred A. Knopf, 1977).

12. For more on moral versus institutional authority, see Ursula King, "Intro duction: Gender and the Study of Religion," in King, *Religion & Gender,* 16.

13. C. Vann Woodward, *Origins of the New South, 1877–1913* (Baton Rouge: Louisiana State University Press, 1951, 1971), 124, 126–29, 136–38; and Edward L. Ayers, *The Promise of the New South: Life after Reconstruction,* 15th anniversary ed. (Oxford: Oxford University Press, 2007), 56, 59, 75, 110–12.

14. Reproduced from Millsaps College, *Bobashela* (1909), 124, Courtesy of Millsaps College Archives, Millsaps-Wilson Library, Millsaps College, Jackson, Mississippi.

15. For a quick account of these issues, see Ayers, *Promise of the New South,* 25, 163, 219–20; and Woodward, *Origins of the New South,* 177, 206–8. For more in-depth accounting of the problems and issues of the sharecropping, lien, and debt peonage systems, see Joe Creech, *Righteous Indignation: Religion and the Populist Revolution* (Champaign: University of Illinois Press, 2006); and Steven Hahn, *A Nation Under Our Feet: Black Political Struggles in the Rural South from Slavery to the Great Migration* (Cambridge, MA: Belknap Press, 2005).

16. For evidences of Holiness teachings in the Mississippi Conference prior to the Civil War, see chapter 5 of this book. Briane K. Turley's *Wheel within a Wheel: Southern Methodism and the Georgia Holiness Association* (Macon, GA: Mercer University Press, 1999) documents the rise of the Georgia Holiness Association after Reconstruction.

17. For one of the now classic works on Reconstruction, see Eric Foner, *Reconstruction: America's Unfinished Revolution, 1863–1877* (New York: Harper Collins Publishers, 2002; originally published by Harper & Row, 1988), xxv, 582. For more on the South redefining itself during this period, see Caroline E. Janney, *Remembering the Civil War: Reunion and the Limits of Reconciliation* (Chapel Hill: University of North Carolina Press, 2013); or Arthur Remillard, *Southern Civil Religions: Imagining the Good Society in the Post-Reconstruction Era* (Athens: University of Georgia Press, 2012).

18. David W. Blight, *Race and Reunion: The Civil War in American Memory* (Cambridge, MA: Harvard University Press, 2001); Edward J. Blum, *Reforging the White Republic: Race, Religion, and American Nationalism, 1865–1898* (Baton Rouge: Louisiana State University Press, 2005); Katharine Du Pre Lumpkin, *The Making of a Southerner* (Athens: University of Georgia Press, 1991), 111–47; and Charles Reagan Wilson, *Baptized in Blood: The Religion of the Lost Cause, 1865–1920* (Athens: University of Georgia Press, 1980).

19. For the most well-known study of the Klan's interaction with gender construction and identity, see Kathleen M. Blee, *Women of the Klan: Racism and Gender in the 1920s* (Los Angeles: University of California Press, 1991). See also Nancy MacLean, *Behind the Mask of Chivalry: The Making of the Second Ku Klux Klan* (Oxford: Oxford University Press, 1994).

20. For more on both the black and white out-migrations from the South, see

James N. Gregory, *The Southern Diaspora: How the Great Migrations of Black and White Southerners Transformed America* (Chapel Hill: University of North Carolina Press, 2005), especially 13–15; Steven Hahn, *A Nation Under Our Feet: Black Political Struggles in the Rural South from Slavery to the Great Migration* (Cambridge, MA: Harvard University Press, 2003); William Cohen, *At Freedom's Edge: Black Mobility and the Southern White Quest for Racial Control, 1861–1915* (Baton Rouge: Louisiana State University Press, 1991); and John M. Giggie, *After Redemption: Jim Crow and the Transformation of African American Religion in the Delta, 1875–1915* (Oxford: Oxford University Press, 2008). See also Ownby, *Subduing Satan*, 194–212; and Ted Ownby, *American Dreams in Mississippi: Consumers, Poverty, and Culture, 1830–1998* (Chapel Hill: University of North Carolina Press, 1999).

21. Certainly, there was an incredible market for religious publications in the antebellum period as well. For more on this, see David Paul Nord, *Faith in Reading: Religious Publishing and the Birth of Mass Media in America* (Oxford: Oxford University Press, 2004). For ways in which these religious publications could influence gender construction and familial relations in the antebellum South, see Christopher A. Graham, "Evangelicals and 'Domestic Felicity' in the Non-Elite South," *Journal of Southern Religion* 15 (2013): http://jsr.fsu.edu/issues/vol15/graham.html.

22. Randall J. Stephens, "There is Magic in Print: The Holiness-Pentecostal Press and the Origins of Southern Pentecostalism," in *Southern Crossroads: Perspectives on Religion and Culture*, ed. Walter H. Conser Jr. and Rodger M. Payne, 194–230 (Lexington: University Press of Kentucky, 2008), 217n8.

23. While various historians have documented the low numbers of evangelical Christians in the South before the American Civil War, after Reconstruction, these numbers rose. For three examples, see Christine Leigh Heyrman, *Southern Cross: The Beginnings of the Bible Belt* (New York: Alfred A. Knopf, 1997); Monica Najar, *Evangelizing the South: A Social History of Church and State in Early America* (Oxford: Oxford University Press, 2008); and E. Brooks Holifield, *The Gentlemen Theologians: American Theology in Southern Culture, 1795–1860* (Durham: Duke University Press, 1978).

24. Department of Commerce and Labor, Bureau of the Census, E. Dana Durand, Director, *Bulletin 103 (Second Edition, Revised and Enlarged): Religious Bodies: 1906*, (Washington, DC: Government Printing Office, 1910). Total population numbers for these states appear on page 38, while total numbers of parishioners appears on page 39. The rise of churchgoers from 1890 to 1900 is demonstrated on page 54.

25. *Religious Bodies: 1906*, 42. Across both the MECS and the SBC, women outnumbered men, by 142 and 146, respectively.

26. For examples of work that concentrate more fully on issues of race and gender during the period, see Gail Bederman's *Manliness & Civilization: A Cultural History of Gender and Race in the United States, 1880–1917* (Chicago: University of Chicago Press, 1996); and Martin Summers, *Manliness & Its Discontents: The Black*

Middle Class & the Transformation of Masculinity, 1900–1930 (Chapel Hill: University of North Carolina Press, 2004). In the volume edited by Craig Thompson Friend titled *Southern Masculinity: Perspectives on Manhood in the South Since Reconstruction* (Athens: University of Georgia Press, 2009), there are several chapters that deal with race and masculinity. See Rose Stremlau, "In Defense of 'This Great Family Government and Estate': Cherokee Masculinity and the Opposition to Allotment," 65–82, and Edward J. Blum, "A Subversive Savior: Manhood and African American Images of Christ in the Early Twentieth-Century South," 150–74. Similarly, in *Black and White Masculinity in the American South, 1800–2000* (Newcastle upon Tyne, England: Cambridge Scholars Publishing, 2009), editors Lydia Plath and Sergio Lussana juxtapose white and black perceptions of masculinity. Interesting discussions are also in Jacquelyn Dowd Hall's *Revolt Against Chivalry: Jesse Daniel Ames and the Women's Campaign Against Lynching*, rev. ed. (New York: Columbia University Press, 1993); Laura Edwards, *Gendered Strife and Confusion: The Political Culture of Reconstruction* (Champaign: University of Illinois Press, 1997); LeeAnn Whites, *The Civil War as a Crisis in Gender: Augusta, Georgia, 1860–1890* (Athens, GA: UGA Press, 1995); and Patricia A. Schecter, *Ida B. Wells-Barnett and American Reform, 1880–1930* (Chapel Hill: University of North Carolina Press, 2001).

27. For more on this, see Andrew Amron, "From Soldier to Street Corner: Martial Imagery in Working Class Black Culture during the World War I Era," PhD dissertation, University of Alabama, 2013.

28. For an excellent example of the ways in which honor, violence, race, and understandings of manhood interacted, see Kris DuRocher's "Violent Masculinity: Learning Ritual and Performance in Southern Lynchings," in *Southern Masculinity*, ed. Friend, 46–64.

29. Bertram Wyatt-Brown, *Honor and Violence in the Old South* (Oxford: Oxford University Press, 1986), 91.

30. For other interpretations of religion in the South, including the idea that southern religion was held captive by the larger culture, see Samuel S. Hill, *Southern Churches in Crisis Revisited* (Tuscaloosa: University of Alabama Press, 1999); and John Lee Eighmy, *Churches in Cultural Captivity: A History of the Social Attitudes of Southern Baptists* (Knoxville: University of Tennessee Press, 1972). See also Donald G. Mathews, "Lynching Is Part of the Religion of Our People: Faith in the Christian South," in *Religion in the American South: Protestants and Others in History and Culture*, ed. Beth Barton Schweiger and Donald G. Mathews, 153–94 (Chapel Hill: University of North Carolina Press, 2004); Daniel Woods, "The Royal Telephone: Early Pentecostalism in the South and the Enthusiastic Practice of Prayer," in *Religion in the American South*, ed. Schweiger and Mathews, 125–52; and Beth Barton Schweiger, "Max Weber in Mount Airy, Or, Revivals and Social Theory in the Early South," in *Religion in the American South*, ed. Schweiger and Mathews, 31–66. See also James B. Bennett, *Religion and the Rise of Jim Crow in New Orleans* (Princeton: Princeton University Press, 2005); Ruel W. Tyson, James L Peacock,

and Daniel W. Patterson, eds., *Diversities of Gifts: Field Studies in Southern Religion* (Champaign: University of Illinois Press, 1988); Daniel Stowell, *Rebuilding Zion: The Religious Reconstruction of the South, 1865–1877* (Oxford: Oxford University Press, 1998); Wayne J. Flynt, *Alabama Baptists: Southern Baptists in the Heart of Dixie* (Tuscaloosa: University of Alabama Press, 1998); and Ralph E. Luker, *The Social Gospel in Black and White: American Racial Reform, 1885–1912* (Chapel Hill: University of North Carolina Press, 1991). For broader interpretations of religion in American life, see Mark A. Noll, David W. Bebbington, and George R. Rawlyk, eds., *Evangelicalism: Comparative Studies of Popular Protestantism in North America, the British Isles, and Beyond, 1700–1900* (Oxford: Oxford University Press, 1994); and Nathan o. Hatch, *The Democratization of American Christianity* (New Haven: Yale University Press, 1989).

31. For a few examples of other types of investigations into southern religious history, see Paul Harvey, *Redeeming the South: Religious Cultures and Racial Identities Among Southern Baptists, 1865–1925* (Chapel Hill: University of North Carolina Press, 1997); Paul Harvey, *Freedom's Coming: Religious Culture and the Shaping of the South from the Civil War through the Civil Rights Era* (Chapel Hill: University of North Carolina Press, 2005); Donald G. Mathews, "Lynching Religion: Why the Old Man Shouted 'Glory!'," in *Southern Crossroads: Perspectives on Religion and Culture*, ed. Walter H. Conser Jr. and Rodger M. Payne, 318–53 (Lexington: University Press of Kentucky, 2008); George C. Rable, *God's Almost Chosen Peoples: A Religious History of the American Civil War* (Chapel Hill: University of North Carolina Press, 2010); Randall J. Stephens, *The Fire Spreads: Holiness and Pentecostalism in the American South* (Cambridge, MA: Harvard University Press, 2008); Samuel S. Hill, *One Name but Several Faces: Varieties of Popular Denominations in Southern History* (Athens: University of Georgia Press, 1996); Rufus B. Spain, *At Ease in Zion: Social History of Southern Baptists, 1865–1900* (Nashville: Vanderbilt University Press, 1967); Christine Leigh Heyrman, *Southern Cross: The Beginnings of the Bible Belt* (Chapel Hill: University of North Carolina Press, 1998); and Hunter Dickinson Farish, *The Circuit Rider Dismounts: A Social History of Southern Methodism, 1865–1900* (Richmond, VA: Dietz, 1938).

32. George Duffield Jr., "Stand Up, Stand Up for Jesus," in *The Methodist Hymnal: Official Hymnal of the Methodist Episcopal Church and the Methodist Episcopal Church, South* (New York: Methodist Book Concern, 1905), 272.

33. For an example of this, see James Hamilton Baxter, "Plan of Salvation," n.d., 20, Box 1, James Hamilton Baxter Papers, Manuscript, Archives, and Rare Book Library, Emory University, Atlanta, Georgia, (JHB).

Chapter 1

1. Edwin Charles Dargan, *Ecclesiology: A Study of the Churches*, 2nd ed. (Louisville, KY: Charles T. Dearing, 1905), 162.

2. See George C. Rable, *God's Almost Chosen Peoples: A Religious History of the*

American Civil War (Chapel Hill: University of North Carolina Press, 2010), 23, for a short account of the split.

3. Department of Commerce and Labor, Bureau of the Census, E. Dana Durand, Director, *Bulletin 103 (Second Edition, Revised and Enlarged): Religious Bodies: 1906* (Washington, DC: Government Printing Office, 1910).

4. C. Vann Woodward argued that in the South, Baptists and Methodists had roughly twice the strength and popularity they had in other parts of the country. C. Vann Woodward, *Origins of the New South, 1877–1913* (Baton Rouge: Louisiana State University Press, 1971), 170.

5. Edward L. Ayers, *The Promise of the New South: Life After Reconstruction*, 15th anniversary ed. (Oxford: Oxford University Press, 2007), 160.

6. For a quick look at some of the shifts in the New South's economy, see Gaines M. Foster, *Ghosts of the Confederacy: Defeat, The Lost Cause, and the Emergence of the New South* (Oxford: Oxford University Press, 1987), 79–87.

7. For a strong case for the presence of progressivism in the religious culture of the New South, see Paul Harvey, *Freedom's Coming: Religious Culture and the Shaping of the South from the Civil War through the Civil Rights Movement* (Chapel Hill: University of North Carolina Press, 2005), 53–77. C. Vann Woodward, among others, argues against this idea and notes the strength of the rural church in the South in *Origins*, 449–50.

8. For examples, see Ayers, *Promise of the New South*, 171.

9. For more, see Ted Ownby's *Subduing Satan: Religion, Recreation, and Manhood in the Rural South, 1865–1920* (Chapel Hill: University of North Carolina Press, 1990), 38–55 and 167–93.

10. Donald G. Mathews, "Lynching Religion: Why the Old Man Shouted 'Glory!,'" in *Southern Crossroads: Perspectives on Religion and Culture*, ed. Walter H. Conser Jr. and Rodger M. Payne, 318–53 (Lexington: University of Kentucky Press, 2008).

11. For some of these works, see Charles Reagan Wilson, *Baptized in Blood: The Religion of the Lost Cause, 1865–1920* (Athens: University of Georgia Press, 1980); Gaines M. Foster, *Ghosts of the Confederacy: Defeat, the Lost Cause, and the Emergence of the New South, 1865–1913* (Oxford: Oxford University Press, 1988); W. Scott Poole, *Never Surrender: Confederate Memory and Conservatism in the South Carolina Upcountry* (Athens: University of Georgia Press, 2004); Gary Gallagher and Alan Nolan, eds., *The Myth of the Lost Cause and Civil War History* (Bloomington: Indiana University Press, 2000); and Arthur Remillard, *Southern Civil Religion: Imagining the Good Society in the Post-Reconstruction Era* (Athens: University of Georgia Press, 2011), 95–103.

12. For more, see Foster, *Ghosts of the Confederacy*, 36–37, 88.

13. Charles B. Galloway, "Jefferson Davis: A Judicial Estimate," given June 3, 1908, in *Bulletin of the University of Mississippi* VI (August 1908): 1–48.

14. See Foster, *Ghosts of the Confederacy*, 124–25, 136–37; and Poole, *Never Surrender*, 68–70.

15. Ayers, *Promise*, 167.

16. Kerfoot, "What We Believe," *The Doctrines of Our Faith: A Convenient Handbook for Use in Normal Classes, Sacred Literature Courses and Individual Study*, ed. Edwin Charles Dargan (Nashville: Sunday School Board Southern Baptist Convention, 1905), 232–33.

17. Dargan, *Ecclesiology*, 229. For more on the relationships between churches and associations, see Dargan, *Ecclesiology*, 218–30. Even when debating women's roles in church, pastors were likely to point out the biblical nature of congregational government, as J. B. Moody did in his book, *Women in the Churches: Their Rights and Restrictions; OR, Paul Harmonized with the Law and the Gospel*, 2nd ed. (Martin, TN: Hall-Moody Institute, 1910), 51.

18. Harvey, *Freedom's Coming*, 23–24.

19. Of course, what Baptists were most known for (and where their name came from) was an emphasis on a believer's baptism. This was the doctrine that only those people who have publicly confessed their faith should be baptized. In and of itself, this theological stance demonstrated one aspect of individual theology. In contrast to the Baptist stance, those who practiced infant baptism, or as the SBC termed it, "paedobaptism," believed that infant baptism was a sign and seal of God's covenant love for families. (See Bryan Chapell, *Why Do We Baptize Infants?* Basics of the Reformed Faith Series [Phillipsburg, NJ: P&R Publishing, 2007], 1–24; also "Westminster Confession," 224–25.) A belief that believer's baptism was the only appropriate type of baptism naturally followed from a strong emphasis on the individual in theology. For more on believer's baptism as the only appropriate type of Christian baptism, see Dargan, *Ecclesiology*, 284–483; E. C. Dargan, *The Doctrines of Our Faith: A Convenient Handbook for Use in Normal Classes, Sacred Literature Courses and Individual Study* (Nashville: Sunday School Board Southern Baptist Convention, 1905), 174–77; and F. H. Kerfoot, "What We Believe According to the Scriptures," in *Doctrines*, ed. Dargan, 231–32. For more on the influence of E. C. Dargan for Southern Baptist theology, see Walter B. Shurden, *Not an Easy Journey: Some Transitions in Baptist Life* (Macon, GA: Mercer University Press, 2005), 80–81.

20. For an example, see George M. Marsden, *Fundamentalism and American Culture*, new ed. (Oxford: Oxford University Press, 2006), 105.

21. Wayne J. Flynt, *Alabama Baptists: Southern Baptists in the Heart of Dixie* (Tuscaloosa: University of Alabama Press, 1998), 83.

22. Flynt, *Alabama Baptists*, 248.

23. Flynt, *Alabama Baptists*, 248–50.

24. Flynt, *Alabama Baptists*, 162.

25. The same years that brought about the split among American Baptists over the issue of slavery, a schism among Methodists occurred over the same issue. The Methodist Bishop James A. Andrew married a woman who owned slaves, and thus became a slave owner himself according to the laws of the day. Northern delegates to the Methodist General Conference objected to the idea of having a slaveholding bishop in the church, while southerners felt that if Andrew were forced

to resign the bishopric or manumit his slaves, all slave owners could eventually be forced to leave the church. In 1844, then, the Methodist Episcopal Church, South, was founded as a separate denomination.

26. For an account by a Southern pastor mourning the schism, see John Griffing Jones, "A Brief Autobiography of J. G Jones and J. A. Jones written for their children," Vol. II, 80–81, John G. Jones papers MS 10, J. B. Cain Archives of Mississippi Methodism, Millsaps-Wilson Library, Millsaps College, Jackson, Mississippi, JGJ. For statistics on the denomination's size, see Mark Noll, *America's God: From Jonathan Edwards to Abraham Lincoln* (Oxford: Oxford University Press, 2002), 169.

27. Noll, *America's God*, 168–69.

28. See chapter 3, "Ministers and Church Officers," in Jno. J. Tigert, ed., *The Doctrines and Discipline of the Methodist Episcopal Church, South* (Nashville: Publishing House of the Methodist Episcopal Church, South, 1902), 48–88, as well as *Minutes of the Annual Conferences of the Methodist Episcopal Church, South*, for the year 1886, (Nashville: Southern Methodist Publishing House, 1887), 119–20. The MECS organized territorial boundaries in order for church officials to better care for the laity. Just as MECS church officials operated within a hierarchy, the denomination's geographic territories ranged in size and responsibilities. In other words, bishops were in charge of large conferences that were often statewide, and assigned pastors to specific, relatively small, districts within those conferences.

29. H. Walter Featherstun, *What We Protest Against: Epworth League Institute Booklet No. 5* (Nashville: Publishing House of the Methodist Episcopal Church, South, n.d., circa 1910), 3.

30. For an example, see the numbers of the North Georgia Conference in *Minutes of the Annual Conferences*, 141–42.

31. Charles B. Galloway, "Christian Experience: Its Supreme Value and Crowning Evidence," *Methodist Times*, September 5, 1901, 644.

32. James Madison Crews, "Regeneration," n.d., circa 1885, n.p. Box 56, JMC.

33. For specific numbers of parishioners from each denomination, see Department of Commerce and Labor, Bureau of the Census, E. Dana Durand, Director, *Bulletin 103 (Second Edition, Revised and Enlarged): Religious Bodies: 1906* (Washington, DC: Government Printing Office, 1910), 42–47, 103–4.

34. Paul Harvey's article on the evangelical campaign for respectable culture at the turn of the century estimates a high level of Methodist and Baptist attendees. See Paul Harvey, "'These Untutored Masses': The Campaign for Respectability among White and Black Evangelicals in the American South, 1870–1930," in *Southern Crossroads: Perspectives on Religion and Culture*, ed. Walter H. Conser Jr. and Rodger M. Payne, 249–52 (Lexington: University Press of Kentucky, 2008). For more on the sacred evangelical culture so pervasive in the South, see Ted Ownby, *Subduing Satan: Religion, Recreation, and Manhood in the Rural South, 1865–1920* (Chapel Hill: University of North Carolina Press, 1990), 122–43, 194–212. See also *Religious Bodies: 1906*, 38–42.

35. Harvey, *Freedom's Coming*, 73–75. See also Alyson Leigh Dickson's work,

"Becoming a Modern Denomination: Gender and Structure in the Southern Baptist Convention." PhD dissertation, Graduate Department of Religion, Vanderbilt University, 2014.

36. Harvey, *Freedom's Coming*, 73–77.

37. Flynt, *Alabama Baptists*, 169–79.

Chapter 2

1. For more on the disruption of household life after the Civil War and Reconstruction, see Laura Edwards, *Gendered Strife and Confusion: The Political Culture of Reconstruction* (Champaign: University of Illinois Press, 1997), 18–20; Elizabeth Hayes Turner, *Women, Culture, and Community: Religion and Reform in Galveston, 1880–1920* (Oxford: Oxford University Press, 1997), 296; and Jane Censer, *The Reconstruction of White Southern Womanhood, 1865–1895* (Baton Rouge: Louisiana State University Press, 2003), 50–51.

2. For more on the ways in which southerners dealt with the New South, see Edward L. Ayers, *The Promise of the New South: Life after Reconstruction*, 15th anniversary ed. (Oxford: Oxford University Press, 2007).

3. Department of Commerce and Labor, Bureau of the Census, E. Dana Durand, Director, *Bulletin 103 (Second Edition, Revised and Enlarged): Religious Bodies: 1906* (Washington, DC: Government Printing Office, 1910), 42.

4. For more on the ways in which kinship ties are expressed through Christian theology, see Janet Martin Soskice, *The Kindness of God: Metaphor, Gender, and Religious Language* (New York: Oxford University Press, 2007), especially 1–34, 52–65, 66–83.

5. William Owen Carver, "The Word Made Flesh," 1904 Sermon Notebook, 7, Box 12, WOC.

6. For more on Eaton's influence in Southern Baptist polity and the Whitsitt controversy, see Gregory A. Wills, *Southern Baptist Theological Seminary, 1859–2009* (Oxford: Oxford University Press, 2009), 192–229; and James H. Slatton, *W.H. Whitsitt: The Man and the Controversy* (Macon, GA: Mercer University Press, 2009).

7. T. T. Eaton, "Babes in Christ," in Sermon Notebooks: Vol. VII, 1883, n.p., Box 2, Thomas Treadwell Eaton Papers, AR. 21, Southern Baptist Historical Library and Archives, Nashville, Tennessee, TTE.

8. Eaton, "Babes in Christ," Vol. II, n.p., TTE.

9. Eaton, "Babes in Christ," Vol. II, n.p., TTE.

10. Rufus W. Weaver, *The Religious Development of the Child: An Evangelical Study from the Scientific View-Point* (New York: Fleming H. Revell Company, 1913), 274.

11. Weaver, *Religious Development*, 217–21.

12. Such prayers for the conversion of sons were not limited merely to southern mothers. Historian Sean Scott's work shows that the idea of wives and mothers urging their male loved ones to repent and give their hearts to God was a major theme for women in the north during the American Civil War. Sean Scott, *A Visi-*

tation of God: Northern Civilians Interpret the Civil War (Oxford: Oxford University Press, 2010), 72, 95.

13. Weaver, *Religious Development*, 220.

14. Weaver, *Religious Development*, 168–70.

15. Weaver, *Religious Development*, 271.

16. Annie Armstrong to Rev. E. L. Compere, February 5, 1894, in *Rescue the Perishing: Selected Correspondence of Annie Armstrong*, ed. Keith Harper, 125 (Macon, GA: Mercer University Press, 2004).

17. Annie Armstrong to Mrs. Burnham, September 7, 1899, in *Rescue the Perishing*, 108.

18. Carver, "Word Made Flesh," 4.

19. Carver, "Word Made Flesh," 7, 9.

20. Edwin Charles Dargan, *The Doctrines of Our Faith: A Convenient Handbook for Use in Normal Classes, Sacred Literature Courses and Individual Study* (Nashville: Sunday School Board Southern Baptist Convention, 1905), 55–56.

21. Dargan, *Doctrines*, 58–59.

22. Dargan, *Doctrines*, 122.

23. Dargan, *Doctrines*, 154–57.

24. For an example of a Social Gospeller's ideas on the Fatherhood of God, see Lyman Abbott, *The Rights of Man: A Study in Twentieth Century Problems* (London: James Clarke, 1901), 343.

25. Lori D. Ginzburg, *Women and the Work of Benevolence: Morality, Politics, and Class in the Nineteenth-Century United States* (New Haven: Yale University Press, 1990), 1.

26. The tension can be seen in Nancy F. Cott's now classic volume *Bonds of Womanhood: "Woman's Sphere" in New England, 1780–1835* (New Haven: Yale University Press, 1977).

27. John L. Johnson, "Emotionalism in Religion," *Proceedings of the Eleventh Baptist Congress, Held in Augusta, Ga., December 1893* (New York: Baptist Congress Publishing, 1894), 20, Baptist Congress Proceedings Collection, AR. 40, Southern Baptist Historical Library and Archives, Nashville, Tennessee, BCPC.

28. Johnson, "Emotionalism," 20, BCPC.

29. William Owen Carver, Diary 1893, 39, Box 11, WOC.

30. Carver, Diary 1893, 39, Box 11, WOC.

31. See Carver, Diary 1893, 40, and Diary 1897, 9, Box 11, WOC.

32. See Carver, Diary 1893, 39, Box 11, WOC.

33. There is, however, some evidence that Carver was well aware that his diary would be read by others, even if not in his lifetime. See Diary 1893, 116–17, Box 11, WOC.

34. E. C. Dargan, "The Story of a Man Scared by a Woman," n.d., Box 6, ECD.

35. Dargan, "Man Scared by a Woman," 1, ECD.

36. See 1 Kings 19 and 21; and 2 Kings 9, Holy Bible.

37. Dargan, "Man Scared by a Woman," 1, ECD.

38. Dargan, *Doctrines*, 122.

39. For more on white women's education in the New South, see Amy Thompson McCandless, *The Past in the Present: Women's Higher Education in the Twentieth Century South* (Tuscaloosa: University of Alabama Press, 1999), 18–57.

40. McCandless, *Past in the Present*, 18.

41. Landrum Pinson Leavell, Untitled Hillman College Commencement Address, 1905, 10, Box 1, 7, Landrum Pinson Leavell Collection, AR. 795–180, Southern Baptist Historical Library and Archives, Nashville, Tennessee, (LPL). Hillman College was a women's college that was eventually bought and absorbed into the SBC-affiliated Mississippi College in Clinton, Mississippi. See the history of Mississippi College at their website: http://www.mc.edu/about/history.

42. Leavell, Untitled Hillman Commencement Address, 7–9, LPL.

43. Leavell, Untitled Hillman Commencement Address, 8, LPL.

44. Leavell, Untitled Hillman Commencement Address, 8, LPL.

45. For more on the ways in which white women's sexuality was protected, see Stephen Kantrowitz, *Ben Tillman and the Reconstruction of White Supremacy* (Chapel Hill: University of North Carolina Press, 2000), 105.

46. For an example of this, see Kris DuRocher, "Violent Masculinity: Learning Ritual and Performance in Southern Lynchings," 55, in *Southern Masculinity*, ed. Friend, 46–64.

47. Leavell, Untitled Hillman Commencement Address, 8, LPL.

48. Leavell, Untitled Hillman Commencement Address, 9, LPL.

49. Jane Censer, *The Reconstruction of White Southern Womanhood, 1865–1895* (Baton Rouge: Louisiana State University Press, 2003), 277.

50. Censer, *Reconstruction of White Southern Womanhood*, 90.

51. For more on the white idea of African American women as laborers outside the home, see Ayers, *Promise of the New South*, 68–70. For more on the African American appropriation of the domestic as a feminine ideal, see Glenda Gilmore, *Gender and Jim Crow: Women and the Politics of White Supremacy in North Carolina* (Chapel Hill: University of North Carolina Press, 1996), 108, 138; and John M. Giggie, *After Redemption: Jim Crow and the Transformation of African American Religion in the Delta, 1875–1915* (Oxford: Oxford University Press, 2008), 139, 148–52.

52. William J. Holtzclaw, *Women of To-day* (Louisville, KY: Baptist Book Concern, 1909), 146.

53. Holtzclaw's sentiments also seemed to echo the ideas of the biblical book of Isaiah, who, when speaking of one who would come to rescue God's chosen people, talked about a suffering servant. Although there was no proof that Holtzclaw had this passage in mind as he penned his ideas that women were "born sufferer[s]," he likely would have recognized the biblical language of the suffering servant. See Isaiah 52:13–53:12, Holy Bible.

54. Annie Armstrong, "Woman's Missionary Union: The General Organization of Southern Baptist Women," 1900(?), *Rescue the Perishing*, 175.

55. Holtzclaw, *Women of To-day*, 16–17.

56. See Nancy F. Cott, *The Grounding of Modern Feminism* (New Haven: Yale University Press, 1987), 117–20.

57. Holtzclaw, *Women of To-day*, 14–16.

58. Holtzclaw, *Women of To-day*, 45.

59. For examples, see J. B. Hawthorne, "John the Baptist," in *Memorial Catalogue: Fiftieth Annual Catalogue and Register of Howard College*, 1892, 57, Box 4, Catherine Allen Sesquicentennial Collection, SC 4090, Special Collection, Samford University Library, Samford University, Birmingham, Alabama, (CASC); Charles B. Galloway, "Progress of the Twentieth Century Fund," *Christian Advocate*, April 6, 1899, 9l; and Joe Creech, "The Price of Eternal Honor: Independent White Christian Manhood in the Late Nineteenth-Century South," in *Southern Masculinity: Perspectives on Manhood in the South Since Reconstruction*, ed. Craig Thompson Friend, 25–45 (Athens: University of Georgia Press, 2009).

60. For an example, see "History of the Week," *Outlook* 109 (May 12, 1915): 56.

61. Holtzclaw, *Women of To-day*, 45.

62. J. B. Moody, *Women in the Churches: Their Rights and Restrictions; OR, Paul Harmonized with the Law and the Gospel*, 2nd ed. (Martin, TN: Hall-Moody Institute, 1910), 42.

63. Moody, *Women in the Churches*, 42.

64. For more on the trope of the virgin or the whore, see Phyllis Marynick Palmer, "White Women/Black Women: The Dualism of Female Identity and Experience in the United States," *Feminist Studies* 9 (Spring 1983): 157–59. For a Southern perspective, see Betina Entzminger, *The Belle Gone Bad: White Southern Women Writers and the Dark Seductress* (Baton Rouge: Louisiana State University Press, 2002), 1–31.

65. McCandless, *Past in the Present*, 50.

66. McCandless, *Past in the Present*, 50–57.

67. J. B. Gambrell, "Call to Universal Conquest of the World," Folder 36, Box 1, SBC.

68. Gambrell, "Universal Conquest," 2, SBC.

69. For more on the founding of the WMU, see David T. Morgan, *Southern Baptist Sisters: In Search of Status, 1845–2000* (Macon, GA: Mercer University Press, 2003).

70. For a quick history of the Woman's Missionary Union from one of its most influential members, see Armstrong, "Woman's Missionary Union The General Organization of Southern Baptist Women," 1900(?), *Rescue the Perishing*, 175–78. For a more detailed history of the Woman's Missionary Union, see T. Laine Scales, *All that Fits a Woman: Training Southern Baptist Women for Charity and Mission, 1907–1926* (Macon, GA: Mercer University Press, 2000), chapter 1; as well as *Souvenir of the Golden Jubilee: Woman's Missionary Union, Auxiliary to Southern Baptist Convention: Commemorating Fifty Years of Missionary Service, 1888–1938* (Woman's Missionary Union, 1938), 5. For a more in-depth analysis of the ways in which the WMU, and other SBC organizations, influenced gender conceptions in the SBC,

see Alyson L. Dickson's dissertation work "Becoming a Modern Denomination: Gender and Structure in the Southern Baptist Convention," PhD dissertation, Graduate Department of Religion, Vanderbilt University, 2014.

71. Mrs. S. A. Chambers, "Women's Work in the Church," 1882, 1, Mrs. S. A. Chambers, SCB 1249, Special Collection, Samford University Library, Samford University, Birmingham, Alabama, (SAC).

72. Chambers, "Women's Work," 1, SAC.

73. Chambers, "Women's Work," 3–4, SAC.

74. Lidd B. Robertson to "Dear Friend and Brother," July 20, 1894 (emphasis in original), 6–7, Box 2, Frost-Bell Papers, AR. 109, Southern Baptist Historical Library and Archives, Nashville, Tennessee, (FBP); emphasis in original. Unfortunately, the sources do not indicate exactly what Robertson did that her pastor opposed, nor do they say what the eventual outcome of her mutiny was.

75. Robertson, July 20, 1894, 7, FBP; emphasis in original.

76. Annie Armstrong to T. P. Bell, April 11, 1894, *Rescue the Perishing*, 101–4.

77. Annie Armstrong to Dr. R. J. Willingham, May 25, 1895, *Rescue the Perishing*, 91–92.

78. For an example, see Lottie Moon to Rev. T. A. Tupper, August 7, 1886, in *Send the Light: Lottie Moon's Letters and Other Writings*, ed. Keith Harper, 91, 133–35 (Macon, GA: Mercer University Press, 2002).

79. For examples, see Lottie Moon to Rev. Tupper, May 10, 1879, *Send the Light*, 91; and then November 6, 1888, and again January 8, 1889, *Send the Light*, 135–38.

80. Lottie Moon to Rev. Tupper, October 5, 1888, *Send the Light*, 133–35.

81. Holtzclaw, *Women of To-day*, 20–21.

82. Annie Armstrong to Dr. J. M. Frost, July 24, 1896, *Rescue the Perishing*, 94–95.

83. For the correspondence covering this issue, see *Rescue the Perishing*, 265–95.

84. W. P. Wilkes, *An Alabama Boy: 1880–1902* (Troy, AL: Self-published, circa 1951), 18.

85. Primitive Baptists were, and are, one of the many varieties of Baptists not a part of the Southern Baptist Convention. Other religious groups sometimes referred to them as "hyper-Calvinists" because of their emphasis on predestination. This emphasis was so strong that they did not participate in evangelistic or missional enterprises because they believed that God would accomplish salvation by calling the elect without human effort.

86. Wilkes, *Alabama Boy*, 11. For a discussion of how architecture reflected and informed theology in America, see Louis P. Nelson, *The Beauty of Holiness: Anglicanism and Architecture in Colonial South Carolina* (Chapel Hill: University of North Carolina Press, 2008).

87. Wilkes, *Alabama Boy*, 19.

88. Moody, *Women in Churches*, 24; the injunction against preaching is discussed in the same work on 20–21.

89. Moody, *Women in Churches*, 27–28.

90. Moody, *Women in Churches*, 69–72.

91. Moody, *Women in Churches*, 77.

92. Moody, *Women in Churches*, 50–51.

93. Leavell, Untitled Hillman Commencement Address, 7, LPL.

94. For more on how the term "lady" epitomizes the feminine, see Robin Lakoff, "Language and Woman's Place," *Language in Society* 2 (April 1973): 45–80; and A. J. Meier, "When Is a Woman a Lady? A Change in Progress?" *American Speech* 74 (Spring 1999): 56–70. For a historical perspective, see McCandless, *Past in the Present*, 12.

95. Elizabeth Hayes Turner, *Women, Culture, and Community: Religion and Reform in Galveston, 1880–1920* (Oxford: Oxford University Press, 1997).

96. Ginzburg, *Women and the Work of Benevolence*; Rebecca Montgomery, "Lost Cause Mythology in New South Reform," in *Negotiating Boundaries of Southern Womanhood: Dealing with the Powers That Be*, ed. Janet L. Coryell, Thomas H. Appleton Jr., Anastatia Sims, and Sandra Gioia Treadway, 174–98 (Columbia: University of Missouri Press, 2000); and Jane Censer, *The Reconstruction of White Southern Womanhood, 1865–1895* (Baton Rouge: Louisiana State University Press, 2003).

97. Censer, *Reconstruction of White Southern Womanhood*, 50–51.

98. For more on the idea of feminine moral authority, see Ursula King, "Introduction: Gender and the Study of Religion," in *Religion & Gender*, ed. Ursula King, 1–40 (Oxford: Blackwell Publishers, 1995).

99. Holtzclaw, *Women of To-day*, 145. For more on the subject of essentializing gender, see Victoria Pruin DeFrancisco and Catherine Helen Palczewski, *Communicating Gender Diversity: A Critical Approach* (Thousand Oaks, CA: Sage, 2007), 18–20; Andreas G. Philaretou, *The Perils of Masculinity: An Analysis of Male Sexual Anxiety, Sexual Addiction, and Relational Abuse* (Lanham, MD: University Press of America, 2004), 39; and for how this might work in the political realm, see Deborah Alexander and Kristi Anderson, "Gender as a Factor in the Attribution of Leadership Traits," *Political Research Quarterly* 46 (September 1993): 527–45.

100. For more on postmillennial thought and its secular offshoots, see Jean B. Quandt, "Religion and Social Thought: The Secularization of Postmillennialism," *American Quarterly* 25 (October 1973): 390–409. Postmillennial thought was stronger in the northern than in the southern part of the United States at the end of the century. For works that examine postmillennial thought in northern mainline denominations in America, see Christopher Hodge Evans, *The Kingdom is Always But Coming: A Life of Walter Rauschenbusch* (Grand Rapids, MI: Wm. B. Eerdmans Publishing, 2004); and Wendy J. Diechmann Edwards, "Manifest Destiny, the Social Gospel and the Coming Kingdom: Josiah Strong's Program of Global Reform, 1885–1916," in *Perspectives on the Social Gospel: Papers from the Inaugural Social Gospel Conference at Colgate Rochester Divinity School*, ed. Christopher H. Evans, 81–116 (Lampeter: The Edwin Mellon Press, 1999).

101. Holtzclaw, *Women of To-day*, 146.

102. See Censer, *Reconstruction of White Southern Womanhood*, 6–7, 50–51; as well as Cott, *Bonds of Womanhood*, 8, 64, 199–204.

103. For examples, see Montgomery, "Lost Cause Mythology in New South

Reform"; and Censer, *Reconstruction of White Southern Womanhood*; Elna C. Green, *Southern Strategies: Southern Women and the Woman Suffrage Question* (Chapel Hill: University of North Carolina Press, 1997); Evelyn A. Kirkley, "'This Work Is God's Cause': Religion in the Southern Woman Suffrage Movement, 1880–1920," *Church History* 59 (December 1990): 507–22; Anne Firor Scott, *The Southern Lady: From Pedestal to Politics, 1830–1930* (Chicago: University of Chicago Press, 1970); and Marjorie Spruill Wheeler, *New Women of the New South: The Leaders of the Woman Suffrage Movement in the Southern States* (Oxford: Oxford University Press, 1993).

104. Holtzclaw, *Women of To-day*, 32.

105. Holtzclaw, *Women of To-day*, 64–66.

106. Holtzclaw, *Women of To-day*, 65.

107. Holtzclaw, *Women of To-day*, 115.

108. For more on the suffrage movement in the South, see Green, *Southern Strategies*; Evelyn A. Kirkley, "'This Work is God's Cause': Religion in the Southern Woman Suffrage Movement, 1880–1920," *Church History* 59 (December 1990): 507–22; Scott, *The Southern Lady*; and Anne Firor Scott, *Making the Invisible Woman Visible* (Champaign: University of Illinois Press, 1984), 212–21.

109. G. W. Bouldin, Autobiographical Materials, 27, written between 1961 and 1963, Box 2, G. W. Bouldin Collection, AR. 193, Southern Baptist Historical Library and Archives, Nashville, Tennessee, (GWB).

110. See Bouldin, Autobiographical Materials, 22–28, GWB.

111. Bouldin, Autobiographical Materials, 27, GWB, emphasis added.

112. W. L. Sanford, "The Credit System," Alumni Oration in *Memorial Catalogue: Fiftieth Annual Catalogue and Register of Howard College*, 1892, 81, Box 4, Catherine Allen Sesquicentennial Collection, SC 4090, Special Collection, Samford University Library, Samford University, Birmingham, Alabama, (CASC). Howard College, in Birmingham, is now known as Samford University.

113. Sanford, "Credit System," 81, CASC.

114. For more on this and how elite white women attempted to turn the politics of domesticity into an opportunity to gain a sense of mastery in their own homes, see Censer, *Reconstruction of White Southern Womanhood*, 90, 277.

115. For examples of this, see Stephen Kantrowitz, *Ben Tillman and the Reconstruction of White Supremacy* (Chapel Hill: University of North Carolina Press, 2000), 1, 3, 94, 110–11.

116. For the rest of his remarks, see Sanford, "The Credit System," *Memorial Catalogue*. For more on the Southern Populists, see Steven Hahn, *The Roots of Southern Populism: Yeoman Farmers and the Transformation of the Georgia Upcountry, 1850–1890*, updated ed. (Oxford: Oxford University Press, 2006); C. Vann Woodward, *Origins of the New South, 1877–1913* (Baton Rouge: Louisiana State University Press, 1971), 235–63; and Ayers, *Promise of the New South*, 249–82.

117. Holtzclaw, *Women of To-day*, 81. Holtzclaw's ideas were very similar to those documented by Nancy Cott. In her work, *The Bonds of Womanhood*, Cott

demonstrated that in the early part of the nineteenth century, women were supposed to remain in very limited roles. There, "they could nurture and maintain their families, . . . provide religious example and inspiration, and . . . affect the world around them by exercising private moral influence." See Cott, *Bonds of Womanhood*, 8.

118. Such ideas were also very similar to those promulgated a century earlier in the ideal of republican motherhood. For more on this, see Linda K. Kerber, *Women of the Republic: Intellect & Ideology in Revolutionary America* (Chapel Hill: University of North Carolina Press, 1980), 265–88; and Rosemarie Zagarri, *Revolutionary Backlash: Women and Politics in the Early American Republic* (Philadelphia: Pennsylvania State University Press, 2007), 5, 19.

119. Holtzclaw, *Women of To-day*, 88.

120. Holtzclaw, *Women of To-day*, 83.

121. Holtzclaw, *Women of To-day*, 117.

122. See Carver, "Baptist Opportunity," n.d., 4, Box 12, WOC.

123. Holtzclaw, *Women of To-day*, 145–46.

124. For more on a woman losing her purity through the actions of her husband, see Holtzclaw, *Women of To-day*, 64–66.

125. Weaver, *Religious Development*, 150, 219–20.

126. Weaver, *Religious Development*, 150.

127. Annie Armstrong to E. L. Compere, February 5, 1894, *Rescue the Perishing*, 125.

128. A. M. Jackson to E. C. Dargan, June 18, 1911, 2, Box 4, ECD.

129. Bouldin, Autobiographical Materials, 2, GWB.

130. Moody, *Women in Churches*, 43.

Chapter 3

1. J. B. Hawthorne, "John the Baptist," in *Memorial Catalogue: Fiftieth Annual Catalogue and Register of Howard College*, 1892, 57, Box 4, Catherine Allen Sesquicentennial Collection, SC 4090, Special Collection, Samford University Library, Samford University, Birmingham, Alabama, (CASC).

2. Hawthorne, "John the Baptist," in *Memorial Catalogue*, 56, Box 4, CASC.

3. Clifford Putney's *Muscular Christianity: Manhood and Sports in Protestant America, 1880–1920* (Cambridge, MA: Harvard University Press, 2001), the standard work on this movement toward hypermasculine Christianity, concentrates almost exclusively on the movement in the Northeast; however, the push for a more muscular Christianity spread throughout the United States. For another example of the manly implications of Christianity in the North, see Gail Bederman, "'The Women Have Had Charge of the Church Work Long Enough': The Men and Religion Forward Movement of 1911–1912 and the Masculinization of Middle-Class Protestantism," *American Quarterly* 41, no. 3 (September 1989): 432–65. Of course, the southern evangelist Sam P. Jones is a prime example of the ways that an ag-

gressively masculine version of Protestant Christianity was also in the South. For a good introduction to the masculine theology of Jones, see Chad Gregory, "Sam Jones: Masculine Prophet of God," in *Georgia Historical Quarterly* 86, no. 2 (Summer 2002): 231–52. Dimensions of Muscular Christianity were not limited to the United States. For a brief look at its development in the United Kingdom, see Neal Garnham, "Both Praying and Playing: 'Muscular Christianity' and the YMCA in North-East County Durham," *Journal of Social History* 35, no. 2 (Winter 2001): 397–407. For masculine influences on Christian mission and practice in West Africa, see Jeremy Rich, "My Matrimonial Bureau: Masculine Concerns and Presbyterian Mission Evangelization in the Gabon Estuary, 1900–1915," *Journal of Religion in Africa* 36, fasc. 2 (2006): 200–223.

4. Putney, *Muscular Christianity*, 6–7, 45–72, 73–98

5. Hawthorne could easily have heard many concerned pastors talking about Muscular Christianity, though, during his time as a pastor at Tabernacle Baptist Church in New York City. For a very brief account of Hawthorne's ministry, including the churches he served in, see William Cathcart, ed., *The Baptist Encyclopaedia: A Dictionary of The Doctrines, Ordinances, Usages, Confessions of Faith, Sufferings, Labors, and Success, and of the General History of the Baptist Denomination in All Lands, with Numerous Biographical Sketches of Distinguished American and Foreign Baptists, and a Supplement*, vol. 2 (Philadelphia: Louis H. Everts, 1880), 511–12.

6. For a few examples of this, see Joe Creech, "The Price of Eternal Honor: Independent White Christian Manhood in the Late Nineteenth-Century South," in *Southern Masculinity: Perspectives on Manhood in the South Since Reconstruction*, ed. Craig Thompson Friend, 25–45 (Athens: University of Georgia Press, 2009); Craig Thompson Friend, "From Southern Manhood to Southern Masculinities: An Introduction," in *Southern Masculinity*, ed. Friend, vii–xxvi; James L. Roark, *Masters without Slaves: Southern Planters in the Civil War and Reconstruction* (New York: W. W. Norton, 1977); W. J. Cash, *The Mind of the South* (New York: Vintage Books, 1991).

7. For demonstrations of this argument, see Elizabeth Grace Hale, *Making Whiteness: The Culture of Segregation in the South, 1890–1940* (New York: Vintage Books, 1998); Donald G. Mathews, "Why the Old Man Shouted 'Glory!'," in *Southern Crossroads: Perspectives on Religion and Culture*, ed. Walter H. Conser Jr. and Rodger M. Payne, 318–53 (Lexington: University Press of Kentucky, 2008); Kris DuRocher, "Violent Masculinity: Learning Ritual and Performance in Southern Lynchings," in *Southern Masculinity*, ed. Friend, 46–64.

8. William Owen Carver, April 7, 1898, Diary 1897–1899, 33, Box 11, William Owen Carver Papers, AR. 76, Southern Baptist Historical Library and Archives, Nashville, Tennessee, (WOC).

9. For more on the honor-driven society of the antebellum South, see Bertram Wyatt-Brown, *Honor and Violence in the Old South* (Oxford: Oxford University Press, 1986).

10. W. Fitzhugh Brundage documents the change in the codes of honor at the

turn of the century in *Lynching in the New South: Georgia and Virginia, 1880–1930* (Champaign: University of Illinois Press, 1993), 50–54.

11. Clay J. Hudson to "Dr. Van Ness," February 3, 1911, 2, Box 15, I. J. Van Ness Papers, AR. 795, Southern Baptist Historical Library and Archives, Nashville, Tennessee, IJVN.

12. "Field Workers, St. Louis, 1913," Box 2, Landrum Pinson Leavell Collection, AR. 795–180, Southern Baptist Historical Library and Archives, Nashville, Tennessee, LPL. The back of the photograph reads "Top Row (Left to Right): Van Ness, Gentry, Hudgins, Joseph Watts. Second Row: Hyman, Rounds, Andrews, L. O. Leavell, C. S. Leavell, F. H. Leavell, L. P. Leavell. Third Row: Strickland, Byrd, Price, Moseley, Middleton, Barnes, Lee, Flake. Bottom Row: Burroughs, Moore, Spilman, Dr. Frost, Foster, Eutzmingen." Image courtesy of Southern Baptist Historical Library and Archives, Nashville, Tennessee.

13. T. T. Eaton, "Sermon to Young Men," in Sermon Notebook Vol. VI: 1871–1878, n.d., 34, Box 1, Thomas Treadwell Eaton Papers, AR. 21, Southern Baptist Historical Library and Archives, Nashville, Tennessee, TTE.

14. Eaton, "Young Men," 47, TTE.

15. T. T. Eaton, "Be Strong and of Good Courage," November 1876, Sermon Vol. VI, 152, TTE.

16. Eaton, "Be Strong," 151, TTE.

17. T. T. Eaton, "Babes in Christ," in Sermon Notebook Vol. VII, n.p., TTE.

18. Eaton, "Babes in Christ," Vol. VII, n.p., TTE.

19. For an example of this, see Gail Bederman, *Manliness & Civilization: A Cultural History of Gender and Race in the United States, 1880–1917*, with forward by Catherine R. Stimpson, (Chicago: University of Chicago Press, 1996), 101–4.

20. Eaton, "Be Strong," 151, TTE, (emphasis added).

21. See Roark, *Masters without Slaves*, especially 68–108 and 156–209.

22. For examples of other religious figures from the time, see Josiah Strong, pocket notepad from South American tour, section on Rio de Janeiro, 1909, Box 1, Josiah Strong Papers by courtesy of the Burke Library at Union Theological Seminary in the City of New York, Columbia University Libraries; Lyman Abbott, "Impressions of a Careless Traveler: Bermuda," *Outlook* 97 (April 15, 1911): 813; Lyman Abbott, "The Message of the Nineteenth Century to the Men of the Twentieth," *Outlook* 102 (October 19, 1912): 350; and Walter Rauschenbusch, "The Belated Races and the Social Problems," 1914, Box 4, Walter Rauschenbusch Papers, American Baptist Historical Society, Rochester, New York.

23. "Landrum Pinson Leavell—First Pair of Long Trousers, 1890," Box 2, LPL. Image courtesy of Southern Baptist Historical Library and Archives, Nashville, Tennessee.

24. For more on the implications of clothing and gender, see Jo B. Paoletti, "Clothing and Gender in America: Children's Fashions, 1890–1920," *Signs* 13, no. 1 (Autumn 1987): 136–43, especially 140–42.

25. Carver, 1897 Diary, January 1, 1897, 1–2, Box 11, WOC.

26. William Owen Carver, "The Complacency of Paul as Illustrated in the Philippian Letter," in 1902 Sermon Notebook, April 11, 1903, 54, Box 12, WOC.

27. William Owen Carver, "Future Leadership of the Churches," in 1902 Sermon Notebook, January 6–8, 1909, 82, Box 12, WOC.

28. W. P. Wilkes, *An Alabama Boy: 1880–1902* (Troy, AL: Self-Published, circa 1951), 21.

29. Ted Ownby's *Subduing Satan: Religion, Recreation, and Manhood in the Rural South, 1865–1920* (Chapel Hill: University of North Carolina Press, 1990), 49–50.

30. Wilkes, *Alabama Boy*, 21.

31. Charles W. Daniel to Dr. Dargan, November 12, 1909, Box 4, E. C. Dargan Collection, AR. 203, Southern Baptist Historical Library and Archives, Nashville, Tennessee, (ECD).

32. For an example, see R. R. Acree to Dear Ed., April 8, 1908, 2, Box 4, ECD.

33. George W. Andrews to I. J. Van Ness, October 5, 1914, 2, Box 1, IJVN; Martin Ball to "My Dear Bro.," October 7, 1914, Box 1, IJVN.

34. For scholarship on homosocial bonds, see Sharon R. Bird, "Welcome to the Men's Club: Homosociality and the Maintenance of Hegemonic Masculinity," *Gender and Society* 10 (April 1996): 120–32; and Jean Lipman-Blumen, "Toward a Homosocial Theory of Sex Roles: An Explanation of the Sex Segregation of Social Institutions," *Signs* 1 (Spring 1976): 15–31.

35. Jonathan Ned Katz's work is very helpful in describing the lack of the gay-straight-bi division during the nineteenth century and the way that men would talk about their relationships to other men. See Jonathan Ned Katz, *Love Stories: Sex Between Men Before Homosexuality* (Chicago: University of Chicago Press, 2001); as well as Jonathan Ned Katz, *The Invention of Heterosexuality* (Chicago: University of Chicago Press, 2007).

36. E. C. Dargan, "The Story of a Man Scared by a Woman," 5, n.d., Box 6, ECD; for the biblical account, see 2 Kings chapter 2.

37. While only a few SBC officials freely used such terms of affection for other men, such expressions were much more prevalent in the Holiness movement.

38. Albert L. Cummings to "Dear Doctor," June 8, 1912, Box 5, ECD.

39. Jerry Sutton, *A Matter of Conviction: A History of the Southern Baptist Engagement with the Culture* (Nashville: B&H Publishing Group, 2008), 88.

40. W. J. Bradley to "Dear Doctor," May 22, 1913, 1, Box 5, ECD.

41. Carver, January 14, 1896, Diary 1896, 9, Box 11, WOC; and Carver, March 25, 1896, Diary 1896, 54, Box 11, WOC.

42. Carver, January 3, 1899, Diary 1897–1899, 38–39, Box 11, WOC.

43. Wilkes, *Alabama Boy*, 37. Emphasis added.

44. Wilkes, *Alabama Boy*, 37.

45. Ida B. Wells often also played on the trope of civilization as she condemned lynching. For an example, see Ida B. Wells, "Southern Horror: Lynch Law in All Its Phases," 49–72, in *Southern Horrors and Other Writings: The Anti-Lynching Campaign*

of Ida B. Wells, 1892–1900, ed. and intro. Jacqueline Jones Royster, 49–72 (Boston: Bedford/St. Martin's, 1997).

46. Rufus W. Weaver, *The Religious Development of the Child: An Evangelical Study from the Scientific View-Point* (New York: Fleming H. Revell Company, 1913), 274.

47. Eaton, "Babes in Christ," Vol. VII, n.p., TTE.

48. D. G. Lyon, "The College Man's Choice of a Profession," Baccalaureate Address, June 8, 1892, in *Memorial Catalogue: Fiftieth Annual Catalogue and Register of Howard College*, 1892, 71, Box 4, Catherine Allen Sesquicentennial Collection, SC 4090, Special Collection, Samford University Library, Samford University, Birmingham, Alabama, (CASC).

49. Lyon, "College Man's Choice," 72, Box 4, CASC.

50. Lyon, "College Man's Choice," 72, Box 4, CASC.

51. Carver, Diary 1893, 136, Box 11, WOC.

52. John L. Johnson, "Emotionalism," *Proceedings of the Eleventh Baptist Congress, Held in Augusta, Ga., December 1893* (New York: Baptist Congress Publishing, 1894), 24–25, Baptist Congress Proceedings Collection, AR. 40, Southern Baptist Historical Library and Archives, Nashville, Tennessee, (BCPC).

53. Johnson, "Emotionalism," 23, BCPC.

54. See Ann Douglas, *The Feminization of American Culture* (New York: Alfred A. Knopf, 1977). There were certainly pastors who felt the need to confront this idea head-on. The idea of Muscular Christianity, as well as the more organized Men and Religion Forward Movement, both attempted to demonstrate the masculine aspects of religion.

55. By the end of the nineteenth century, many Southern Baptists largely had dropped such a connection between masculine emotion and religious fervor. Earlier that century, though, many evangelical groups, and Methodists and Baptists in particular, were known for their emotive revivals and camp meetings. Yet as evangelicals became a larger part of southern culture, their unique styles of worship and gendered expressions began to meld with the rest of society. By the time Reconstruction was over, in 1877, the transition was almost complete and most Baptists criticized Holiness groups for their expressive displays of emotion in worship. For more, see Monica Najar, *Evangelizing the South: A Social History of Church and State in Early America* (Oxford: Oxford University Press, 2008), 62; and Christine Leigh Heyrman, *Southern Cross: The Beginnings of the Bible Belt* (New York: Alfred A. Knopf, 1997), 205–15, 252. Many whites also believed that African Americans engaged in emotional worship, and so thought that staid, controlled worship was not just a mark of proper decorum but a racial trait as well. For more on this, see "Letter from Natchez, Miss.," *Baptist and Reflector* (Nashville), June 25, 1896, 4; J. W. Rush, "Fair Play," *Alabama Christian Advocate*, January 17, 1895, 1; J. W. Rush, "Shut Out," *Alabama Christian Advocate*, July 11, 1895, 1. See also Randall J. Stephens, *The Fire Spreads: Holiness and Pentecostalism in the American South* (Cambridge, MA: Harvard University Press, 2008), 82–93.

56. Fernando Coello McConnell, "The Doctrine of Missions," 1902, 3, Folder

46, Box 1, Southern Baptist Convention Sermon Collection, AR. 638, Southern Baptist Historical Library and Archives, Nashville, Tennessee, (SBC).

57. McConnell, "Doctrine of Missions," 12, Box 1, SBC.

58. For more on Baptists and temperance, see Sutton, *A Matter of Conviction*, 84–91; Wayne J. Flynt, *Alabama Baptists: Southern Baptists in the Heart of Dixie* (Tuscaloosa: University of Alabama Press, 1998), 210–19. See also Joe L. Coker, *Liquor in the Land of the Lost Cause: Southern White Evangelicals and the Prohibition Movement* (Lexington: University of Kentucky Press, 2007), 199–231.

59. Eaton, "Be Strong," 154, TTE.

60. William J. Holtzclaw, *Women of To-day* (Louisville, KY: Baptist Book Concern, 1909), 119.

61. Wilkes, *Alabama Boy*, 19.

62. Officials in the Southern Baptist Convention were not the only ones who viewed alcohol as a potential threat to manhood. For more, see Elaine Frantz Parsons, *Manhood Lost: Fallen Drunkards and Redeeming Women in the Nineteenth Century United States* (Baltimore: Johns Hopkins University Press, 2003).

63. Carver, "Future Leadership," 83, Box 12, WOC.

64. *Memorial Catalogue*, 1892, 24–25, Box 4, CASC.

65. *Memorial Catalogue*, 1892, 30, Box 4, CASC.

66. Sanford, "The Credit System," 1892, 82, Box 4, CASC.

67. Creech, "Price of Eternal Honor," 25–45.

68. For an excellent discussion on the language of independence, see Creech, "Price of Eternal Honor," 25–45.

69. For examples of this, see Stephen Kantrowitz, *Ben Tillman and the Reconstruction of White Supremacy* (Chapel Hill: University of North Carolina Press, 2000), 1, 3, 94, 110–11.

70. There were other issues that split the Populist movement as well, though perhaps none had quite the saliency of racial politics. For more on the Southern Populists, see Steven Hahn, *The Roots of Southern Populism: Yeoman Farmers and the Transformation of the Georgia Upcountry, 1850–1890*, updated ed. (Oxford: Oxford University Press, 2006); C. Vann Woodward, *Origins of the New South, 1877–1913* (Baton Rouge: Louisiana State University Press, 1971), 235–63; Edward L. Ayers, *The Promise of the New South: Life after Reconstruction*, 15th anniversary ed. (Oxford: Oxford University Press, 2007), 249–82. For more on specifically Baptist engagement with Populist ideas, see Flynt, *Alabama Baptists*, 219–27.

71. For more on the warrior image in the American South, see Craig Thompson Friend, "From Southern Manhood to Southern Masculinities: An Introduction," in *Southern Masculinity*, ed. Friend, xi–xii.

72. A. J. Dickinson in Flynt, *Alabama Baptists*, 271.

73. T. T. Eaton, "Faith as Opposed to Doubt," 1882, 13, Folder 26, Box 1, SBC.

74. Eaton, "Babes in Christ," Vol. VII, n.p., TTE.

75. Eaton, "Sermon to Young Men," 42, Vol. 1, TTE.

76. J. B. Gambrell, "Call to Universal Conquest of the World," 1, 1892, Folder

36, Box 1, Southern Baptist Convention Sermon Collection, Southern Baptist Historical Library and Archives, Nashville, Tennessee, (SBC).

77. Gambrell, "Universal Conquest," 1, Box 1, SBC.

78. Fernando Coello McConnell, "The Doctrine of Missions," 1902, 9, Folder 46, Box 1, SBC; see also Carver, "Future Leadership," 80, Box 12, WOC.

79. Rufus W. Weaver, "Sermon Subjects," preached in July 1911 and December 1912, respectively, Box 11, Rufus W. Weaver Collection, AR. 99, Southern Baptist Historical Library and Archives, Nashville, Tennessee, (RWW).

80. Eaton, "Be Strong," 152–53.

Chapter 4

1. Historian Ted Ownby's study of the connections between religion and manly recreation in the New South is particularly helpful in showing how different geographic spaces were cordoned off from various models of manhood. See Ted Ownby, *Subduing Satan: Religion, Recreation, and Manhood in the Rural South, 1865–1920* (Chapel Hill: University of North Carolina Press, 1990).

2. Sam P. Jones, "Quite Your Meanness," in *Sam Jones' Own Book: A Series of Sermons: Collected and Edited Under the Author's own Supervision with An Autobiographical Sketch* (Cincinnati: Cranston and Stowe, 1887), 58–59.

3. Jno. J. Tigert, ed., *The Doctrines and Discipline of the Methodist Episcopal Church, South* (Nashville: Publishing House of the Methodist Episcopal Church, South, 1902), 347.

4. James Madison Crews, "Dancing," n.p., August 1884, in Sermon Book, Box 56, JMC.

5. Ninth International Sunday School Convention program, n.p., April 26–30, 1899, in Box 3, Asa Griggs Candler Papers, Manuscript, Archives, and Rare Book Library, Emory University, Atlanta, Georgia, (AGCP).

6. For more on the idea of Christianity as a "feminizing" force in American life, see Ann Douglass, *The Feminization of American Culture* (New York: Alfred A. Knopf, 1977).

7. For more on the Spanish-American and Philippine-American wars and their influence on gender in the United States, see Kristin L. Hoganson, *Fighting for American Manhood: How Gender Politics Provoked the Spanish-American and Philippine-American Wars* (New Haven: Yale University Press, 1998); and Matthew Frye Jacobson, *Barbarian Virtues: The United States Encounters Foreign Peoples at Home and Abroad, 1876–1917* (New York: Hill and Wang, 2000).

8. *The Book of Common Prayer from the Original Manuscript Attached to the Act of Uniformity of 1662, and now Preserved in the House of Lords* (London: Eyre & Spottiswoode, 1892), 264.

9. Charles Reagan Wilson, *Baptized in Blood: The Religion of the Lost Cause, 1865–1920* (Athens: University of Georgia Press, 1980) 36–57, especially 44.

10. For more on the ways in which images of African American soldiers began

to work into black culture, see Andrew Amron's "From Soldier to Street Corner: Martial Imagery in Working Class Black Culture during the World War I Era," PhD dissertation, University of Alabama, 2013.

11. For more on how this happened in North Carolina, see Glenda Gilmore, *Gender and Jim Crow: Women and the Politics of White Supremacy in North Carolina, 1896–1920* (Chapel Hill: University of North Carolina Press, 1996), 78–82.

12. For more on the uniforms and martial parades of African American fraternal orders, see John Giggie, *After Redemption: Jim Crow and the Transformation of African American Religion in the Delta, 1875–1915* (Oxford: Oxford University Press, 2008), 70–73. See also Amron, "From Soldier to Street Corner."

13. "Negro Veteran Lynched for Refusing to Doff Uniform," *Chicago Defender*, April 5, 1919, quoted in Ralph Ginzburg, *100 Years of Lynching* (Baltimore: Black Classic Press, 1962), 118.

14. Sam P. Jones, "Fighting the Devil," in *Sam Jones' Gospel Sermons As Delivered by the Great Preacher* (Chicago: Rhodes & McClure Publishing Company, 1898), 71.

15. Jones, "The Christian light," in *Sam Jones' Gospel Sermons*, 29–30.

16. See Wilson, *Baptized in Blood*, 109.

17. Charles B. Galloway, "Progress of the Twentieth Century Fund," *Christian Advocate*, April 6, 1899, 9.

18. For a brief comparison of Baptist (congregational) and Methodist (episcopal) styles of church government and the resultant ways in which organizations were able to thrive in the two denominations, see Anne Firor Scott, *Making the Invisible Woman Visible* (Champaign: University of Illinois Press, 1984), 200–203.

19. For more on this point, see Wilson's *Baptized in Blood*, 109.

20. Charles B. Galloway, "Methodism of Tomorrow: An Address Delivered by Bishop Galloway," January 11, 1904, 2, in Box 3, AGCP.

21. Galloway, "Methodism of Tomorrow," 3.

22. Charles B. Galloway, "Christian Experience: Its Supreme Value and Crowning Evidence," *The Methodist Times*, September 5, 1901, 644.

23. For more on the idea that evangelical Christianity was opposed to rough-and-tumble masculine culture, see Ted Ownby, *Subduing Satan: Religion, Recreation, and Manhood in the Rural South, 1865–1920* (Chapel Hill: University of North Carolina Press, 1990). For the idea of Christianity as a domesticated faith, see Ann Douglass, *The Feminization of American Culture* (New York: Alfred A. Knopf, 1977).

24. Craig Thompson Friend, "From Southern Manhood to Southern Masculinities: An Introduction," in *Southern Masculinity: Perspectives on Manhood in the South Since Reconstruction*, ed. Craig Thompson Friend, xi–xii (Athens: University of Georgia Press, 2009).

25. For further examples of the ways in which communal and individual masculinity was used in the American South at this time, see Joe Creech, "The Price of Eternal Honor: Independent White Christian Manhood in the Late Nineteenth-Century South," in *Southern Masculinity*, ed. Friend, 25–45.

26. Galloway, "Christian Experience," 644.

27. James Madison Crews, "An Autobiography," 1885, 10, Box 56, JMC.

28. James Madison Crews to Ora Elizabeth Askew (reproduced and typeset for JMC), "An Epistle of Love," 1875, 1, JMC; emphasis in original.

29. C. E. D. to John Davis Gray, March 17, 1879, 1, Box 2, Burge Family Papers, 1832–1952, Manuscript, Archives, and Rare Book Library, Emory University, Atlanta, Georgia, BFP.

30. Jones, "Autobiography," Vol. 1, 1830–1833, 1, JGJ.

31. Jones, "Autobiography," Vol. II, 163, JGJ.

32. Jones, "Autobiography," Vol. II, 173 and 175, JGJ.

33. Retaining mastery in the midst of great personal loss was one way southern men could demonstrate their manhood. See James L. Roark, *Masters without Slaves: Southern Planters in the Civil War and Reconstruction* (New York: W. W. Norton, 1977), especially 68–108 and 156–209.

34. John Massey, "Character," n.d., 13–14, emphasis in original, Tuskegee Female College and Alabama Conference Female College H1, Methodist Archives Center, Huntington College Library, Huntington College, Montgomery, Alabama, ACFC.

35. John Massey, "Beauty," 2, 1882 Commencement at Alabama Conference Female College, ACFC; emphasis in original.

36. Massey, "Beauty," 8, 11, ACFC.

37. Massey, "Beauty," 11, ACFC.

38. Massey, "Beauty," 8, 17, ACFC.

39. For examples of these things, see Mark 11:12–19; Luke 24; Mark 10:13–16; John 11:32–36, Holy Bible.

40. James Osgood Andrew Clark, "They that wait upon the Lord shall renew their strength," n.d., 5–6, Box 3, James Osgood Andrew Clark papers, Manuscript, Archives, and Rare Book Library, Emory University, Atlanta, Georgia, JOAC.

41. James Madison Crews, Untitled Sermon on Hebrews 4:16, n.d., n.p., Box 56, JMC.

42. Asa Griggs Candler to Charles Howard Candler, February 24, 1903, Box 1, AGC.

43. Asa Griggs Candler to Lucy Candler, September 9, 1899, 1, Box 18, AGC.

44. For examples, see Isaac D. Borders papers, Box 1, "Letters to his wife" folder, IDB.

45. Borders to "My Beloved," November 26, 1912, 1, IDB. In Borders's letters to his wife, he often addresses her in the third person ("My heart hungers so for her").

46. Borders to "My well beloved sweetheart-wife," December 15, 1912, 3, IDB.

47. Borders to "My Precious Wife," March 1, 1913, 1, IDB.

48. For more on his desire to be a good father, see letters dated December 13, 1912; December 15, 1912; and December 25, 1912, IDB.

49. James Hamilton Baxter, "The Active and the Passive in Religious Life," n.d., 3, Box 1, James Hamilton Baxter Papers, Manuscript, Archives, and Rare Book Library, Emory University, Atlanta, Georgia, (JHB).

50. Baxter, "Active and Passive," 5–6, JHB.

51. James Hamilton Baxter, "The Church's Care of the Young," January 31, 1882, 5 (page added to end and repaginated), JHB.

52. Atticus G. Haygood, "Work out your own salvation," October 5, 1884, 7, Box 2, AGH.

53. Atticus G. Haygood, "David and His Sling," January 6, 1883, Box 2, AGH.

54. Haygood, "David," 2, AGH.

55. Haygood, "David," 3, AGH.

56. Haygood, "David," 4, AGH.

57. Sam P. Jones, "The Virtue of Honesty," in *Sam Jones' Gospel Sermons*, 62.

58. Sam P. Jones, "Fighting the Devil," in *Sam Jones' Gospel Sermons*, 68.

59. For more on the discourse of civilization, see Bederman, *Manliness & Civilization*, 31–41, 48.

60. Gail Bederman, *Manliness & Civilization: A Cultural History of Gender and Race in the United States, 1880–1917* (Chicago: University of Chicago Press, 1996), 48.

61. John Massey, "The Vital Point in Education," given July 20, 1895, 2, Dr. John Massey Personal Papers H71, Methodist Archives Center, Huntington College Library, Huntington College, Montgomery, Alabama, JMPP.

62. Massey, "Character," 4, emphasis in original, ACFC.

63. Massey, "Character," 5, emphasis in original, ACFC.

64. Charles B. Galloway, "Inflexibility of Purpose," n.d., 1, Box 5, Charles B. Galloway Papers M14, J. B. Cain Archives of Mississippi Methodism, Millsaps-Wilson Library, Millsaps College, Jackson, Mississippi (CBG).

65. Charles B. Galloway, "The Mother of the Wesleys," n.d., 2–5, Box 5, CBG.

66. Charles B. Galloway, "Stability of Character," n.d., Box 5, CBG.

67. Charles B. Galloway, "Jefferson Davis: A Judicial Estimate," given June 3, 1908, in *Bulletin of the University of Mississippi* VI (August 1908): 1–48.

68. For more on how the idea of a Christian gentleman became an archetype in the postwar South, see Friend, "Southern Manhood to Southern Masculinities," in *Southern Masculinity*, ed. Friend, x–xii.

69. Galloway, "Jefferson Davis," 36–41.

70. Galloway, "Jefferson Davis," 47.

71. Historian Charles Reagan Wilson notes that Bishop Galloway was "perhaps the best-known Lost-Cause paternalist in the post-1900 period." For more, see Wilson, *Baptized in Blood*, 109.

72. For more on the development of the Lost Cause and its popularity, see David W. Blight, *Race and Reunion: The Civil War in American Memory* (Cambridge, MA: Harvard University Press, 2001); Edward J. Blum, *Reforging the White Republic: Race, Religion, and American Nationalism, 1865–1898* (Baton Rouge: Louisiana State University Press, 2005); Katharine Du Pre Lumpkin, *The Making of a Southerner* (Athens: University of Georgia Press, 1991), 111–47; Wilson, *Baptized in Blood*; and W. Scott Poole, *Never Surrender: Confederate Memory and Conservatism in the South Carolina Upcountry* (Athens: University of Georgia Press, 2004).

73. Certainly, the Methodist bishop from Mississippi was not the only religious leader to portray Davis as a messianic figure. In fact, historians have documented that from 1890 to 1920, Davis rivaled Robert E. Lee as the most revered "Southern Saint" in the pantheon of Lost Cause iconography. Bishop Galloway's portrayal of Davis was thus not unusual during the period, but it did offer a window into the vision of southern white Christian manliness that the Methodist leader tried to imprint on his audience. For more, see Wilson, *Baptized in Blood*, 50–51; and Lloyd A. Hunter, "The Immortal Confederacy: Another Look at Lost Cause Religion," in *The Myth of the Lost Cause and Civil War History*, ed. Gary W. Gallagher and Alan T. Nolan, 196–98 (Bloomington: Indiana University Press, 2000).

74. Galloway, "Jefferson Davis," 30–31.

75. Charles B. Galloway, "Bishop Galloway's Work," *Southern Methodist Recorder*, March 2, 1899, 4.

76. Stephen Kantrowitz, *Ben Tillman and the Reconstruction of White Supremacy* (Chapel Hill: University of North Carolina Press, 2000), 5, 110–11. See also C. Vann Woodward, *Origins of the New South, 1877–1913* (Baton Rouge: Louisiana State University Press, 1971), 240–63.

77. Charles B. Galloway, "My First Visit to Cuba," *Christian Advocate*, March 15, 1907, 10.

78. Josiah Strong, *Our Country: Its Possible Future and Its Present Crisis* (New York: American Home Missionary Society, 1885), 46–58.

79. For more on the anti-Catholic secret societies and rhetoric in the United States during this time, see John Higham's *Strangers in the Land: Patterns of American Nativism, 1860–1925*, 2nd ed. (New Brunswick, NJ: Rutgers University Press, 1992), 77–87.

80. The ideas linking race with masculinity have been explored by historian Gail Bederman and numerous other scholars who have shown the multitudinous ways that white males linked their racial and gender identities. For examples, see Gail Bederman, *Manliness & Civilization*, 77–120, 170–216; Kristin L. Hoganson, *Fighting for American Manhood: How Gender Politics Provoked the Spanish-American and Philippine-American Wars* (New Haven: Yale University Press, 1998), 24–30; Matthew Frye Jacobson, *Barbarian Virtues: The United States Encounters Foreign Peoples at Home and Abroad, 1876–1917* (New York: Hill and Wang, 2000), 3–4, 222–23; and Colin B. Chapell, "The Third Strand: Race, Gender, and Self-Government in the Mind of Lyman Abbott," *Fides et Historia* 42 (Fall 2010): 27–54.

81. Galloway, "My First Visit to Cuba," 10.

82. Lewis gave this sermon thirty times between June 1912 and July 1927. Barney Washington Lewis, "The Search for a Man," June 9, 1912, Folder 2, BWL.

83. Lewis, "Search for a Man," 1, BWL.

84. Lewis, "Search for a Man," 3–5, BWL.

85. Lewis, "Search for a Man," 6, 3, BWL.

86. James Osgood Andrew Clark, "They that wait upon the Lord shall renew their strength," n.d., 11, Box 3, JOAC.

87. Barney Washington Lewis, "The Wise Men Worship Christ," February 16, 1914, 3, BWL; and Clark, "They that wait," 3–5, JOAC.

88. For more on the argument, and the resultant ideas about "chaos" in African American spirituality, see Wilson, *Baptized in Blood*, 103.

89. See Daniel chapter 3, Holy Bible.

90. James Osgood Andrew Clark, "Shadrack, Meshack, and Abed-Nego," n.d., 5, Box 4, JOAC.

91. Isaac D. Borders to "My Beloved," November 26, 1912, 14, IDB.

92. Isaac D. Borders to "My Well Beloved Wife," December 13, 1912, 2, IDB.

93. Borders, December 13, 1912, 4, IDB.

94. Isaac D. Borders to "My very tenderly beloved sweetheart," February 8, 1913, 12, IDB.

95. Borders, February 8, 1913, 13, IDB.

96. For more on Borders's desire that God would grant him manly qualities, see Borders, December 13, 1912, 4; Borders, February 8, 1913, 13; and Isaac D. Borders to "My Precious Sweetheart Wife," December 18, 1912, 4, IDB.

Chapter 5

1. Charles B. Galloway, "Christian Experience: Its Supreme Value and Crowning Evidence," *The Methodist Times*, September 5, 1901, 644.

2. For examples of remarks on regeneration and the conversion experience, see James Osgood Andrew Clark, "They that wait upon the Lord shall renew their strength," n.d., 11, Box 3, James Osgood Andrew Clark papers, Manuscript, Archives, and Rare Book Library, Emory University, Atlanta, Georgia, (JOAC); and Isaac D. Borders, "Regeneration," 1907, Isaac D. Borders M17, J. B. Cain Archives of Mississippi Methodism, Millsaps-Wilson Library, Millsaps College, Jackson, Mississippi, (IDB).

3. James Hamilton Baxter, "The Atonement: Its Extent," November 4, 1880, Box 1, James Hamilton Baxter Papers, Manuscript, Archives, and Rare Book Library, Emory University, Atlanta, Georgia, (JHB); and Barney Washington Lewis, "The Plan of Salvation," 2, September 17, 1902, Folder 2, Barney Washington Lewis Papers M58, J. B. Cain Archives of Mississippi Methodism, Millsaps-Wilson Library, Millsaps College, Jackson, Mississippi, (BWL); and H. Walter Featherstun, *What We Protest Against: Epworth League Institute Booklet No. 5* (Nashville: Publishing House of the Methodist Episcopal Church, South, n.d., circa 1910), 3–6.

4. For some of the tensions inherent in this view, see Amy Thompson McCandless, *The Past in the Present: Women's Higher Education in the Twentieth Century South* (Tuscaloosa: University of Alabama Press, 1999).

5. *Clergyman's Pocket Diary and Visiting Book*, arranged by James Porter (New York: Nelson & Philips, 1876), 14–15.

6. James Osgood Andrew Clark, "Therefore, you shall lay up my words," n.d., 23, Box 4, JOAC.

7. Clark, "Therefore," 11, JOAC.

8. Historian Sean Scott's study of religion in the North during the American Civil War supports this idea and demonstrates that the fathers of soldiers took great pains to impart spiritual lessons to their sons. Sean Scott, *A Visitation of God: Northern Civilians Interpret the Civil War* (Oxford: Oxford University Press, 2010), 140. Perhaps more germane is Charity Rakestraw Carney's work, *Ministers and Masters: Methodism, Manhood, and Honor in the Old South* (Baton Rouge: Louisiana State University Press, 2011), 12–13. Quote from Clark, "Therefore," 23, JOAC.

9. For examples, see Leviticus chapters 8–9, 16, 21–22, Holy Bible.

10. Jno. J. Tigert, ed., *The Doctrines and Discipline of the Methodist Episcopal Church, South* (Nashville: Publishing House of the Methodist Episcopal Church, South, 1902), 1–2, 4–5, 10–11.

11. For a different view, one that emphasized the priesthood of all believers, see Walter B. Shurden, *Not an Easy Journey: Some Transitions in Baptist Life* (Macon, GA: Mercer University Press, 2005), 80–87.

12. Proverbs 22:6, Holy Bible.

13. Charles B. Galloway, "Inflexibility of Purpose," n.d., 1, Box 5, Charles B. Galloway Papers M14, J. B. Cain Archives of Mississippi Methodism, Millsaps-Wilson Library, Millsaps College, Jackson, Mississippi, (CBG).

14. John Griffing Jones, "A Brief Autobiography of J. G. Jones and J. A. Jones written for their children," vol. II, 1833–1887, 185–87, John G. Jones papers MS10, J. B. Cain Archives of Mississippi Methodism, Millsaps-Wilson Library, Millsaps College, Jackson, Mississippi, JGJ.

15. John Massey, "The Education of Our Girls," n.d., probably around 1895, 14, Box H71, Dr. John Massey Personal Papers H71, Methodist Archives Center, Huntington College Library, Huntington College, Montgomery, Alabama, JMPP.

16. John Massey, "The Higher Education of Man," 1878, n.p., Box 1, Tuskegee Female College and Alabama Conference Female College H1, Methodist Archives Center, Huntington College Library, Huntington College, Montgomery, Alabama, ACFC.

17. John Massey, "Home," 1879, n.p., Box 1, ACFC.

18. John Massey, "Education of Our Girls," 5, JMPP. A similar sentiment is found in Massey's article, "Woman's Highest Sphere of Influence," *The* (Alabama Conference Female College) *Sagastoan* 3 (March 1903): 12–14.

19. Massey, "Education of Our Girls," 12, JMPP.

20. For more on this, see John M. Giggie, *After Redemption: Jim Crow and the Transformation of African American Religion in the Delta, 1875–1915* (Oxford: Oxford University Press, 2008), 139, 148–52.

21. McCandless, *Past in the Present*, 32–34.

22. John Massey, "Woman's Place in Civilization," 1886, n.p., Box 1, ACFC; emphasis in original.

23. Some of these ideas took their cues from the notion of republican motherhood. For more on that concept, see Nancy F. Cott, *The Bonds of Womanhood: "Wom-*

an's Sphere" in New England, 1780–1835 (New Haven: Yale University Press, 1977), 8; Linda K. Kerber, *Women of the Republic: Intellect & Ideology in Revolutionary America* (Chapel Hill: University of North Carolina Press, 1980), 265–88; and Rosemarie Zagarri, *Revolutionary Backlash: Women and Politics in the Early American Republic* (Philadelphia: Pennsylvania State University Press, 2007), 5, 19.

24. Massey's speech came thirty-four years before the passage of the Nineteenth Amendment, although there were southern suffragists working toward women's suffrage by that point in time. For more on the southern suffrage movement, see Elna C. Green, *Southern Strategies: Southern Women and the Woman Suffrage Question* (Chapel Hill: University of North Carolina Press, 1997); Evelyn A. Kirkley, "'This Work is God's Cause': Religion in the Southern Woman Suffrage Movement, 1880–1920," *Church History* 59 (December 1990): 507–22; and Anne Firor Scott, *The Southern Lady: From Pedestal to Politics, 1830–1930* (Chicago: University of Chicago Press, 1970).

25. Atticus G. Haygood, "Jesus and the Woman of Samaria," March 3, 1889, 2, Box 2, Atticus G. Haygood Family Papers, Manuscript, Archives, and Rare Book Library, Emory University, Atlanta, Georgia, (AGH).

26. Haygood, "Woman of Samaria," 3, Box 2, AGH.

27. Atticus G. Haygood to W. L. Chambers, June 12, 1889, reprinted in *Southern Christian Advocate*, June 26, 1889, in Bound Volume 10, 25, AGH.

28. Massey, "Education of Our Girls," 16–18, JMPP.

29. Women's colleges frequently provided curriculums based on literature and fine arts rather than on science and business, as found at men's schools. For a comparison of men's and women's education, see the *1905 Annual Catalogue of the Alabama Conference Female College*, in Methodist Archives Center, Huntington College Library, Huntington College, Montgomery, Alabama; and compare with the *Millsaps College Register, 1906–1907*, in J. B. Cain Archives of Mississippi Methodism, Millsaps-Wilson Library, Millsaps College, Jackson, Mississippi.

30. Massey, "Education of Our Girls," 18–19, JMPP.

31. McCandless, *Past in the Present*, 18, 20, 26, 34.

32. See Massey, "Education of Our Girls," 24–25, JMPP; and Massey, "Higher Education of Man," 3, ACFC. The biblical reference comes from Psalm 144:12.

33. For more on this, see Laura Edwards, *Gendered Strife and Confusion: The Political Culture of Reconstruction* (Champaign: University of Illinois Press, 1997), 18.

34. Massey, *Reminiscences*, 287, 289–90.

35. Asa Griggs Candler to "My Dear Son," April 24, 1902, 1, Box 1, (emphasis in original), Asa Griggs Candler Papers, Manuscript, Archives, and Rare Book Library, Emory University, Atlanta, Georgia, (AGC).

36. Barney Washington Lewis, "The Plan of Salvation," September 21, 1902, 3, BWL.

37. For more on Lewis's belief that all are equally helpless before a holy God and his rejection of distinctions, see Lewis, "Plan of Salvation," 2–5, BWL.

38. For more on this ideal, see Edward J. Blum, *Reforging the White Republic: Race,*

Religion, and American Nationalism, 1865–1898 (Baton Rouge: Louisiana State University Press, 2005), 38–39, 47–48, 92–104, 108; and Curtis J. Evans, *The Burden of Black Religion* (Oxford: Oxford University Press, 2008). See also Katharine Du Pre Lumpkin, *The Making of a Southerner* (Athens: University of Georgia Press, 1991), 136–37.

39. *Fifty-Third Annual Catalogue and Announcement of Grenada College and Conservatory of Music, Art, and Elocution*, 1904–1905 (Grenada, MS: Sentinel Book and Job Print., 1904), 6.

40. *Catalogue and Announcement of Grenada College*, 53.

41. Galloway, "Mother of the Wesleys," 18, Box 5, CBG; emphasis in original.

42. Galloway, "Mother of the Wesleys," 20–21, Box 5, CBG.

43. John Milford Williams, *The Education of Women for the New Age: A Plea for Greater Liberality for Women's Colleges* (Nashville: Board of Education [of the] Methodist Episcopal Church, South, n.d., circa 1910), 4.

44. Williams, *Education of Women*, 8.

45. Williams, *Education of Women*, 6–8.

46. McCandless, *Past in the Present*, 34.

47. For examples of these types of educational offerings, see *Fifty-Third Annual Catalogue and Announcement of Grenada College and Conservatory of Music, Art, and Elocution, 1904–1905* (Grenada, MS: Sentinel Book and Job Print., 1904); *Annual Catalogue: Alabama Conference Female College, Tuskegee, Alabama, 1899* (Cincinnati: Elm Street Printing Works, 1899).

48. See Whitworth Female College's *LeFost* I (1911), n.p.

49. For more on the Womanless Wedding, see Craig Thompson Friend, "The Womanless Wedding: Masculinity, Cross-Dressing, and Gender Inversions in the Modern South," in *Southern Masculinity: Perspectives on Manhood in the South Since Reconstruction*, ed. Craig Thompson Friend, 219–45 (Athens: University of Georgia Press, 2009).

50. Friend, "Womanless Wedding," 222–24, 226–27.

51. "Votes For Women" Club, (Millsaps College) *Bobashela* IX (Columbus, Ohio: The Champlin Press, 1913), 120.

52. *Belles and Pomegranates* (Montgomery, AL: The Students of the Woman's College of Alabama, 1915), n.p. Image courtesy of the Methodist Archives Center, Huntington College Library, Huntington College, Montgomery, Alabama.

53. *The Southron* (Greensboro, AL: The Student Body of Southern University, 1914), n.p. Southern University eventually moved to Birmingham and merged with Birmingham College to become what is now known as Birmingham-Southern College.

54. Images from *The Southron* courtesy of Birmingham-Southern College Archives.

55. James Osgood Andrew Clark to "My Precious Wife," June 25, 1878, reprinted in the *Baltimore Episcopal Methodist* and found in the Clark Scrapbook, n.p., Box 7, JOAC.

56. Clark to "My Precious Wife," n.p., JOAC.

57. For more on the idea that politics were "unladylike," see Mary G. Dietz and James Farr, "'Politics would undoubtedly unwoman her': Gender, Suffrage, and American Political Science," in *Gender and American Social Science: The Formative Years*, ed. Helene Silverberg, 61–85 (Princeton: Princeton University Press, 1998); and Lyman Abbott, *America in the Making* (New Haven: Yale University Press, 1911), 155–57.

58. Jones, "Autobiography," Vol. II, 162, JGJ.

59. Anthea D. Butler, *Women in the Church of God in Christ: Making a Sanctified World* (Chapel Hill: University of North Carolina Press, 2007), 12.

60. Butler, *Women in the Church of God in Christ*, 15, 31.

61. "The First Mile Post: Being a History of the Sunday School of Wesley Memorial Church, Corner Ivy and Auburn Streets, Atlanta, Georgia" (Atlanta, GA: Wesley Memorial Church, 1904), Box 3, AGC.

62. "The First Mile Post," 6, Box 3, AGC.

63. Image courtesy of Manuscript, Archives, and Rare Book Library, Emory University, Atlanta, Georgia.

64. Elizabeth Hayes Turner, *Women, Culture, and Community: Religion and Reform in Galveston, 1880–1920* (Oxford: Oxford University Press, 1997), 66–71.

65. Isaac D. Borders to "My Precious Sweetheart Wife," December 18, 1912, 2, Box 1, IDB.

66. See folder marked "Borders-Lipscomb Controversy," in Box 1, IDB.

67. R. A. Meek to Isaac D. Borders, March 12, 1913, Box 1, IDB.

68. Jones, "Autobiography," 217, JGJ. Even though Jones used the same terms and had much of the same theology as those in the Holiness movement, he never identified himself as anything but a Southern Methodist. It is for this reason that this author has kept him in the ranks of the MECS, though more will be said about him in the chapter 6, which examines the Holiness movement.

69. Isaac D. Borders, "Credo," n.d., 2, Box 1, IDB. Traditional understandings of Trinitarian theology, soteriology, and other basic elements of the Christian faith were all attacked in this document.

Chapter 6

1. The formation of both the Wesleyan Methodist Church, in 1843, and the Free Methodist Church, in 1860, provide two counter examples of the move away from the doctrines of Christian perfection in Methodism during this period. However, neither of these two denominations had a significant influence in the American South, as they both opposed slavery. For more on this, see Mark Noll, *America's God: From Jonathan Edwards to Abraham Lincoln* (Oxford: Oxford University Press, 2002), 169; and Jon Butler, Grant Wacker, and Randall Balmer, *Religion in American Life: A Short History* (Oxford: Oxford University Press, 2008), 239.

2. Throughout this work, I will follow the lead of the Holiness movement and

use the terms "holiness," "entire sanctification," "Christian perfection," "second blessing," and "perfect love" interchangeably. For an understanding of how these terms relate, see W. B. Godbey, *Divine Healing* (Greensboro, NC: Apostolic Messenger Office, 1909), 7.

3. For an excellent study of Holiness in the African American churches during the time, see John M. Giggie, *After Redemption: Jim Crow and the Transformation of African American Religion in the Delta, 1875–1915* (Oxford: Oxford University Press, 2008). For ease of reading, the racial marker "white" has been dropped through the rest of the text.

4. Beverly Carradine, *The Sanctified Life* (Cincinnati: M. W. Knapp, 1897), 114.

5. Beverly Carradine, *Sanctification* (Nashville: Publishing House of the Methodist Episcopal Church, South, 1891), 30, 20; W. B. Godbey, *Spiritual Gifts and Graces* (Cincinnati: God's Revivalist Office, 1895), 11.

6. "Holiness," *Christian Index* 64, (August 12, 1886): 31.

7. W. B. Godbey, *Autobiography of Rev. W.B. Godbey, A.M.* (Cincinnati: God's Revivalist Office, 1909), 102.

8. W. B. Godbey, *Work of the Holy Spirit* (Louisville, KY: Pickett Publishing, 1902), 52. Some scholars interpret the Holiness movement as primarily a way of demonstrating self-mastery and discipline. Such an interpretation can be found in Benton Johnson, "Do Holiness Sects Socialize in Dominant Values?" *Social Forces* 39 (May 1961): 309–16, especially 313–16.

9. Kenneth O. Brown, "William Asbury Dodge," in *William Asbury Dodge: Southern Holiness Pioneer*, comp. Kenneth O. Brown, xi–xii (Hazleton, PA: Holiness Archives, 2001).

10. J. Lawrence Brasher, *The Sanctified South: John Lakin Brasher and the Holiness Movement* (Champaign: University of Illinois Press, 1994), 178–80. The Salvation Army also believed in entire sanctification.

11. Godbey, *Autobiography*, 94–95.

12. Brasher, *Sanctified South*, 177.

13. Brasher, *Sanctified South*, 176.

14. See Mary Lee Cagle, *Life and Work of Mary Lee Cagle: An Autobiography* (Kansas City, MO: Nazarene Publishing House, 1928), 21; and Brasher, *Sanctified South*, 176–77.

15. Brown, *William Asbury Dodge*, xii.

16. Cagle, *Life and Work*, 21.

17. Brasher, *Sanctified South*, 177, 180.

18. Brown, *William Asbury Dodge*, xii.

19. Carradine, *Sanctification*, 49; emphasis in original.

20. Cagle, *Life and Work*, 21; Godbey, *Autobiography*, 94–97, 101–2; and Brasher, *Sanctified South*, 177, 180.

21. See Randall J. Stephens, *The Fire Spreads: Holiness and Pentecostalism in the American South* (Cambridge, MA: Harvard University Press, 2008); Brasher, *Sanctified South*; and Briane K. Turley, *Wheel within a Wheel: Southern Methodism and the*

Georgia Holiness Association (Macon, GA: Mercer University Press, 1999). For how the doctrines of entire sanctification were retained throughout the early part of the nineteenth century in American Methodism, see Allan Coppedge, "Entire Sanctification in Early Methodism: 1812–1835," *Wesleyan Theological Journal* 13 (Spring 1978): 34–50.

22. Godbey, *Autobiography*, 118.

23. John Griffing Jones, "A Brief Autobiography of J. G. Jones and J. A. Jones written for their children," Vol. II, 217–18, John G. Jones papers MS10, J. B. Cain Archives of Mississippi Methodism, Millsaps-Wilson Library, Millsaps College, Jackson, Mississippi, JGJ.

24. Jones, "Autobiography," Vol. I, 213–14; also recounted at the time of her death in Vol. II 1833–1887, 184–85, JGJ. See also Jones, "Autobiography," Vol. I, 27, 52–53, 58.

25. Jones recounts receiving the second blessing again in "Autobiography," Vol. I, 47, 50, 98–100.

26. Jones, "Autobiography," Vol. I, 93, 96, 97.

27. "State of Religion on the Mississippi District. Extract of a letter from the Rev. William Winans, Presiding Elder of the Mississippi District," *The Methodist Magazine* 7 (April 1, 1824), 156; and "State of Religion in the Mississippi District. Extract of a letter from the Rev. William Winans." Dated October 20, 1824, *The Methodist Magazine* 8 (January 1, 1825), 39. For more examples of the doctrines of Holiness in American Methodism during the early part of the nineteenth century, see Coppedge, "Entire Sanctification in Early Methodism." While Coppedge does argue that these doctrines remained in American Methodism, very few of his examples come from the South.

28. Jones, "Autobiography," Vol. II, 106.

29. According to Jones's account, numerous "leading ministers arose in quick succession and asserted not only their unqualified belief in the doctrine of Christian perfection . . . , but testified to their personal experience of a clean heart." Jones, "Autobiography," Vol. II, 106–7.

30. John Griffing Jones, *A Complete History of Methodism As Connected with the Mississippi Conference of the Methodist Episcopal Church, South*, vol. I, (Nashville: Publishing House of the Methodist Episcopal Church, South, 1908), 5.

31. Historians who examine the Holiness movement in the South have typically overlooked this fact. One of the most recent works on the Holiness and Pentecostal movements in the South, *Fire Spreads*, briefly glanced over those in the region who held to Holiness beliefs prior to the Civil War but concluded that they were in the minority within the Methodist fold and actually had their roots outside of the American South. See Stephens, *Fire Spreads*, particularly chapter 2, "Angels from the North," 15–55. As noted in footnote 19, Coppedge argues a very different case in his article in the *Wesleyan Theological Journal*. However, Coppedge's evidence in the South is far from conclusive.

32. For more on self-identification, see Carl J. Couch, "Self-Identification and

Alienation," *The Sociological Quarterly* 7 (Summer 1966): 255–64; and Norman A. Chance, "Acculturation, Self-Identification, and Personality Adjustment," *American Anthropologist* New Series 67 (April 1965): 372–93. Respectful of Jones's identification with the MECS rather than the Holiness movement, I have continued to include him primarily in the Methodist chapters rather than the Holiness ones.

33. For more, see Stephens, *Fire Spreads*, 15–55.

34. *W.A. Dodge*, 123–24. As noted earlier, though, the heaviest concentrations of Holiness teachings were in north Georgia.

35. Mark K. Bauman, *Warren Akin Candler: The Conservative as Idealist* (Metuchen, NJ: Scarecrow Press, 1981), 46–50; and Harold W. Mann, *Atticus Greene Haygood: Methodist Bishop, Editor, and Educator* (Athens: University of Georgia Press, 1965), 163.

36. Bauman, *Candler*, 46–50; and Mann, *Haygood*, 159, 163.

37. For more on Candler's evolving opposition to Holiness or second blessing theology, see Alfred M. Pierce, *Giant Against the Sky: The Life of Bishop Warren Akin Candler* (New York: Abingdon-Cokesbury Press, 1948), 47–48; Bauman, *Candler*, 46–50; Turley, *Wheel within a Wheel*, 15; and Stephens, *Fire Spreads*, 140, 154.

38. Mann, *Haygood*, 159, 166; Stephens, *Fire Spreads*, 153–54; Turley, *Wheel within a Wheel*, 144–47.

39. While Haygood's biographer, Harold Mann, downplays the relationship between Jarrell, Dodge, and Haygood, more recent accounts of the Holiness movement in Georgia indicate a friendship between the men in the years before the American Civil War. For more, see Mann, *Haygood*, 41–43, 71–72; Turley, *Wheel within a Wheel*, 298–99.

40. Turley, *Wheel within a Wheel*, 312; Stephens, *Fire Spreads*, 154; Turley, *Wheel Within A Wheel*, 146.

41. Stephens, *Fire Spreads*, 158–61; Charles Brougher Jernigan, *Pioneer Days of the Holiness Movement in the Southwest* (Kansas City, MO: Pentecostal Nazarene Publishing House, 1919), 109–24.

42. Stephens, "There is Magic in Print," 194–230; Stephens, *Fire Spreads*, 99–135.

43. "The Holiness People in Georgia," *St. Louis Globe-Democrat*, April 16, 1885.

44. For the defining popular portrayal of revival and Holiness religion in the early twentieth century, see Sinclair Lewis's novel *Elmer Gantry* (New York: Harcourt, Brace, 1927).

45. Godbey, *Autobiography*, 73.

46. Carradine, *Sanctified Life*, 211.

47. Cagle, *Life and Work*, 29–31.

48. M. W. Knapp, "Pentecostal Preachers," in *The Full Salvation Quarterly* III (July 1897): 10.

49. Knapp, "Pentecostal Preachers," 23.

50. See also Knapp, "Pentecostal Preachers," 7, 9, and 21.

51. For examples, see Godbey, *Spiritual Gifts and Graces*, 6, 7, and 19–20

52. Godbey, *Spiritual Gifts and Graces*, 7.

53. Godbey, *Autobiography*, 72–73 and 75.

54. Godbey, *Autobiography*, 75.

55. For more on how the Holiness movement was made up of all classes and types of people throughout the South, see Stephens, *Fire Spreads*, 62–66.

56. W. S. Harrison, "Christian Perfection—What It Is," (New Orleans) *Christian Advocate*, November 5, 1896, 1.

57. For an example of the wide-ranging work of these traveling evangelists of Holiness, see Stephens, *Fire Spreads*, 47–52, 75, 99.

58. Stephens, *Fire Spreads*, 101, 135.

59. Stephens, *Fire Spreads*, 99–135.

60. Stephens, *Fire Spreads*, 221–27.

61. Stephens, *Fire Spreads*, 223–24.

62. Vinson Synan, *The Holiness-Pentecostal Tradition: Charismatic Movements in the Twentieth Century*, 2nd ed., (Grand Rapids, MI: Wm. B. Eerdmans Publishing, 1997), 146.

63. Stephens, *Fire Spreads*, 221–27.

Chapter 7

1. For similar findings within an African American Holiness denomination, see Anthea D. Butler, *Women in the Church of God in Christ: Making a Sanctified World* (Chapel Hill: University of North Carolina Press, 2007).

2. While I do not rely solely on Thomas Tweed's theory of religion, I do find it helpful in retaining ideas of movement and change. For more on these notions, and the aquatic metaphors that he uses to describe religion and culture, see Thomas A. Tweed, *Crossing and Dwelling: A Theory of Religion* (Cambridge, MA: Harvard University Press, 2006), especially 54–79.

3. For more on this, see Elizabeth Grace Hale, *Making Whiteness: The Culture of Segregation in the South, 1890–1940* (New York: Vintage Books, 1998), 85–119, especially 94–98; and Amy Thompson McCandless, *The Past in the Present: Women's Higher Education in the Twentieth Century South* (Tuscaloosa: University of Alabama Press, 1999), 6, 12, 18, 34.

4. William Baxter Godbey, *Shall the Women Preach?* (Louisville, KY: Pentecostal Publishing, 1891; reprinted by Holiness Data Ministry, Digital Edition, 1999), 7.

5. For more on the southern women's suffrage movement, see Marjorie Spruill Wheeler, *New Women of the New South: The Leaders of the Woman Suffrage Movement in the Southern States* (Oxford: Oxford University Press, 1993); Evelyn A. Kirkley, "'This Work Is God's Cause': Religion in the Southern Woman Suffrage Movement, 1880–1920," *Church History* 59 (December 1990): 507–22; and Elna C. Green, *Southern Strategies: Southern Women and the Woman Suffrage Question* (Chapel Hill: University of North Carolina Press, 1997).

6. Godbey, *Shall the Women Preach*? 4.

7. W. B. Godbey, *Work of the Holy Spirit* (Louisville, KY: Pickett Publishing, 1902), 55.

8. W. B. Godbey, *Spiritual Gifts and Graces* (Cincinnati: God's Revivalist Office, 1895), 7.

9. Godbey, *Shall the Women Preach?* 4–5.

10. Godbey, *Spiritual Gifts and Graces*, 19.

11. Though Godbey did not quote the reference, the most likely source is 1 Corinthians 1–3, Holy Bible.

12. W. B. Godbey and Seth C. Rees, *The Return of Jesus* (Cincinnati: God's Revivalist Office, 1898), 14.

13. Godbey, *Spiritual Gifts and Graces*, 20.

14. Mrs. J. Wm. Garbutt, comp. *Rev. W.A. Dodge as We Knew Him with Sketches of His Life, Diary, Consecration and Sermons* (Atlanta, GA: Franklin Printing and Publishing Company, 1906), 111, in *William Asbury Dodge: Southern Holiness Pioneer*, comp. Kenneth O. Brown, (Hazleton, PA: Holiness Archives, 2001).

15. Randall J. Stephens, *The Fire Spreads: Holiness and Pentecostalism in the American South* (Cambridge, MA: Harvard University Press, 2008), 82–92.

16. Charles Reagan Wilson, *Baptized in Blood: The Religion of the Lost Cause, 1865–1920* (Athens: University of Georgia Press, 1980); Edward J. Blum, *Reforging the White Republic: Race, Religion, and American Nationalism, 1865–1898* (Baton Rouge: Louisiana State University Press, 2005); and David W. Blight, *Race and Reunion: The Civil War in American Memory* (Cambridge, MA: Harvard University Press, 2001),

17. Eventually, Knapp, Godbey, and many other Southern Holiness leaders would separate themselves from the Pentecostal movement and become harsh critics of those who spoke in tongues. Stephens, *Fire Spreads*, 223–29.

18. M. W. Knapp, "Pentecostal Preachers," in *The Full Salvation Quarterly* III (July 1897): 1–77, (Cincinnati, Ohio: Revivalist Office, 1897), 21.

19. Knapp, "Pentecostal Preachers," 42; emphasis in original.

20. Charles Brougher Jernigan, *Pioneer Days of the Holiness Movement in the Southwest* (Kansas City, MO: Pentecostal Nazarene Publishing House, 1919), 17.

21. Jernigan, *Pioneer Days*, 33.

22. Jernigan, *Pioneer Days*, 34.

23. Jernigan, *Pioneer Days*, 146–49.

24. Jernigan, *Pioneer Days*, 146.

25. Mary Lee Cagle, "Woman's Right to Preach," in *Life and Work of Mary Lee Cagle: An Autobiography* (Kansas City, MO: Nazarene Publishing House, 1928), 169.

26. Cagle, "Woman's Right," in *Life and Work*, 171.

27. Cagle, "Woman's Right," in *Life and Work*, 171.

28. Cagle, "Woman's Right," in *Life and Work*, 167.

29. Cagle, *Life and Work*, 21.

30. Cagle, *Life and Work*, 34–39. Jernigan, *Pioneer Days*, 116–21, and 147 tracks

her work as an evangelist through parts of Arkansas, Texas, New Mexico, and Arizona.

31. Grant Wacker, *Heaven Below: Early Pentecostals and American Culture* (Cambridge, MA: Harvard University Press, 2001), 162–65.

32. See A. J. Jarrell, *The Key to the Storehouse; OR, Faith in God the Secret of All Triumph* (New York: Palmer and Hughes, n.d. 188?), 29–31.

33. See Stephens, *Fire Spreads*, 31–34.

34. J. C. Morris, "Woman's Rights," *Alabama Christian Advocate*, August 1, 1895, 1; G. G. Smith, "Georgia Letter," *Southern Christian Advocate*, August 9, 1888, 1; "Misreading the Scriptures," *Christian Advocate*, June 11, 1896, 1; "Women Cannot Preach," *The Watchman and the Southron*, December 11, 1895, 1; and J. B. Moody, *Women in the Churches: Their Rights and Restrictions; OR, Paul Harmonized with the Law and the Gospel*, 2nd ed. (Martin, TN: Hall-Moody Institute, 1910), 21, 76–79.

35. Jernigan, *Pioneer Days*, 33–34.

36. Cagle, *Life and Work*, 20–22.

37. J. Lawrence Brasher, *The Sanctified South: John Lakin Brasher and the Holiness Movement* (Champaign: University of Illinois Press, 1994), 140–41.

38. For more, see Jernigan, *Pioneer Days*, 33–34; Cagle, *Life and Work*, 22; and Stephens, *Fire Spreads*, 92–97.

39. See Nancy F. Cott, *The Bonds of Womanhood: "Woman's Sphere" in New England, 1780–1835* (New Haven: Yale University Press, 1977), 8, 64, 199–200; Jane Censer, *The Reconstruction of White Southern Womanhood, 1865–1895* (Baton Rouge: Louisiana State University Press, 2003), 51, 90, 276–77.

40. Cagle, *Life and Work*, 22. During the time, a pure woman frequently meant a chaste woman, and there were even those who suggested that a woman might lose her purity through the actions of a sexually unfaithful husband. See William J. Holtzclaw, *Women of To-day*, (Louisville, KY: Baptist Book Concern, 1909), 64–66.

41. See Leigh Eric Schmidt, "'A Church-Going People Are a Dress-Loving People': Clothes, Communication, and Religious Culture in Early America," *Church History* 58 (March 1989): 36–51. African American women had to deal not only with what was perceived as a gendered problem but also with the ways in which fashion and dress were described in racialized terms. For more on this, see Pamela E. Klassen, "The Robes of Womanhood: Dress and Authenticity among African American Methodist Women in the Nineteenth Century," *Religion and American Culture: A Journal of Interpretation* 14 (Winter 2004): 39–82.

42. Klassen, "Robes of Womanhood," 39.

43. Jernigan records that it was not just the women who removed outward signs of adornment, but all those in the Holiness movement. Jernigan, *Pioneer Days*, 7–8.

44. B. S. Taylor, "The Gibeonites: A Scriptural Allegory," *The Full Salvation Quarterly* II (October 1896): 81, (Cincinnati, Ohio: Revivalist Office, 1896).

45. Taylor, "Gibeonites," 82.

46. Taylor did mention that he thought there was a "clearly defined line be-

tween the dress of a real Christian gentleman or lady, and the worldly fashion, the carnal display, the affection and sham of 'society.'" ("Gibeonites," 81). However, this remark was mild compared to the rebuke that women received for their dress.

47. Beverly Carradine, *The Sanctified Life* (Cincinnati: M. W. Knapp, 1897), 159.

48. Carradine, *Sanctified Life*, 164.

49. For examples of how this worked in other religious traditions, see Beryl Satter, *Each Mind a Kingdom: American Women, Sexual Purity, and the New Thought Movement, 1875–1920* (Los Angeles: University of California Press, 1999), 22–26, 30–32.

50. Cagle, *Life and Work*, 32.

51. Cagle, *Life and Work*, 32–33.

52. For more on these narratives, see Schmidt, "Church-Going People," 49.

53. Cagle, *Life and Work*, 20.

54. For more on how spiritual identity was demonstrated through discipline practices such as modest dress, see Anthea D. Butler, "Observing the Lives of the Saints: Sanctification as Practice in the Church of God in Christ," in *Practicing Protestants: Histories of Christian Life in America, 1630–1965*, ed. Laurie F. Maffly-Kipp, Leigh E. Schmidt, and Mark Valeri, 158–76 (Baltimore: Johns Hopkins University Press, 2006).

55. This presents a clear example of the ways that Holiness theology altered, but did not create, understandings of gender.

56. For just two examples from the eighteenth century of vanity as a feminine sin, see Gilbert Crokatt, *Scotch Presbyterian Eloquence Displayed: Or, The Folly of Their Teaching Discovered from Their Books, Sermons, & Prayers: Interspersed with Some Genuine Adventures, in Love, &c.* (England: Printed for Richard Baldwin, 1748), 98, 109; Thomas Brown, *A Legacy for the Ladies. Or, Characters of the Women of the Age* (London: Printed by H. Meere, 1705), 2, 12, 39, 79, 83 (most of the text is a diatribe against women).

57. Godbey, *Autobiography*, 37.

58. Godbey, *Autobiography*, 43.

59. Godbey, *Autobiography*, 25–26. For Godbey's mother, this meant that she took each of her sons individually during the 1830s and 1840s and told them that she was consecrating them for the Lord's service and that they were to become preachers. Godbey's mother would have fit well into the model shown by many Christian women of the evangelist's youth prior to the American Civil War. Many women of the period believed that it was their duty to encourage the religious affections of their children. For more, see Sean Scott, *A Visitation of God: Northern Civilians Interpret the Civil War* (Oxford: Oxford University Press, 2010).

60. Godbey, *Autobiography*, 73.

61. For an example, see Godbey, *Spiritual Gifts and Graces*, 66–69.

62. Cagle, *Life and Work*, 15–17.

63. Godbey, *Autobiography*, 13.

64. Jernigan, *Pioneer Days*, 10–11.

65. Beverly Carradine, *Sanctification* (Nashville: Publishing House of the Methodist Episcopal Church, South, 1891), 138.

66. Godbey and Rees, *The Return of Jesus*, 101.

67. For one example of this, see Taylor, "Gibeonites," 81–82.

68. For examples, see Taylor, "Gibeonites," 84–86; and Carradine, *Sanctification*, 138.

69. Taylor, "Gibeonites," 84–86.

70. In Jernigan's *Pioneer Days*, this idea is discussed and argued against, saying that this false idea of "marital purity" hurt "many once happy homes" and even brought about the "separation of husbands and wives" (154).

71. Taylor, "Gibeonites," 85.

72. Jernigan, *Pioneer Days*, 154.

73. Godbey, *Autobiography*, 428.

74. See Ephesians 5:22–23 and Revelation 21:9–10, Holy Bible.

75. For preachers and pastors from other traditions, see Fernando Coello McConnell, "The Doctrine of Missions," 1902, 3, Folder 46, Box 1, Southern Baptist Convention Sermon Collection, AR. 638, Southern Baptist Historical Library and Archives, Nashville, Tennessee, SBC; Holtzclaw, *Women of To-day*; and James Madison Crews, "Regeneration," n.d., circa 1885, Box 56, Personal Papers of James Madison Crews MC87, Methodist Archives Center, Huntington College Library, Huntington College, Montgomery, Alabama, JMC.

76. W. B. Godbey, *Church—Bride—Kingdom* (Cincinnati: God's Revivalist Office, 1905), 111.

77. Godbey, *Church—Bride—Kingdom*, 103.

78. Godbey and Rees, *The Return of Jesus*, 19. Those in the Holiness movement were certainly not the first to have spiritual ideals tinged with erotic language. There is a long history of erotic language used in Christianity, perhaps none more famous than Teresa of Ávila, who claimed that an angel appeared to her and plunged a golden spear into her "innermost core." She noted that this left her "utterly consumed with the love of God. The pain was so intense that it made me moan. The sweetness this anguish carries with it is so bountiful that I could never wish for it to cease." For more on Teresa of Ávila, see Mirabai Starr, trans., *Teresa of Ávila: The Book of My Life* (Boston: New Seed Books, 2007), 224–26. For more on love and eros in Christianity, see Virginia Burrus and Catherine Keller, *Toward a Theology of Eros: Transfiguring Passion at the Limits of Discipline* (New York: Fordham University Press, 2006), and Simon May, *Love: A History* (New Haven: Yale University Press, 2011), 96–100.

79. For examples, see Godbey, *Autobiography*, 103, 108–9.

80. Godbey, *Spiritual Gifts and Graces*, 66.

81. Godbey, *Autobiography*, 416; and Godbey, *Church—Bride—Kingdom*, 81.

82. Godbey, *Autobiography*, 88.

83. Godbey, *Autobiography*, 89.

84. For more on marriage in the American South, see Carol Bleser, ed., *In Joy and Sorrow: Women, Family, and Marriage in the Victorian South, 1830–1900* (Oxford: Oxford University Press, 1991).

85. Godbey, *Autobiography*, 53.

86. See Maureen Fitzgerald, "The Religious is Personal is Political: Foreword to the 1993 edition of *The Woman's Bible*," in *The Woman's Bible*, ed. Elizabeth Cady Stanton, foreword by Maureen Fitzgerald (Ann Arbor, MI: Northeastern University Press, 1993), iii.

87. For more on this interpretation, see Josh Remington, "Recovering a Creation Mythology: Reading Genesis in the 21st Century," unpublished paper presented at the 2008 Urshan Graduate School of Theology Symposium, "Standing Together for Truth," (November 7–9, 2008): 6; and Robert Alter, *Genesis: Translation and Commentary* (New York City: W. W. Norton, 1996), 9.

88. Kathleen M. Brown's "Beyond the Great Debates: Gender and Race in Early America," *Reviews in American History* 26 The Challenge of American History (March 1998): 96–123 looks at a few of the ways in which the ideal of the "helpmeet" has been debated and discussed by historians, though it does not deal specifically with the theological interpretations. A brief look at the different theological interpretations can be found in Judith S. Antonelli, *In the Image of God: A Feminist Commentary on the Torah* (Northvale, NJ: Jason Aronson, 1995), 5–7.

89. See Censer, *Reconstruction of White Southern Womanhood*, 51, 90, 276–77.

90. Godbey, *Autobiography*, 89.

91. "Peculiar people" is a reference to 1 Peter 2:9, which (in the King James Version) talks about a "peculiar people" set apart from other nations. It is a phrase frequently referenced by Holiness folks.

Chapter 8

1. For more on the notions of honor in the South, see Bertram Wyatt-Brown, *Southern Honor: Ethics and Behavior in the Old South* (Oxford: Oxford University Press, 1982). See also Ted Ownby, *Subduing Satan: Religion, Recreation, and Manhood in the Rural South, 1865–1920* (Chapel Hill: University of North Carolina Press, 1990), 12–13; and Craig Thompson Friend, "From Southern Manhood to Southern Masculinities: An Introduction," in *Southern Masculinity: Perspectives on Manhood in the South Since Reconstruction*, ed. Craig Thompson Friend, xi–xii (Athens: University of Georgia Press, 2009). Similar ideas of manhood and masculinity permeated other parts of the country, and Victorian notions of manly self-control and restraint were challenged by notions of "barbarian virtues" and "the strenuous life." For more on these issues, see Gail Bederman, *Manliness & Civilization: A Cultural History of Gender and Race in the United States, 1880–1917* (Chicago: University of Chicago Press, 1996), 78–80, 100–101, 184–96.

2. Ownby, *Subduing Satan*, 93; and Elliot J. Gorn, "Gouge and Bite, Pull Hair and Scratch: The Social Significance of Fighting in the Southern Backcountry," *American Historical Review* 90 (February 1985): 18–43.

3. W. McDonald, *Scriptural Views of Holiness* (Philadelphia: National Publishing Association for the Promotion of Holiness, 1877), 11.

4. A. J. Jarrell, *Christian Perfection: An Address* (La Grange, GA: A. J. Jarrell, n.d., presumed 1880s), 13.

5. For more on dominant ideas of southern manhood, see Bederman, *Manliness & Civilization*, 77–120; and Ownby, *Subduing Satan*, 38–55, 89–99. See also Friend, *Southern Masculinity*, ed. Friend, vii–xxvi. Certainly, there were other forms of masculinity that incorporated sentimentality, but the dominant ideas in the Deep South did not.

6. For more on African American religious practices, see Anthea D. Butler, *Women in the Church of God in Christ: Making a Sanctified World* (Chapel Hill: University of North Carolina Press, 2007); and John M. Giggie, *After Redemption: Jim Crow and the Transformation of African American Religion in the Delta, 1875–1915* (Oxford: Oxford University Press, 2008). Studies documenting early southern evangelicalism and its more emotive forms of worship include Monica Najar, *Evangelizing the South: A Social History of Church and State in Early America* (Oxford: Oxford University Press, 2008); and Christine Leigh Heyrman, *Southern Cross: The Beginnings of the Bible Belt* (New York: Alfred A. Knopf, 1997). For more on the ways in which the Southern Baptist Convention and the Methodist Episcopal Church, South, accepted many cultural notions of masculinity, see Colin Brett Chapell, "Recasting the Image of God: How Faith Shaped Identity in the Deep South," PhD dissertation, University of Alabama, 2011.

7. A. J. Jarrell, *Faint-Heartedness* (New York: Palmer and Hughes, n.d., presumed 1880s), 6–8.

8. Jarrell, *Faint-Heartedness*, 15–16.

9. B. S. Taylor, "The Gibeonites: A Scriptural Allegory," in *The Full Salvation Quarterly* 2 (October 1896): 28. For the biblical text, see Joshua 9–10, Holy Bible.

10. Taylor, "Gibeonites," 34–35.

11. For examples of people who did not use this type of language, see Charles B. Galloway Papers M14 at J. B. Cain Archives of Mississippi Methodism, Millsaps-Wilson Library, Millsaps College, Jackson, Mississippi; the James Osgood Andrew Clark Papers at Manuscript, Archives, and Rare Book Library, Emory University, Atlanta, Georgia; Dr. John Massey Personal Papers H71, and Personal Papers of James Madison Crews MC87 at Methodist Archives Center, Huntington College Library, Huntington College, Montgomery, Alabama; and I. J. Van Ness Papers, AR. 795, Landrum Pinson Leavell Collection, AR. 795–180, Thomas Treadwell Eaton Papers, AR. 21, and William Owen Carver Papers, AR. 76, all at Southern Baptist Historical Library and Archives, Nashville, Tennessee.

12. Jonathan Ned Katz's work is very helpful in describing the lack of the gay-straight-bi division during the nineteenth century. See Jonathan Ned Katz, *Love*

Stories: Sex Between Men Before Homosexuality (Chicago: University of Chicago Press, 2001); as well as his *The Invention of Heterosexuality* (Chicago: University of Chicago Press, 2007). See also Martin Baum Duberman's helpful (though dated) review essay, "Reclaiming the Gay Past," *Reviews in American History* 16 (December 1988): 515–25. Benjamin E. Wise's recent biography of William Alexander Percy challenges this point, arguing that, though often hidden and fragile, there were understandings of identity based on sexual orientation in the American South during this period. For more see Benjamin E. Wise, *William Alexander Percy: The Curious Life of a Mississippi Planter and Sexual Freethinker* (Chapel Hill: University of North Carolina Press, 2012).

13. The evidence for this goes back at least to the 1826 letters between James Henry Hammond and Jeff Withers. For more on this, see Martin Duberville, "'Writhing Bedfellows' in Antebellum South Carolina: Historical Interpretation and the Politics of Evidence," in *Carryin' On in the Lesbian and Gay South*, ed. John Howard, 15–33 (New York: New York University Press, 1997).

14. Wise's *William Alexander Percy* is also helpful in examining some of the tensions between same-sex desire and other markers of personal identity.

15. For more on homosociality, see Jean Lipman-Blumen, "Toward a Homosocial Theory of Sex Roles: An Explanation of the Sex Segregation of Social Institutions," *Signs* 1 (Spring 1976): 15–31; and Sharon R. Bird, "Welcome to the Men's Club: Homosociality and the Maintenance of Hegemonic Masculinity," *Gender and Society* 10 (April 1996): 120–32. Lipman-Blumen defines homosocial engagement as the "seeking, enjoyment, and/or preference for the company of the same sex" (16). As an example of hostility toward gay culture in the Deep South at the turn of the century, see Benjamin E. Wise, "The Cosmopolitanism of William Alexander Percy," in *Southern Masculinity*, ed. Friend, 129–49.

16. Mary Lee Cagle, *Life and Work of Mary Lee Cagle: An Autobiography* (Kansas City, MO: Nazarene Publishing House, 1928), 25.

17. I Samuel 20, Holy Bible.

18. Many pastors in the Southern Baptist Convention and in the Methodist Episcopal Church, South, reserved emotive language for their families. For examples, see Charles B. Galloway Papers M14, and John G. Jones Papers MS10 both at J. B. Cain Archives of Mississippi Methodism, Millsaps-Wilson Library, Millsaps College, Jackson, Mississippi; the James Osgood Andrew Clark Papers at Manuscript, Archives, and Rare Book Library, Emory University, Atlanta, Georgia; Dr. John Massey Personal Papers H71, and Personal Papers of James Madison Crews MC87 at Methodist Archives Center, Huntington College Library, Huntington College, Montgomery, Alabama; and I. J. Van Ness Papers, AR. 795, Landrum Pinson Leavell Collection, AR. 795–180, Thomas Treadwell Eaton Papers, AR. 21, and William Owen Carver Papers, AR. 76, all at Southern Baptist Historical Library and Archives, Nashville, Tennessee.

19. For more on the practices of sanctification, see Anthea D. Butler, "Observing the Lives of the Saints: Sanctification as Practice in the Church of God in

Christ," in *Practicing Protestants: Histories of Christian Life in America, 1630–1965*, ed. Laurie F. Maffly-Kipp, Leigh E. Schmidt, and Mark Valeri, 158–76 (Baltimore: Johns Hopkins University Press, 2006). For examples of those in the Holiness movement who believed that they had a new identity because of purity, see Beverly Carradine, *The Sanctified Life* (Cincinnati: M. W. Knapp, 1897), 13; McDonald, *Scriptural Views of Holiness*, 12–13; and A. J. Jarrell, "Christian Perfection," 11–13.

20. John L. Johnson, "Emotionalism in Religion," *Proceedings of the Eleventh Baptist Congress, Held in Augusta, Ga., December 1893* (New York: Baptist Congress Publishing, 1894), 20, Baptist Congress Proceedings Collection, AR. 40, Southern Baptist Historical Library and Archives, Nashville, Tennessee.

21. Landrum Pinson Leavell, Untitled Hillman College Commencement Address, 1905, 10, Box 1, Landrum Pinson Leavell Collection, AR. 795–180, Southern Baptist Historical Library and Archives, Nashville, Tennessee, (LPL), 7–9.

22. William J. Holtzclaw, *Women of To-day* (Louisville, KY: Baptist Book Concern, 1909), 32, 64–66, 115.

23. Eventually, Knapp, Godbey, and many other Southern Holiness leaders would separate themselves from the Pentecostal movement and become harsh critics of those who spoke in tongues. Randall J. Stephens, *The Fire Spreads: Holiness and Pentecostalism in the American South* (Cambridge, MA: Harvard University Press, 2008), 223–29.

24. M. W. Knapp, "Pentecostal Preachers," in *The Full Salvation Quarterly* III (July 1897): 13, 16, 20–22.

25. Knapp, "Pentecostal Preachers," 55.

26. Samuel A. Cowan, "Holiness or Entire Sanctification," (New Orleans) *Southwestern Christian Advocate*, February 16, 1899, 2.

27. Godbey, *Church—Bride—Kingdom* (Cincinnati: God's Revivalist Office, 1905), 104–5.

28. Godbey, *Church—Bride—Kingdom*, 88.

29. Godbey, *Church—Bride—Kingdom*, 93.

30. Godbey, *Church—Bride—Kingdom*, 89.

31. Godbey, *Autobiography of Rev. W.B. Godbey, A.M.* (Cincinnati: God's Revivalist Office, 1909), 416.

32. Godbey, *Church—Bride—Kingdom*, 89.

33. For more on how white masculinity relied on ideas of race, power, and mastery, see Joe Creech, "The Price of Eternal Honor: Independent White Christian Manhood in the Late Nineteenth-Century South," in *Southern Masculinity*, ed. Friend, 28; and Kris DuRocher, "Violent Masculinity: Learning Ritual and Performance in Southern Lynchings," in *Southern Masculinity*, ed. Friend, 46–82.

34. For examples of this in the Old South see Wyatt-Brown, *Southern Honor*; and Gorn, "Gouge and Bite." For a study of how this continued beyond the Civil War and Reconstruction, see Edward L. Ayers, *Vengeance and Justice: Crime and Punishment in the 19th-Century American South* (Oxford: Oxford University Press, 1984).

35. Diane Winston, *Red-Hot and Righteous: The Urban Religion of the Salvation Army* (Cambridge, MA: Harvard University Press, 1999), 82–83.

36. Winston, *Red-Hot and Righteous*, 83.

37. For examples, see Charles B. Galloway, "Progress of the Twentieth Century Fund," *Christian Advocate*, April 6, 1899, 9; James Madison Crews, "Dancing," n.p., August 1884, in Sermon Book, Box 56, James Madison Crews MC87, Methodist Archives Center, Huntington College Library, Huntington College, Montgomery, Alabama; and J. B. Gambrell, "Call to Universal Conquest of the World," Folder 36, Box 1, Southern Baptist Convention Sermon Collection, AR. 638, Southern Baptist Historical Library and Archives, Nashville, Tennessee.

38. W. B. Godbey, *Spiritual Gifts and Graces* (Cincinnati: God's Revivalist Office, 1895), 46.

39. J. T. Morris, "Remarks by Rev. J. T. Morris at Service Held in Memory of Rev. A. J. Jarrell," August 30, 1896, Box 6, Charles Crawford Jerrell, MSS 428, Manuscript, Archives, and Rare Book Library, Emory University, Atlanta, Georgia, (CCJ); Jarrell, *Faint-Heartedness*, 8.

40. Carradine, *The Sanctified Life*, 64.

41. Knapp, "Pentecostal Preachers," 47.

42. Many people in the Holiness movement did their utmost to remain in their home denominations despite internal opposition to Holiness theology. For many adherents, this meant they stayed in the MECS, where the writings of John Wesley (1703–1791), one of the founders of Methodism, taught that Christians might have their hearts cleansed of all indwelling sin. For the Wesleyan teachings on entire sanctification, see John Wesley, "A Plain Account of Christian Perfection," in *The Works of Rev. John Wesley in Ten Volumes*, vol. VIII, 1st American ed. (New York: J. &J. Harper, 1827), 5–67. Even so, many officials in the MECS argued that Christian perfection did not come through an instantaneous second blessing of the Holy Ghost and bitterly opposed Holiness teachings. For an example, see Atticus G. Haygood, "Disputing about Holiness," 1888 in Bound Volume 8, Atticus G. Haygood Family Papers, Manuscript, Archives, and Rare Book Library, Emory University, Atlanta, Georgia, (AGH).

43. Godbey, *Autobiography*, 349–51.

44. Godbey, *Autobiography*, 185.

45. Godbey, *Autobiography*, 108–9.

46. For examples of fighting other denominations, see Godbey, *Autobiography*, 108–9, 185, 349–51.

47. Godbey, *Autobiography*, 175.

48. Knapp, "Pentecostal Preachers," 41.

49. Knapp, "Pentecostal Preachers," 7.

50. Godbey, *Work of the Holy Spirit*, 74.

51. Godbey, *Autobiography*, 191.

52. Godbey, *Autobiography*, 480.

53. Godbey, *Autobiography*, 287–88.

54. Godbey, *Autobiography*, 276.

55. Cagle, *Life and Work*, 30. Throughout her autobiography, Cagle referred to herself in the third person.

56. Winston, *Red-Hot and Righteous*, 82–83.

57. See Stephens, *Fire Spreads*, 49.

58. Carradine, *Sanctification*, 121.

59. Taylor, "Gibeonites," 51–53.

60. For examples of historians and others who have taken note of the violent nature of southern masculinity, see W. J. Cash, *The Mind of the South*, with a new introduction by Bertram Wyatt-Brown (New York: Vintage Books, 1991); Bryant Simon, *Fabric of Defeat: The Politics of South Carolina Millhands, 1910–1948* (Chapel Hill: University of North Carolina Press, 1998); Ben Kantrowitz, *Ben Tillman and the Reconstruction of White Supremacy* (Chapel Hill: University of North Carolina Press, 2000); and Wyatt-Brown, *Southern Honor*.

61. E. M. Bounds, "A Man of Prayer," in *Rev. W.A. Dodge*, 23.

62. Bounds, "Man of Prayer," in *Rev. W.A. Dodge*, 25.

63. Cagle, *Life and Work*, 85.

64. Cagle eventually states this very thought in her sermon on "Women's Right to Preach." *Life and Work*, 160–62.

65. See Bederman, *Manliness & Civilization*, 1–45; John F. Kasson, *Houdini, Tarzan, and the Perfect Man: The White Male Body and The Challenge of Modernity in America* (New York: Hill and Wang, 2001), 3–19 and 21–75; and Ownby, *Subduing Satan*, 70–75.

66. The most articulate demonstration of the argument for a divide between the ideas of secular masculine culture and quiet, self-controlled evangelical life is found in Ted Ownby's *Subduing Satan*.

Conclusion

1. For more on Sikh identity in general, see Paramjit S. Judge, "The Politics of Sikh Identity and Its Fundamentalist Assertion," *Economic and Political Weekly* 39, no. 35 (August 28–September 3, 2004): 3947–54; for an analysis of gender identity within Sikhism, see Doris R. Jakobsh, "Relocating Gender in Sikh History: Transformation, Meaning and Identity," PhD dissertation, University of British Columbia, 1999. For more on the general complications of religious identity, see Nathan Katz, "Identity of a Mystic: The Case of Sa'id Sarmad, a Jewish-Yogi-Sufi Courtier of the Mughals," *Numen* 47, fasc. 2 (2000): 142–60.

2. For a discussion of clothing and its religious significance within Roman Catholic religious orders, see Susan O. Michelman, "Changing Old Habits: Dress of Women Religious and Its Relationship to Personal and Social Identity," *Sociological Inquiry* 67, no. 3 (July 1997): 350–63. A discussion of the changing costs of identifying with Catholic religious orders after Vatican II (including the fact that

many orders dropped the requirement for initiates to take a new name) is explored in Roger Finke, "An Orderly Return to Tradition: Explaining the Recruitment of Members into Catholic Religious Orders," *Journal for the Scientific Study of Religion* 36, no. 2 (June 1997): 218–30.

3. According to its website, the evangelical group Promise Keepers has "directly reached more than 6 million men through men's conferences" since 1990. http://www.promisekeepers.org/about, accessed December 4, 2013.

4. http://actlikemen.com/, accessed February 24, 2015; http://www.mightymenusa.org, accessed December 4, 2013. For a directory listing these and other groups, see http://mensteppingup.com/stepping-up-strategic-allies/, accessed December 4, 2013.

5. David Murrow, *Why Men Hate Going to Church* (Nashville: Thomas Nelson, 2005), 11.

6. For more on this remark, Driscoll's insistence that it was said in jest, and the controversy surrounding it, see http://sojo.net/blogs/2013/05/09/mark-driscoll-gas-guzzlers-mark-masculinity, accessed September 6, 2013.

7. *Fight Church*, directed by Daniel Junge and Bryan Storkel (2014; Santa Monica, CA: Lions Gate Entertainment), Amazon Instant Video, http://smile.amazon.com/dp/B00MYL09TA.

8. For the article in the *Atlantic*, see Emma Green, "The Warrior Wives of Evangelical Christianity," *Atlantic*, November 9, 2014, http://www.theatlantic.com/national/archive/2014/11/the-warrior-wives-of-evangelical-christianity/382365/. For Elizabeth's blog, see thewarriorwives.net, quote from http://www.thewarriorwives.net/p/why-this-blog.html.

9. Eric Mason, *Manhood Restored: How the Gospel Makes Men Whole* (Nashville: B&H Books, 2013); Beth Impson, *Called to Womanhood: The Biblical View for Today's World* (Wheaton, IL: Crossway Books, 2001); Darrin Patrick, *The Dude's Guide to Manhood: Finding True Manliness in a World of Counterfeits* (Nashville: Thomas Nelson, 2014); Wendy Horger Alsup, *The Gospel-Centered Woman: Understanding Biblical Womanhood through the Lens of the Gospel* (Seattle: CreateSpace Independent Publishing Platform, 2013); and John Piper, *What's the Difference?: Manhood and Womanhood Defined According to the Bible* (Wheaton, IL: Crossway Books, 2008), and *The Journal for Biblical Manhood and Womanhood* (Louisville, KY: Council on Biblical Manhood and Womanhood). Other examples include Dennis Rainey, *Stepping Up: A Call to Courageous Manhood* (Little Rock: Family Life Publishing, 2011); Carolyn McCulley, *Radical Womanhood: Feminine Faith in a Feminist World* (Chicago: Moody Publishing, 2008); Dan Doriani, *The Life of a God-Made Man: Becoming a Man After God's Heart* (Wheaton, IL: Crossway Books, 2001); and Rebecca Jones, *Does Christianity Squash Women?: A Christian Look at Womanhood* (Nashville: Broadman & Holman Publishers, 2005).

10. John Eldredge, *Wild at Heart: Discovering the Secret of a Man's Soul* (Nashville: Thomas Nelson, 2001). See Rachel Donadio, "Faith-Based Publishing," *New York Times* (November 28, 2004) for publishing numbers through 2004.

11. For more on the Eldredges' ministries, workbooks, and conferences, see RansomedHeart.com, the website of John Eldredge and Stasi Eldredge. There is certainly a backlash against the model of Christian masculinity that John Eldredge promotes, though none have had the publishing success that Eldredge has enjoyed and most are represented in blogs and websites. For examples of the backlash against this model of evangelical masculinity, see http://thegospelcoalition.org/blogs/tgc/2013/09/04/prove-your-gender/, accessed September 5, 2013; http://www.christianpiatt.com/#!blog/c151g, accessed December 6, 2013; http://sojo.net/blogs/2013/05/09/mark-driscoll-gas-guzzlers-mark-masculinity, accessed May 9, 2013; http://thegospelcoalition.org/blogs/tgc/2013/04/16/gospel-centered-manhood-three-correctives/, accessed April 19, 2013.

12. See John Eldredge and Stasi Eldredge, *Captivating: Unveiling the Mystery of a Woman's Soul* (Nashville: Thomas Nelson, 2005); and Stasi Eldredge, *You Are Captivating: Celebrating a Mother's Heart* (Nashville: Thomas Nelson, 2007).

Bibliography

Archival and Manuscript Collections and Their Abbreviations

American Baptist Historical Society, Rochester, New York (now housed at Mercer University, Macon, Georgia).

Rauschenbusch, Walter, Papers

Burke Library, Union Theological Seminary, New York, New York, and Columbia University Libraries, New York, New York.

Strong, Josiah, Papers

J. B. Cain Archives of Mississippi Methodism, Millsaps-Wilson Library, Millsaps College, Jackson, Mississippi.

Lewis, Barney Washington, Papers, (BWL).
Galloway, Charles B., Papers, (CBG).
Borders, Isaac D., (Papers), (IDB).
Jones, John G., Papers, (JGJ).

Manuscript, Archives, and Rare Book Library, Emory University, Atlanta, Georgia.

Candler, Asa Griggs, Papers, (AGCP).
Haygood, Atticus G., Family Papers, (AGH).
Burge Family Papers, 1832–1952, (BFP).
Crawford, Charles, Papers, (CCJ).
Baxter, James Hamilton, Papers, (JHB).
Clark, James Osgood Andrew, Papers, (JOAC).

The Methodist Archives Center, Huntington College Library, Huntington College, Montgomery, Alabama.

Tuskegee Female College and Alabama Conference Female College H1, (ACFC).
Massey, Dr. John, Personal Papers, (JMPP).
Crews, James Madison, Personal Papers, (JMC).

Millsaps College Archives, Millsaps-Wilson Library, Millsaps College, Jackson, Mississippi.

Berry, Mary J., Collection, Whitworth College.

Special Collection, Samford University Library, Samford University, Birmingham, Alabama.

Catherine Allen Sesquicentennial Collection, (CASC).
Mrs. S. A. Chambers, (SAC).

Southern Baptist Historical Library and Archives, Nashville, Tennessee.

Baptist Congress Proceedings Collection, (BCPC).
Dargan, E. C., Collection, (ECD).
Frost-Bell Papers, (FBP).
Bouldin, G. W., Collection, (GWB).
Van Ness, I. J., Papers, (IJVN).
Leavell, Landrum Pinson, Collection, (LPL).
Burrows, Lansing, Papers, (LBP).
Weaver, Rufus W., Collection, (RWW).
Southern Baptist Convention Sermon Collection, (SBC).
Eaton, Thomas Treadwell, Papers, (TTE).
Carver, William Owen, Papers, (WOC).

Periodicals

Alabama Christian Advocate
Atlanta Constitution
Baptist and Reflector (Nashville)
Belles and Pomegranates (Woman's College of Alabama)
Bulletin of the University of Mississippi
Bobashela (Millsaps College)
Christian Advocate
Christian Index (Philadelphia, Pennsylvania)
Entre Nous (Howard College)
Full Salvation Quarterly
Globe-Democrat (St. Louis)
Journal for Biblical Manhood and Womanhood
Journal of Southern History
LeFost (Whitworth Female College)
Methodist Magazine
Methodist Times
New York Times
Outlook
Proceedings of the Eleventh Baptist Congress, Held in Augusta, Ga., December 1893

Sagastoan (Alabama Conference Female College Quarterly)
Southern Christian Advocate
Southern Methodist Recorder
Southron (Southern University)
Southwestern Christian Advocate (New Orleans, Louisiana)
Watchman and the Southron

Articles and Papers

Alexander, Deborah, and Kristi Anderson. "Gender as a Factor in the Attribution of Leadership Traits." *Political Research Quarterly* 46 (September 1993): 527–45.

Becker, William H. "The Black Church: Manhood and Mission." *Journal of the American Academy of Religion* 40 (September 1972): 316–33.

Bederman, Gail. "'The Women Have Had Charge of the Church Work Long Enough': The Men and Religion Forward Movement of 1911–1912 and the Masculinization of Middle-Class Protestantism." *American Quarterly* 41 (September 1989): 432–65.

Bird, Sharon R. "Welcome to the Men's Club: Homosociality and the Maintenance of Hegemonic Masculinity." *Gender and Society* 10 (April 1996): 120–32.

Brown, Kathleen M. "Beyond the Great Debates: Gender and Race in Early America." *Reviews in American History* 26 The Challenge of American History (March 1998): 96–123.

Chance, Norman A. "Acculturation, Self-Identification, and Personality Adjustment." *American Anthropologist* New Series 67 (April 1965): 372–93.

Chapell, Colin B. "The Third Strand: Race, Gender, and Self-Government in the Mind of Lyman Abbott." *Fides et Historia* 42 (Summer/Fall 2010): 27–54.

——. "Sanctified Manhood: Theology and Identity in the Southern Holiness Movement." *Journal of the Historical Society* 13 (December 2013): 465–90.

Coppedge, Allan. "Entire Sanctification in Early Methodism: 1812–1835." *Wesleyan Theological Journal* 13 (Spring 1978): 34–50.

Couch, Carl J. "Self-Identification and Alienation." *The Sociological Quarterly* 7 (Summer 1966): 255–64.

Duberman, Martin Baum. "Reclaiming the Gay Past." *Reviews in American History* 16 (December 1988): 515–25.

Edwards, Wendy J. Diechmann. "Manifest Destiny, the Social Gospel and the Coming Kingdom: Josiah Strong's Program of Global Reform, 1885–1916." In *Perspectives on the Social Gospel: Papers from the Inaugural Social Gospel Conference at Colgate Rochester Divinity School*, ed. Christopher H. Evans 1, 81–116. Lampeter: Edwin Mellon Press, 1999.

Finke, Roger. "An Orderly Return to Tradition: Explaining the Recruitment of Members into Catholic Religious Orders." *Journal for the Scientific Study of Religion* 36, no. 2 (June 1997): 218–30.

Garnam, Neal. "Both Praying and Playing: 'Muscular Christianity' and the YMCA in North-East County Durham." *Journal of Social History* 35 (Winter 2001): 397–407.

Gorn, Elliot J. "Gouge and Bite, Pull Hair and Scratch: The Social Significance of Fighting in the Southern Backcountry." *American Historical Review* 90 (February 1985): 18–43.

Graham, Christopher A. "Evangelicals and 'Domestic Felicity' in the Non-Elite South." *Journal of Southern Religion* 15 (2013): http://jsr.fsu.edu/issues/vol15/graham.html.

Gregory, Chad. "Sam Jones: Masculine Prophet of God." *Georgia Historical Quarterly* 86 (Summer 2002): 231–52.

Hackett, David G. "Gender and Religion in American Culture, 1870–1930." *Religion and American Culture* 5 (Summer 1995): 127–57.

Johnson, Benton. "Do Holiness Sects Socialize in Dominant Values?" *Social Forces* 39 (May 1961): 309–16.

Judge, Paramjit S. "The Politics of Sikh Identity and Its Fundamentalist Assertion." *Economic and Political Weekly* 39, no. 35 (August 28–September 3, 2004): 3947–54.

Katz, Nathan. "Identity of a Mystic: The Case of Sa'id Sarmad, a Jewish-Yogi-Sufi Courtier of the Mughals." *Numen* 47, fasc. 2 (2000): 142–60.

Kirkley, Evelyn A. "'This Work Is God's Cause': Religion in the Southern Woman Suffrage Movement, 1880–1920." *Church History* 59 (December 1990): 507–22.

Klassen, Pamela E. "The Robes of Womanhood: Dress and Authenticity among African American Methodist Women in the Nineteenth Century." *Religion and American Culture: A Journal of Interpretation* 14 (Winter 2004): 39–82.

Lakoff, Robin. "Language and Woman's Place." *Language in Society* 2 (April 1973): 45–80.

Lipman-Blumen, Jean. "Toward a Homosocial Theory of Sex Roles: An Explanation of the Sex Segregation of Social Institutions." *Signs* 1 (Spring 1976): 15–31.

Lynch, James R. "Baptist Women in Ministry through 1920." *American Baptist Quarterly* 13 (December 1994): 304–18.

Marsh, Charles. "What is Lived Theology?" Unpublished Paper presented at the Conference on Lived Theology and Civil Courage, (June 12–14, 2003).

McLean, Nancy. "The Leo Frank Case Reconsidered: Gender and Sexual Politics in the Making of Reactionary Populism." *Journal of American History* 78 (December 1991): 917–48.

Meier, A. J. "When Is a Woman a Lady? A Change in Progress?" *American Speech* 74 (Spring 1999): 56–70.

Michelman, Susan O. "Changing Old Habits: Dress of Women Religious and Its Relationship to Personal and Social Identity." *Sociological Inquiry* 67, no. 3 (July 1997): 350–63.

Moore, James Tice. "Redeemers Reconsidered: Change and Continuity in the Democratic South, 1870–1900." *Journal of Southern History* 44 (1978): 357–78.

Palmer, Phyllis Marynick. "White Women/Black Women: The Dualism of Female Identity and Experience in the United States." *Feminist Studies* 9 (Spring 1983): 151–70.

Paoletti, Jo B. "Clothing and Gender in America: Children's Fashions, 1890–1920." *Signs* 13 (Autumn 1987): 136–43.

Payne, Roger M. "Editor's Column." *Journal of Southern Religion* 1 (1998): http://jsr.fsu.edu/payne.htm.

Quandt, Jean B. "Religion and Social Thought: The Secularization of Postmillennialism." *American Quarterly* 25 (October 1973): 390–409.

Raboteau, Albert J. "Holy Ordinary: Locating the Sacred in Literature and Life." The Sixth Annual Capps Lecture in Christian Theology at the University of Virginia, (November 4, 2009).

Rich, Jeremy. "My Matrimonial Bureau: Masculine Concerns and Presbyterian Mission Evangelization in the Gabon Estuary, 1900–1915." *Journal of Religion in Africa* 36 (2006): 200–223.

Remington, Josh. "Recovering a Creation Mythology: Reading Genesis in the 21st Century." Unpublished Paper presented at the 2008 Urshan Graduate School of Theology Symposium, "Standing Together for Truth." (November 7–9, 2008).

Schmidt, Leigh Eric. "'A Church-Going People Are a Dress-Loving People': Clothes, Communication, and Religious Culture in Early America." *Church History* 58 (March 1989): 36–51.

Scott, Joan W. "Gender: A Useful Category of Historical Analysis." *American Historical Review* 91 (December 1986): 1053–75.

——. "Fantasy Echo: History and the Construction of Identity." *Critical Inquiry* 27 (Winter 2001): 284–304.

Stivers, William. "Woodrow Wilson and the Arab World: The Liberal Dilemma." *Colorado College Studies* 20 (1984): 106–23.

Taylor, B. S. "The Gibeonites: A Scriptural Allegory." *The Full Salvation Quarterly* II (October 1896): 1–86.

Books, Dissertations, and Pamphlets

Abbott, Lyman. *America in the Making*. New Haven: Yale University Press, 1911.

——. *The Rights of Man: A Study in Twentieth Century Problems*. London: James Clarke, 1901.

Alsup, Wendy Horger. *The Gospel-Centered Woman: Understanding Biblical Womanhood through the Lens of the Gospel*. CreateSpace Independent Publishing Platform, 2013.

Alter, Robert. *Genesis: Translation and Commentary*. New York: W. W. Norton, 1996.

Amron, Andrew. "From Soldier to Street Corner: Martial Imagery in Working Class Black Culture during the World War I Era." PhD dissertation, University of Alabama, 2013.

Antonelli, Judith S. *In the Image of God: A Feminist Commentary on the Torah*. Northvale, NJ: Jason Aronson, 1995.

Annual Catalogue: Alabama Conference Female College, Tuskegee, Alabama, 1899. Cincinnati: Elm Street Printing Works, 1899.

Ayers, Edward L. *The Promise of the New South: Life after Reconstruction*. 15th Anniversary Edition. Oxford: Oxford University Press, 2007.

——. *Vengeance and Justice: Crime and Punishment in the 19th-Century American South*. Oxford: Oxford University Press, 1984.

Bauman, Mark K. *Warren Akin Candler: The Conservative as Idealist*. Metuchen, NJ: Scarecrow Press, 1981.

Bebbington, David W. *Evangelicalism in Modern Britain: A History from the 1730s to the 1980s*. Cambridge: Cambridge University Press, 1993.

Bederman, Gail. *Manliness & Civilization: A Cultural History of Gender and Race in the United States, 1880–1917*. Forward by Catherine R. Stimpson. Chicago: University of Chicago Press, 1996.

Bendroth, Margaret Lamberts. *Fundamentalism & Gender, 1875 to the Present*. New Haven: Yale University Press, 1993.

Bennett, James B. *Religion and the Rise of Jim Crow in New Orleans*. Princeton: Princeton University Press, 2005.

Blee, Kathleen M. *Women of the Klan: Racism and Gender in the 1920s*. Los Angeles: University of California Press, 1991.

Bleser, Carol, ed. *In Joy and Sorrow: Women, Family, and Marriage in the Victorian South, 1830–1900*. Introduction by C. Vann Woodward. Oxford: Oxford University Press, 1991.

Blight, David W. *Race and Reunion: The Civil War in American Memory*. Cambridge, MA: Harvard University Press, 2001.

Blum, Edward J. *Reforging the White Republic: Race, Religion, and American Nationalism, 1865–1898*. Baton Rouge: Louisiana State University Press, 2005.

Boles, John B. *The Great Revival: Beginnings of the Bible Belt*. Lexington: University Press of Kentucky, 1996.

Book of Common Prayer from the Original Manuscript Attached to the Act of Uniformity of 1662, *and now Preserved in the House of Lords*. London: Eyre & Spottiswoode, 1892.

Boswell, Angela, and Judith N. McArthur, eds. *Women Shaping the South: Creating and Confronting Change*. Columbia: University of Missouri Press, 2006.

Brasher, Brenda E. *Godly Women: Fundamentalism & Female Power*. New Brunswick, NJ: Rutgers University Press, 1998.

Brasher, J. Lawrence. *The Sanctified South: John Lakin Brasher and the Holiness Movement*. Champaign: University of Illinois Press, 1994.

Brown, Kenneth O., compiler. *William Asbury Dodge: Southern Holiness Pioneer*. Hazleton, PA: Holiness Archives, 2001.

Brown, Thomas. *A Legacy for the Ladies: Or, Characters of the Women of the Age*. London: Printed by H. Meere, 1705.

Brundage, W. Fitzhugh. *Lynching in the New South: Georgia and Virginia, 1880–1930*. Champaign: University of Illinois Press, 1993.

Burrus, Virginia, and Catherine Keller. *Toward a Theology of Eros: Transfiguring Passion at the Limits of Discipline.* New York: Fordham University Press, 2006.

Butler, Anthea D. *Women in the Church of God in Christ: Making a Sanctified World.* Chapel Hill: University of North Carolina Press, 2007.

Butler, Jon, Grant Wacker, and Randall Balmer. *Religion in American Life: A Short History.* Oxford: Oxford University Press, 2008.

Cagle, Mary Lee. *Life and Work of Mary Lee Cagle: An Autobiography.* Kansas City, MO: Nazarene Publishing House, 1928.

Carnes, Mark C., and Clyde Griffen, eds. *Meanings for Manhood: Constructions of Masculinity in Victorian America.* Chicago: University of Chicago Press, 1990.

Carney, Charity Rakestraw. *Ministers and Masters: Methodism, Manhood, and Honor in the Old South.* Baton Rouge: Louisiana State University Press, 2011.

Carradine, Beverly. *Sanctification.* Introduction by L. L. Pickett. Nashville: Publishing House of the Methodist Episcopal Church, South, 1891.

———. *The Sanctified Life.* Cincinnati: M. W. Knapp, 1897.

Cash, W. J. *The Mind of the South.* New Introduction by Bertram Wyatt-Brown. New York: Vintage Books, 1991.

Cathcart, William, ed. *The Baptist Encyclopaedia: A Dictionary of The Doctrines, Ordinances, Usages, Confessions of Faith, Sufferings, Labors, and Success, and of the General History of the Baptist Denomination in All Lands, with Numerous Biographical Sketches of Distinguished American and Foreign Baptists, and a Supplement.* Philadelphia: Louis H. Everts, 1880.

Censer, Jane. *The Reconstruction of White Southern Womanhood, 1865–1895.* Baton Rouge: Louisiana State University Press, 2003.

Chapell, Bryan. *The Wonder of It All: Rediscovering the Treasures of Your Faith.* Wheaton, IL: Crossway Books, 1999.

———. *Why Do We Baptize Infants?* Basics of the Reformed Faith Series. Phillipsburg, NJ: P&R Publishing, 2007.

Chapell, Colin Brett. "Recasting the Image of God: How Faith Shaped Identity in the Deep South." PhD dissertation, University of Alabama, 2011.

Clendenin, Daniel B., ed. *Eastern Orthodox Theology.* Second edition. Grand Rapids, MI: Paternoster Press, 2003.

Clergyman's Pocket Diary and Visiting Book. Arranged by James Porter. New York: Nelson & Philips, 1876.

Cohen, William. *At Freedom's Edge: Black Mobility and the Southern White Quest for Racial Control, 1861–1915.* Baton Rouge: Louisiana State University Press, 1991.

Coker, Joe L. *Liquor in the Land of the Lost Cause: Southern White Evangelicals and the Prohibition Movement.* Lexington: University of Kentucky Press, 2007.

Conser Jr., Rodger M. and Walter H. Payne, eds. *Southern Crossroads: Perspectives on Religion and Culture.* Lexington: University Press of Kentucky, 2008.

Coryell, Janet L., Thomas H. Appleton Jr., Anastatia Sims, and Sandra Gioia Treadway, eds. *Negotiating Boundaries of Southern Womanhood: Dealing with the Powers That Be.* Columbia: University of Missouri Press, 2000.

Cott, Nancy F. *Bonds of Womanhood: "Woman's Sphere" in New England, 1780–1835*. New Haven: Yale University Press, 1977.

——. *The Grounding of Modern Feminism*. New Haven: Yale University Press, 1987.

Creech, Joe. *Righteous Indignation: Religion and the Populist Revolution*. Champaign: University of Illinois Press, 2006.

Creeds of the Churches: A Reader in Christian Doctrine from the Bible to the Present. Edited by John H. Leith. Third Edition. Louisville, KY: John Knox Press, 1982.

Crokatt, Gilbert. *Scotch Presbyterian Eloquence Displayed: Or, the Folly of Their Teaching Discovered from Their Books, Sermons, & Prayers: Interspersed with Some Genuine Adventures, in Love, & c*. England: Printed for Richard Baldwin, 1748.

Dargan, Edwin Charles. *The Doctrines of Our Faith: A Convenient Handbook for Use in Normal Classes, Sacred Literature Courses and Individual Study*. Nashville: Sunday School Board Southern Baptist Convention, 1905.

——. *Ecclesiology: A Study of the Churches*. Second edition. Louisville, KY: Charles T. Dearing, 1905.

DeBurg, Betty A. *Ungodly Women: Gender and the First Wave of American Fundamentalism*. Minneapolis: Fortress, 1990.

DeFrancisco, Victoria Pruin, and Catherine Helen Palczewski. *Communicating Gender Diversity: A Critical Approach*. Thousand Oaks, CA: Sage, 2007.

Delamont, Sarah, and Lorna Duffin, eds. *The Nineteenth-Century Woman: Her Cultural and Physical World*. London: Croom Helm, 1978.

Department of Commerce and Labor, Bureau of the Census. *Bulletin 103 (Second Edition, Revised and Enlarged): Religious Bodies: 1906*. Washington, DC: Government Printing Office, 1910.

Dickson, Alyson L. "Becoming a Modern Denomination: Gender and Structure in the Southern Baptist Convention, 1870–1920." PhD dissertation, Vanderbilt University, 2014.

Dore, Elizabeth, and Maxine Molyneux, eds. *Hidden Histories of Gender and the State in Latin America*. Durham: Duke University Press, 2000.

Doriani, Dan. *The Life of a God-Made Man: Becoming a Man After God's Heart*. Wheaton, IL: Crossway Books, 2001.

Douglass, Ann. *The Feminization of American Culture*. New York: Alfred A. Knopf, 1977.

Doyle, Don H. *New Men, New Cities, New South: Atlanta, Nashville, Charleston, Mobile, 1860–1910*. Chapel Hill: University of North Carolina Press, 1990.

Du Pre Lumpkin, Katharine. *The Making of a Southerner*. Foreword by Darlene Clark Hine. Athens: University of Georgia Press, 1991.

Edwards, Laura. *Gendered Strife and Confusion: The Political Culture of Reconstruction*. Champaign: University of Illinois Press, 1997.

Eighmy, John Lee. *Churches in Cultural Captivity: A History of the Social Attitudes of Southern Baptists*. Knoxville: University of Tennessee Press, 1972.

Eire, Carlos M. N. *A Very Brief History of Eternity*. Princeton: Princeton University Press, 2010.

Eldredge, John. *Wild at Heart: Discovering the Secret of a Man's Soul*. Nashville: Thomas Nelson, 2001.

Eldredge, John, and Stasi Eldredge. *Captivating: Unveiling the Mystery of a Woman's Soul*. Nashville: Thomas Nelson, 2005.

Eldredge, Stasi. *You Are Captivating: Celebrating a Mother's Heart*. Nashville: Thomas Nelson, 2007.

Elwell, Walter, ed. *Evangelical Dictionary of Theology*. Second edition. Grand Rapids, MI: Baker Book House Company, 2001.

Emerson, Michael O., and Christian Smith. *Divided by Faith: Evangelical Religion and the Problem of Race in America*. Oxford: Oxford University Press, 2000.

Entzminger, Betina. *The Belle Gone Bad: White Southern Women Writers and the Dark Seductress*. Baton Rouge: Louisiana State University Press, 2002.

Evans, Christopher Hodge. *The Kingdom is Always But Coming: A Life of Walter Rauschenbusch*. Grand Rapids, MI: Wm. B. Eerdmans Publishing, 2004.

Evans, Curtis J. *The Burden of Black Religion*. Oxford: Oxford University Press, 2008.

Farish, Hunter Dickinson. *The Circuit Rider Dismounts: A Social History of Southern Methodism, 1865–1900*. Richmond, VA: Dietz, 1938.

Featherstun, H. Walter. *What We Protest Against: Epworth League Institute Booklet No. 5*. Nashville: Publishing House of the Methodist Episcopal Church, South, n.d., ca. 1910.

Fifty-Third Annual Catalogue and Announcement of Grenada College and Conservatory of Music, Art, and Elocution, 1904–1905. Grenada, MS: Sentinel Book and Job Print, 1904.

Fitzgerald, Maureen. "The Religious is Personal is Political: Foreword to the 1993 Edition of *The Woman's Bible*." in *The Woman's Bible*. Edited by Elizabeth Cady Stanton. Foreword by Maureen Fitzgerald. Ann Arbor, MI: Northeastern University Press, 1993.

Flynt, Wayne J. *Alabama Baptists: Southern Baptists in the Heart of Dixie*. Tuscaloosa: University of Alabama Press, 1998.

Foner, Eric. *Reconstruction: America's Unfinished Revolution, 1863–1877*. New York: Harper Collins Publishers, 2002; originally published by Harper & Row, 1988.

Foster, Gaines M. *Ghosts of the Confederacy: Defeat, the Lost Cause, and the Emergence of the New South, 1865–1913*. Oxford: Oxford University Press, 1988.

Friend, Craig Thompson, ed. *Southern Masculinity: Perspectives on Manhood in the South Since Reconstruction*. Athens: University of Georgia Press, 2009.

Friend, Craig Thompson, and Lorri Glover, eds. *Southern Manhood: Perspectives on Masculinity in the Old South*. Athens: University of Georgia Press, 2004.

Gallagher, Gary, and Alan T. Nolan, eds. *The Myth of the Lost Cause and Civil War History*. Bloomington: Indiana University Press, 2010.

Garbutt, Mrs. J. Wm., compiler. *Rev. W.A. Dodge as We Knew Him with Sketches of His Life, Diary, Consecration and Sermons*. Atlanta, GA: Franklin Printing and Publishing Company, 1906.

Gedge, Karin E. *Without Benefit of Clergy: Women and the Pastoral Relationship in Nineteenth-Century America.* Oxford: Oxford University Press, 2003.

Genter, Dedre, and S. Goldin-Meadow, eds. *Language in Mind: Advances in the Study of Language and Thought.* Boston: MIT Press, 2003.

Giggie, John M. *After Redemption: Jim Crow and the Transformation of African American Religion in the Delta, 1875–1915.* Oxford: Oxford University Press, 2008.

Gilmore, Glenda Elizabeth. *Gender and Jim Crow: Women and the Politics of White Supremacy in North Carolina, 1896–1920.* Chapel Hill: University of North Carolina Press, 1996.

Ginzberg, Lori D. *Women and the Work of Benevolence: Morality, Politics, and Class in the Nineteenth-Century United States.* New Haven: Yale University Press, 1990.

Ginzburg, Ralph. *100 Years of Lynching.* Baltimore: Black Classic Press, 1962.

Godbey, W. B. *Autobiography of Rev. W. B. Godbey, A.M.* Cincinnati: God's Revivalist Office, 1909.

———. *Church—Bride—Kingdom.* Cincinnati: God's Revivalist Office, 1905.

———. *Divine Healing.* Greensboro, NC: Apostolic Messenger Office, 1909.

———. *Happy Nonagenarian.* Zarephath, NJ: Pillar of Fire, 1919.

———. *Shall the Women Preach?* Louisville, KY: Pentecostal Publishing, 1891; reprinted by Holiness Data Ministry, Digital Edition, 1999.

———. *Spiritual Gifts and Graces.* Cincinnati: God's Revivalist Office, 1895.

———. *Work of the Holy Spirit,* Louisville, KY: Pickett Publishing, 1902.

Godbey, W. B., and Seth C. Rees. *The Return of Jesus.* Cincinnati, OH: God's Revivalist Office, 1898.

Green, Elna C. *Southern Strategies: Southern Women and the Woman Suffrage Question.* Chapel Hill: University of North Carolina Press, 1997.

Gregory, James N. *The Southern Diaspora: How the Great Migrations of Black and White Southerners Transformed America.* Chapel Hill: University of North Carolina Press, 2005.

Groothuis, Rebecca Merrill. *The Feminist Bogeywoman: Questions and Answers about Evangelical Feminism.* Grand Rapids, MI: Baker Books, 1995.

Hahn, Steven. *A Nation Under Our Feet: Black Political Struggles in the Rural South from Slavery to the Great Migration.* Cambridge, MA: Harvard University Press, 2003.

———. *The Roots of Southern Populism: Yeoman Farmers and the Transformation of the Georgia Upcountry, 1850–1890.* Updated edition. Oxford: Oxford University Press, 2006.

Hale, Elizabeth Grace. *Making Whiteness: The Culture of Segregation in the South, 1890–1940.* New York: Vintage Books, 1998.

Hall, Jacquelyn Dowd. *Revolt Against Chivalry: Jesse Daniel Ames and the Women's Campaign Against Lynching.* Revised edition. New York: Columbia University Press, 1993.

Haller John S., and Robin M. Haller. *The Physician and Sexuality in Victorian America.* New York: W. W. Norton, 1977.

Harrison, W. P., ed. *Doctrines and Discipline of the Methodist Episcopal Church, South.* Nashville: Publishing House of the M.E. Church, South, 1892.

Harper, Keith, ed. *Rescue the Perishing: Selected Correspondence of Annie Armstrong.* Macon, GA: Mercer University Press, 2004.

——. *Send the Light: Lottie Moon's Letters and Other Writings.* Macon, GA: Mercer University Press, 2002.

Harvey, Paul. *Freedom's Coming: Religious Culture and the Shaping of the South from the Civil War through the Civil Rights Era.* Chapel Hill: University of North Carolina Press, 2005.

——. *Redeeming the South: Religious Cultures and Racial Identities among Southern Baptists, 1865–1925.* Chapel Hill: University of North Carolina Press, 1997.

Hatch, Nathan O. *The Democratization of American Christianity.* New Haven: Yale University Press, 1989.

Heyrman, Christine Leigh. *Southern Cross: The Beginnings of the Bible Belt.* New York: Alfred A. Knopf, 1997.

Heriot, M. Jean. *Blessed Assurance: Assessing Religious Beliefs through Actions in a Carolina Baptist Church.* Knoxville: University of Tennessee Press, 1994.

Higginbotham, Evenlyn Brooks. *Righteous Discontent: The Women's Movement in the Black Baptist Church.* Cambridge, MA: Harvard University Press, 1993.

Higham, John. *Strangers in the Land: Patterns of American Nativism, 1860–1925.* Second edition. New Brunswick, NJ: Rutgers University Press, 1992.

Hill, Samuel S. *One Name but Several Faces: Varieties of Popular Denominations in Southern History.* Athens: University of Georgia Press, 1996.

——. *Southern Churches in Crisis.* New York: Holt, Rinehart and Winston, 1966.

——. *Southern Churches in Crisis Revisited.* Tuscaloosa: University of Alabama Press, 1999.

Hoganson, Kristin L. *Fighting for American Manhood: How Gender Politics Provoked the Spanish-American and Philippine-American Wars.* New Haven: Yale University Press, 1998.

Holifield, E. Brooks. *The Gentlemen Theologians: American Theology in Southern Culture, 1795–1860.* Durham: Duke University Press, 1978.

Holtzclaw, William J. *Women of To-day.* Introduction by J. A. Leavitt. Louisville, KY: Baptist Book Concern, Publishers, 1909.

Howard, John, ed. *Carryin' On in the Lesbian and Gay South.* New York: New York University Press, 1997.

Impson, Beth. *Called to Womanhood: The Biblical View for Today's World.* Wheaton, IL: Crossway Books, 2001.

Jacobson, Matthew Frye. *Barbarian Virtues: The United States Encounters Foreign Peoples at Home and Abroad, 1876–1917.* New York: Hill and Wang, 2000.

Jakobsh, Doris R. "Relocating Gender in Sikh History: Transformation, Meaning and Identity." PhD dissertation, University of British Columbia, 1999.

Janney, Caroline E. *Remembering the Civil War: Reunion and the Limits of Reconciliation.* Chapel Hill: University of North Carolina Press, 2013.

Jarrell, A. J. *Faint-Heartedness*. New York: Palmer and Hughes, n.d. [188?].

——. *Christian Perfection: An Address*. La Grange, GA: A. J. Jarrell, n.d. 188?.

——. *The Key to the Storehouse; OR, Faith in God the Secret of All Triumph*. New York: Palmer and Hughes, n.d. [188?].

Jernigan, Charles Brougher. *Pioneer Days of the Holiness Movement in the Southwest*. Kansas City, MO: Pentecostal Nazarene Publishing House, 1919.

Johnson, John J. *Latin America in Caricature*. Austin: University of Texas Press, 1980.

Jones, John Griffing. *A Complete History of Methodism As Connected with the Mississippi Conference of the Methodist Episcopal Church, South*. Vol. I. Nashville: Publishing House of the Methodist Episcopal Church, South, 1908.

Jones, Rebecca. *Does Christianity Squash Women?: A Christian Look at Womanhood*. Nashville: Broadman & Holman Publishers, 2005.

Jones, Sam P. *Sam Jones' Gospel Sermons As Delivered by the Great Preacher*. Chicago: Rhodes & McClure, 1898.

——. *Sam Jones' Own Book: A Series of Sermons: Collected and Edited Under the Author's Own Supervision with an Autobiographical Sketch*. Cincinnati: Cranston and Stowe, 1887.

Kantrowitz, Stephen. *Ben Tillman and the Reconstruction of White Supremacy*. Chapel Hill: University of North Carolina Press, 2000.

Kasson, John F. *Houdini, Tarzan, and the Perfect Man: The White Male Body and the Challenge of Modernity in America*. New York: Hill and Wang, 2001.

Katz, Jonathan Ned. *Love Stories: Sex Between Men Before Homosexuality*. Chicago: University of Chicago Press, 2001.

——. *The Invention of Heterosexuality*. Chicago: University of Chicago Press, 2007.

Kerber, Linda. *Women of the Republic: Intellect & Ideology in Revolutionary America*. Chapel Hill: University of North Carolina Press, 1980.

King, Ursula, ed. *Religion & Gender*. Oxford: Blackwell Publishers, 1995.

Knapp, M. W. "Pentecostal Preachers." *The Full Salvation Quarterly* III (July 1897): 1–77. Cincinnati, OH: Revivalist Office, 1897.

Kostlevy, William. *Holy Jumpers: Evangelicals and Radicals in Progressive Era America*. Oxford: Oxford University Press, 2010.

Lazenby, Marion Elias. *History of Methodism in Alabama and West Florida: Being an Account of the Amazing March of Methodism through Alabama and West Florida*. Nashville: Parthenon, 1960.

Lewis, Sinclair. *Elmer Gantry*. New York: Harcourt, Brace, 1927.

Lippy, Charles H. *Do Real Men Pray?: Images of the Christian Man and Male Spirituality in White Protestant America*. Knoxville: University of Tennessee Press, 2005.

Luker, Ralph E. *The Social Gospel in Black and White: American Racial Reform, 1885–1912*. Chapel Hill: University of North Carolina Press, 1991.

MacLean, Nancy. *Behind the Mask of Chivalry: The Making of the Second Ku Klux Klan*. Oxford: Oxford University Press, 1994.

Maffly-Kipp, Laurie F., Leigh E. Schmidt, and Mark Valeri, eds. *Practicing Protestants: Histories of Christian Life in America, 1630–1965*. Baltimore: Johns Hopkins University Press, 2006.

Mann, Harold W. *Atticus Greene Haygood: Methodist Bishop, Editor, and Educator*. Athens: University of Georgia Press, 1965.

Marsden, George M. *Fundamentalism and American Culture*. New edition. Oxford: Oxford University Press, 2006.

Martin, Dale B. *Sex and the Single Savior: Gender and Sexuality in Biblical Interpretation*. Louisville, KY: Westminster John Knox Press, 2006.

Mason, Eric. *Manhood Restored: How the Gospel Makes Men Whole*. Nashville: B&H Books, 2013.

Massey, John. *Reminiscences: Giving Sketches of Scenes Through Which the Author Has Passed and Pen Portraits of People Who Have Modified His Life*. Nashville: Publishing House of the Methodist Episcopal Church, South, 1916.

May, Simon. *Love: A History*. New Haven: Yale University Press, 2011.

McCandless, Amy Thompson. *The Past in the Present: Women's Higher Education in the Twentieth Century South*. Tuscaloosa: University of Alabama Press, 1999.

McCulley, Carolyn. *Radical Womanhood: Feminine Faith in a Feminist World*. Chicago: Moody Publishing, 2008.

McDonald, W. *Scriptural Views of Holiness*. Philadelphia: National Publishing Association for the Promotion of Holiness, 1877.

McDowell, Linda. *Gender, Identity, and Place: Understanding Feminist Geographies*. Minneapolis: University of Minnesota Press, 1999.

Methodist Hymnal: Official Hymnal of the Methodist Episcopal Church and the Methodist Episcopal Church, South, The. New York: Methodist Book Concern, 1905.

Moody, J. B. *Women in the Churches: Their Rights and Restrictions; OR, Paul Harmonized with the Law and the Gospel*. Second edition. Martin, TN: Hall-Moody Institute, 1910.

Morgan, David T. *Southern Baptist Sisters: In Search of Status, 1845–2000*. Macon, GA: Mercer University Press, 2003.

Murrow, David. *Why Men Hate Going to Church*. Nashville: Thomas Nelson, 2005.

Najar, Monica. *Evangelizing the South: A Social History of Church and State in Early America*. Oxford: Oxford University Press, 2008.

Nelson, Louis P. *The Beauty of Holiness: Anglicanism and Architecture in Colonial South Carolina*. Chapel Hill: University of North Carolina Press, 2008.

Nichols, Stephen J. *The Reformation: How a Monk and a Mallet Changed the World*. Wheaton, IL: Crossway Books, 2007.

Noll, Mark A. *America's God: From Jonathan Edwards to Abraham Lincoln*. Oxford: Oxford University Press, 2002.

Noll, Mark A., David W. Bebbington, and George R. Rawlyk, eds. *Evangelicalism: Comparative Studies of Popular Protestantism in North America, the British Isles, and Beyond, 1700–1900*. Oxford: Oxford University Press, 1994.

Nord, David Paul. *Faith in Reading: Religious Publishing and the Birth of Mass Media in America*. Oxford: Oxford University Press, 2004.

O'Brien, Micheal. *Rethinking the South: Essays in Intellectual History*. Athens: University of Georgia Press, 2003.

Owen, Christopher H. *Sacred Flame of Love: Methodism and Society in Nineteenth-Century Georgia*. Athens: University of Georgia Press, 1998.

Ownby, Ted. *American Dreams in Mississippi: Consumers, Poverty, and Culture, 1830–1998*. Chapel Hill: University of North Carolina Press, 1999.

——. *Subduing Satan: Religion, Recreation, and Manhood in the Rural South, 1865–1920*. Chapel Hill: University of North Carolina Press, 1990.

Park, James William. *Latin America Underdevelopment: A History of Perspectives in the United States, 1870–1965*. Baton Rouge: Louisiana State University Press, 1995.

Parsons, Elaine Frantz. *Manhood Lost: Fallen Drunkards and Redeeming Women in the Nineteenth Century United States*. Baltimore: Johns Hopkins University Press, 2003.

Patrick, Darrin. *The Dude's Guide to Manhood: Finding True Manliness in a World of Counterfeits*. Nashville: Thomas Nelson, 2014.

Philaretou, Andreas G. *The Perils of Masculinity: An Analysis of Male Sexual Anxiety, Sexual Addiction, and Relational Abuse*. Lanham, MD: University Press of America, 2004.

Pierce, Alfred M. *Giant Against the Sky: The Life of Bishop Warren Akin Candler*. New York: Abingdon-Cokesbury Press, 1948.

Pike, Frederick B. *The United States and Latin America: Myths and Stereotypes of Civilization and Nature*. Austin: University of Texas Press, 1992.

Piper, John. *What's the Difference?: Manhood and Womanhood Defined According to the Bible*. Wheaton, IL: Crossway Books, 2008.

Piper, John, and Wayne Gruden, eds. *Recovering Biblical Manhood and Womanhood: A Response to Evangelical Feminism*. Wheaton, IL: Crossway Books, 1991.

Plath, Lydia, and Sergio Lussana, eds. *Black and White Masculinity in the American South, 1800–2000*. Newcastle upon Tyne, England: Cambridge Scholars Publishing, 2009.

Poole, W. Scott. *Never Surrender: Confederate Memory and Conservatism in the South Carolina Upcountry*. Athens: University of Georgia Press, 2004.

Putney, Clifford. *Muscular Christianity: Manhood and Sports in Protestant America, 1880–1920*. Cambridge, MA: Harvard University Press, 2001.

Rable, George C. *God's Almost Chosen Peoples: A Religious History of the American Civil War*. Chapel Hill: University of North Carolina Press, 2010.

Rainey, Dennis. *Stepping Up: A Call to Courageous Manhood*. Little Rock: Family Life Publishing, 2011.

Remillard, Arthur. *Southern Civil Religions: Imagining the Good Society in the Post-Reconstruction Era*. Athens: University of Georgia Press, 2012.

Riesebrodt, Martin. *The Promise of Salvation: A Theory of Religion*. Translated by Steven Randell. Chicago: University of Chicago Press, 2012.

Roark, James L. *Masters without Slaves: Southern Planters in the Civil War and Reconstruction*. New York: W. W. Norton, 1977.

Rotundo, E. Anthony. *American Manhood: Transformations in Masculinity from the Revolution to the Modern Era*. New York: Basic Books, 1993.

Satter, Beryl. *Each Mind a Kingdom: American Women, Sexual Purity, and the New Thought Movement, 1875–1920*. Los Angeles: University of California Press, 1999.

Scales, T. Laine. *All that Fits a Woman: Training Southern Baptist Women for Charity and Mission, 1907–1926*. Macon, GA: Mercer University Press, 2000.

Schecter, Patricia A. *Ida B. Wells-Barnett and American Reform, 1880–1930*. Chapel Hill: University of North Carolina Press, 2001.

Schneider, A. Gregory. *The Way of the Cross Leads Home: The Domestication of American Methodism*. Bloomington: Indiana University Press, 1993.

Schweiger, Beth Barton, and Donald G. Mathews, eds. *Religion in the American South: Protestants and Others in History and Culture*. Chapel Hill: University of North Carolina Press, 2004.

Scott, Anne Firor. *The Southern Lady: From Pedestal to Politics, 1830–1930*. Chicago: University of Chicago Press, 1970.

———. *Making the Invisible Woman Visible*. Champaign: University of Illinois Press, 1984.

Scott, Sean. *A Visitation of God: Northern Civilians Interpret the Civil War*. Oxford: Oxford University Press, 2010.

Shelley, Bruce L. *Church History in Plain Language*. Foreword by Mark Noll. Second edition. Dallas: Word Publishing, 1995.

Shurden, Walter B. *Not an Easy Journey: Some Transitions in Baptist Life*. Macon, GA: Mercer University Press, 2005.

Silverberg, Helene, ed. *Gender and American Social Science: The Formative Years*. Princeton: Princeton University Press, 1998.

Simon, Bryant. *Fabric of Defeat: The Politics of South Carolina Millhands, 1910–1948*. Chapel Hill: University of North Carolina Press, 1998.

Slatton, James H. *W. H. Whitsitt: The Man and the Controversy*. Macon, GA: Mercer University Press, 2009.

Soskice, Janet Martin. *The Kindness of God: Metaphor, Gender, and Religious Language*. Oxford: Oxford University Press, 2007.

Souvenir of the Golden Jubilee: Women's Missionary Union, Auxiliary to Southern Baptist Convention: Commemorating Fifty Years of Missionary Service, 1888–1938. Published by the Women's Missionary Union, 1938.

Spain, Rufus B. *At Ease in Zion: Social History of Southern Baptists, 1865–1900*. Nashville: Vanderbilt University Press, 1967.

Starr, Mirabai, trans. *Teresa of Ávila: The Book of My Life*. Foreword by Tessa Bielecki. Boston: New Seed Books, 2007.

Stephens, Randall J. *The Fire Spreads: Holiness and Pentecostalism in the American South*. Cambridge, MA: Harvard University Press, 2008.

———. "'The Fire Spreads': The Origins of the Southern Holiness and Pentecostal Movements." PhD dissertation, University of Florida, 2003.

Stowell, Daniel. *Rebuilding Zion: The Religious Reconstruction of the South, 1865–1877*. Oxford: Oxford University Press, 1998.

Strong, Josiah. *Our Country: Its Possible Future and Its Present Crisis.* Introduction by Austin Phelps. New York: American Home Missionary Society, 1885.

Summers, Martin. *Manliness & Its Discontents: The Black Middle Class & the Transformation of Masculinity, 1900–1930.* Chapel Hill: University of North Carolina Press, 2004.

Sutton, Jerry. *A Matter of Conviction: A History of the Southern Baptist Engagement with the Culture.* Foreword by James T. Draper Jr. Nashville: B&H Publishing Group, 2008.

Synan, Vinson. *The Holiness-Pentecostal Tradition: Charismatic Movements in the Twentieth Century.* Second edition. Grand Rapids, MI: Wm. B. Eerdmans Publishing, 1997.

Tigert, Jno. J., ed. *The Doctrines and Discipline of the Methodist Episcopal Church, South.* Nashville: Publishing House of the Methodist Episcopal Church, South, 1902.

Turley, Briane K. *A Wheel within a Wheel: Southern Methodism and the Georgia Holiness Association.* Macon, GA: Mercer University Press, 1999.

Turner, Elizabeth Hayes. *Women, Culture, and Community: Religion and Reform in Galveston, 1880–1920.* Oxford: Oxford University Press, 1998.

Tweed, Thomas. *Crossing and Dwelling: A Theory of Religion.* Cambridge, MA: Harvard University Press, 2006.

Tyson, Ruel W., James L Peacock, and Daniel W. Patterson, eds. *Diversities of Gifts: Field Studies in Southern Religion.* Champaign: University of Illinois Press, 1988.

Van Leeuwen, Mary Stewart. *Gender and Grace: Love, Work, & Parenting in a Changing World.* Downers Grove, IL: InterVarsity Press, 1990.

Wacker, Grant. *Heaven Below: Early Pentecostals and American Culture.* Cambridge, MA: Harvard University Press, 2001.

Walters, Ronald G., ed. *Primers for Prudery: Sexual Advice to Victorian America.* Updated edition. Baltimore: Johns Hopkins University Press, 2000.

Weaver, Rufus W. *The Religious Development of the Child: An Evangelical Study from the Scientific View-Point.* Introduction by John Richard Sampey. New York: Fleming H. Revell Company, 1913.

Wells, Ida B. *Southern Horrors and Other Writings: The Anti-Lynching Campaign of Ida B. Wells, 1892–1900.* Edited and with an Introduction by Jacqueline Jones Royster. Boston: Bedford/St. Martin's, 1997.

Wesley, John. *The Works of Rev. John Wesley in Ten Volumes.* Vol. VIII, first American edition. New York: J. & J. Harper, 1827.

Wesley Memorial Church. "The First Mile Post: Being a History of the Sunday School of Wesley Memorial Church, Corner Ivy and Auburn Streets, Atlanta, Georgia." Atlanta, GA: Wesley Memorial Church, 1904.

Wheeler, Marjorie Spruill. *New Women of the New South: The Leaders of the Woman Suffrage Movement in the Southern States.* Oxford: Oxford University Press, 1993.

Whites, LeeAnn. *The Civil War as a Crisis in Gender: Augusta, Georgia, 1860–1890.* Athens: University of Georgia Press, 1995.

Wiener, Jonathan. *Social Origins of the New South, Alabama, 1860–1895*. Baton Rouge: Louisiana State University Press, 1978.

Wilkes, W[illiam] P[ughes]. *An Alabama Boy: 1880–1902*. Troy, AL: Self-published, circa 1951.

Williams, John Milford. *The Education of Women for the New Age: A Plea for Greater Liberality for Women's Colleges*. Nashville: Board of Education [of the] Methodist Episcopal Church, South, n.d., circa 1910.

Wills, Gregory A. *Southern Baptist Theological Seminary, 1859–2009*. Oxford: Oxford University Press, 2009.

Wilson, Charles Reagan. *Baptized in Blood: The Religion of the Lost Cause, 1865–1920*. Athens: University of Georgia Press, 1980.

Winston, Diane. *Red-Hot and Righteous: The Urban Religion of the Salvation Army*. Cambridge, MA: Harvard University Press, 1999.

Wise, Benjamin E. *William Alexander Percy: The Curious Life of a Mississippi Planter and Sexual Freethinker*. Chapel Hill: University of North Carolina Press, 2012.

Woodward, C. Vann. *Origins of the New South, 1877–1913*. Baton Rouge: Louisiana State University Press, 1951, 1971.

Wyatt-Brown, Bertram. *Honor and Violence in the Old South*. Oxford: Oxford University Press, 1986.

———. *Southern Honor: Ethics and Behavior in the Old South*. Oxford: Oxford University Press, 1982.

Zagarri, Rosemarie. *Revolutionary Backlash: Women and Politics in the Early American Republic*. Philadelphia: Pennsylvania State University Press, 2007.

Index

Act Like Men, 144
African Americans, 10–11, 29, 49, 82, 92, 114, 135, 147; veterans, 64
Aiken, S. C., 92–93
Alabama, 1, 6, 8, 15, 19, 35, 40, 46, 52, 54–56, 58, 68, 74, 79, 81–85, 88–89, 101, 136, 140
Alabama Conference Female College, 72, 81–82, 85, 88–89
Alabama Education Association, 72
American Civil War, 18–19, 45, 49, 60–61, 64, 104, 117
Anti-Suffrage League, 90
Arkansas, 116
Armstrong, Annie, 23–24, 30, 33–35, 42
Ayers, Edward, 158n2, 160n51, 192n34
Azusa Street Revivals, 110

Ball, Martin, 53
Baptism: believer's, 17–18; of fire, 101–3, 134; infant, 80
Barton, Clara, 81
Baxter, James Hamilton, 70–71
Bederman, Gail, 72, 175n80, 190n5
Belles and Pomegranates, 89
Birmingham-Southern College, 90, 179n53
Bobashela, 7, 88
Borders, Isaac D., 69–70, 77–78, 94–95, 173n45, 176n96
Bouldin, G. W., 39, 42
Bounds, E. M., 142
Bourbon Democrats, 40
Bradley, W. J., 54
Brasher, John Lakin, 101–2, 118
Burroughs, Moore, 46
Butler, Anthea, 92, 184n1, 187n54, 190n6, 191n19

Cagle, Mary Lee, 102, 116–18, 120–22, 133, 140, 142–43, 194n55, 194n64
California, 69, 77, 94
Campbell, Alexander, 138
Candler, Asa Griggs, 69, 85–86
Candler, Warren, 7, 105–6, 109, 183n37
Carradine, Beverly, 102–3, 107, 119, 123–24, 138, 141, 192n19
Carver, William Owen, 24–26, 45, 50–52, 54, 56–58, 159n33
Censer, Jane, 29, 36, 164n114
Chambers, S. A., 33
Chicago Defender, 64
China, 34–35
Christ in the Rockies, 144
Christian Soldier, 5, 60, 62–64, 66, 70, 132, 137
"Church Militant," 64, 130
Church of England, 64
Church of God in Christ, 92
civil religion, 16

Clark, Ela Reed, 39
Clark, James Osgood Andrew, 68, 76–77, 80, 90–91, 176n2
class identity, 2, 11, 18, 27, 29, 50, 56, 68, 70, 72, 88, 100, 114, 119–20, 122
Confederate States of America (also Confederacy), 16, 64, 73–74
conversion, 4, 17–20, 22–23, 79–80, 82, 84, 91, 95, 101, 103, 123, 146, 147
Coulson, Amanda, 116, 117
Cowan, Samuel A., 135
Crews, James Madison, 19, 67–68
Cuba, 75
Cummings, Albert, 53

Daniel, Charles, 52–53
Dargan, E. C., 24, 26, 52–54, 156n17, 156n19
David (King of Israel), 71, 133
Davis, Jefferson, 16, 73–74
Deep South, 4, 6, 9, 12, 17, 19, 27, 40, 73, 80, 83, 103, 110–11, 113, 120
Dickinson, A. J., 60
Dodge, W. A., 101–3, 105–6, 114, 142, 183n39
domestic ideal, 11, 27, 29, 40–42, 81, 84–85, 93–94, 118, 128
Driscoll, Marc, 144, 195n6
Duffield, George, 12
Duncan, William W., 94

Eaton, Thomas Treadwell, 22, 24, 47–50, 55–56, 58, 60–61, 158n6
Eldrddge, John and Stasi, 145, 196n11
Elijah, 53
Elisha, 53
Elizabeth I, 27–28
emancipation, 10
Emory College, 7, 69, 71
entire sanctification, 3, 5–7, 81, 94, 99–101, 103–10, 112–14, 116–17, 119–22, 127, 130, 132, 134–38, 143, 147, 150n10, 181n2, 181n10, 182n21, 193n42
Equal Suffrage Club, 89–90

Fatherhood of God, 24–25
female preachers, 113–14, 116–18, 140
Flynt, Wayne J., 18, 170n70
Frost, James Marion, 46

Galloway, Charles C., 7, 16, 19, 65–68, 70, 72–75, 78–80, 87, 174n71, 175n73
Galloway Women's College, 87
Gambrell, J. B., 32, 61
Garbutt, Mrs. S. S., 114
Georgia, 6–7, 9, 15, 19, 29, 42, 57, 64, 67–71, 74, 76, 79, 80, 88, 91, 93, 105, 107, 109, 114, 136–37, 140, 142
Georgia Holiness Association, 105, 117, 131, 142
Giggie, John, xii, 29, 172n12, 181n3, 190n6
Ginzberg, Lori, 36
Godbey, William Baxter, 101–3, 107–8, 110, 113–14, 121, 122, 125–28, 135–40, 185n11, 185n17, 187n59, 192n23
Grant, Posey, 56–57
Gray, John David, 67
Grenada College, 86

Hall-Moody Institute, 31
Harris, R. L., 133
Harrison, H. S., 109
Hawthorne, J. B., 44–45
Hayes, Lucy Webb, 90–91
Haygood, Atticus G., 7, 71, 83, 105–6, 183n39, 193n42
"helpmeet," 127, 189n88
Hillman College, 27, 36, 134
Holiness movement, 3–11, 19, 95, 99–143, 147–48
Holtzclaw, William J., 29–31, 34, 36–42, 58, 134, 160n53, 164n117, 165n124
Holy Spirit (also Holy Ghost), 45, 48, 50–51, 58, 60, 99–102, 104, 107, 110, 113–14, 116, 125–26, 128, 130–35, 138–39, 141, 147
Howard College, 40, 44, 56, 58–59
Huntington College, xi, 72, 89

Imago Dei, 4
Indian Springs Camp Meeting, 101
International Sunday School Convention, 63–64
Iron Sharpens Iron, 144

Jackson, A. M., 42
Jackson, Thomas J. "Stonewall," 1
Japan, 39
Jarrell, A. J., 105–6, 117, 131–32, 137, 183n39
Jernigan, Charles, 116–117, 123, 125, 186n43, 188n70
Jesus, xii, 3, 4–5, 12, 19–20, 22–25, 33, 36, 46–48, 51, 57, 60–61, 67–68, 70, 74, 77–81, 84, 86, 95, 100–101, 113–14, 137, 141, 146; conqueror, 3, 5, 62, 65–66, 68, 78, 147; groom, 123–27; shepherd, 3, 62, 66, 68, 78, 147
Jezebel, 26
Johnson, John L., 25, 57
Jonathan, 133
Jones, John Griffing, 67–68, 70, 81, 91–92, 94–95, 99, 104–5, 157n26, 180n68, 182n25, 182n29, 183n32
Jones, Sam, 63, 65–66, 71–72, 165n3

Kantrowitz, Stephen, 59, 160n45
Kentucky, 17, 24, 34, 47, 138
Kingdom of God, 1, 5, 33, 35, 37, 78, 113, 138
kinship, 21–22, 24, 158n4
Knapp, M. W., 107–8, 115, 134, 138–39, 185n17, 192n23
Kolb, Rueben T., 74
Ku Klux Klan, 8, 151n19

Landmark Baptists (also Landmarkism), 17–18
Lazenby, Marion E., 1–2
Leavell, Landrum Pinson, 26–29, 36–37, 46, 50–51, 134, 167n12
LeFost, 88
Lewis, Barney, 75–76, 86, 175n82, 178n37
Lost Cause, 8, 16, 27, 65, 73
lynching, 16, 45, 55, 64
Lyon, D. G., 56

Maria Teresa, 27–28
marriage (also marital), 6, 38, 52, 123, 128, 134, 145; as a model relationship, 112, 123–26, 128, 143; roles in, 127–28; sex in, 38, 124–25
Massey, John, 68, 72, 81–85, 178n24
mastery, 4, 10–11, 21, 29, 44–45, 47–60, 68, 76, 136, 147, 164n114, 173n33, 181n8, 192n33
McConnell, Fernando, 57–58
McDonald, W., 131
McWhirter, Martha, 116
Meek, R. A., 94
Mercer University, 53, 55
Methodist Episcopal Church, South (also MECS and Methodist), 1, 3–5, 7, 9–11, 15–16, 18–20, 57, 62–68, 70–72, 75–83, 85–89, 92, 94–95, 99, 103–7, 109, 123, 129–30, 132, 135, 137–38, 146–48
Methodist Magazine, 104
Mighty Men Conference USA, 144
Millsaps College, xi, 7, 86, 88–89, 178n29
Mississippi, 6–16, 19, 25–27, 32, 50, 53, 57, 65, 67, 69, 73–75, 77–81, 86, 88, 91, 94, 95, 119, 134, 136
Mississippi Conference of the MECS, 77, 104
Missouri, 1, 106
Montgomery, Rebecca, 36
Moody, J. B., 31, 35–36, 42, 156n17, 162n88
Moon, Lottie, 34–35
mother(s), 23–26, 81, 87, 91, 93, 95, 145; role in spiritual formation, 23–24, 42, 73, 81, 92, 122
Murrow, David, 144
"Muscular Christianity," 44, 60, 65, 72, 165n3, 166n5, 169n54

New Orleans Christian Advocate, 94, 109
New South, 2–6, 8, 10–11, 15–20, 25, 28, 37, 44–45, 50, 53, 60, 65, 70, 80, 82, 84, 86, 92, 94–95, 100, 104, 109, 113, 117, 120–21, 127–28, 130, 135–36, 138, 140, 142–43, 146
North Georgia Conference, 105–6

Ohio, 103, 109

Palmer, Phoebe, 117
Pentecostals, 109–10, 115, 117, 134
Philippines, 64
Populists, 40, 59, 74
postmillennialism, 37, 163n100
Primitive Baptists, 25, 35
Promise Keepers, 144
Protestant, 6, 10, 37, 66, 75, 95, 100, 117
purity, 25–28, 31, 36–38, 41–43, 45, 52, 64, 82, 91, 118, 120, 124, 131, 133–35, 143, 165n124, 186n40, 188n70, 192n19

Quantrill, William, 1

racial ideology, 10, 27, 29
Reconstruction, 8, 17, 20, 76, 99, 105
Robertson, Lidd, 33, 162n74
Roman Catholic, 16, 75, 144
Ryan, Father Abram, 16

Salvation Army, 102, 114, 136
sanctification, 100–104, 108–9, 112–17, 119–20, 123–26, 128–30, 133, 135, 137, 141. *See also* entire sanctification
Sanford, W. L., 40, 59
Satan, 62, 110, 131, 136–137, 139, 140
slave (also slavery), 10, 15, 42, 45, 49, 54, 58, 64, 76, 132, 156n25, 180n1
Smith, Amanda Berry, 114
Social Gospel, 24
Social Service Commission, 54
South Alabama Educational Association, 84
South Carolina, 33, 109
South Georgia Conference, 106
Southern Baptist Convention (also SBC and Baptist), 3–5, 9–11, 15–27, 29–37, 39, 41–52, 54–61, 71, 99, 106–7, 109, 123, 132, 134, 137, 146–48
Southern Baptist Historical Library and Archives, xi
Southern Baptist Historical Society, 24
Southern Baptist Theological Seminary, 17, 22, 24–25
"Southern Lady," 10, 20
Southron, 89–90, 179n53
Southwestern Christian Advocate, 135
Spanish-American War, 63
spiritual warfare, 60–61, 64, 131, 137–39,
Stephens, Randall, 115
Stepping Up, 144
Strong, Josiah, 75, 167n22
Suffragette Club, 89–90
Sunday School, 22, 33, 63–64, 92–93, 116

Taylor, B. S., 119, 124–25, 132, 141, 186n46
Tennessee, 31, 35, 46
Texas, 35–36, 93, 116, 125
Tillman, "Pitchfork" Ben, 40, 59, 74
Turner, Elizabeth Hayes, 36, 93
Tweed, Thomas, 2–3, 150n7, 184n2
Twentieth Century Fund, 65

Van Ness, I. J., 46, 53
Virginia, 1, 109

Wacker, Grant, 117
Warrior Wives, 145
Watson, Tom, 74
Weaver, Rufus W., 22–23, 42, 55, 61
Wells, Ida B., 55, 168n45
Wesley, Charles, 73, 87
Wesley, John, 73, 87, 193n42
Wesley, Suzanna, 73, 87

Whitsitt, William H., 17–18, 22, 158n6
Whitworth Female College, 88
Wilkes, William, 35, 52, 54, 58
Willard, Frances, 81
Williams, John, 87–88
Winans, William, 104
women preachers. *See* female preachers
Woman's College of Alabama, 89
women's education, 5, 27, 30–32, 43, 79, 81–87, 95, 146
Women's Missionary Union (WMU), 20, 23–24, 30, 32–34
Women's Moral Authority, 5, 36–39, 82, 84, 91
women's suffrage (also woman suffrage), 38–39, 41, 83, 89–90, 113, 164n108, 178n24, 184n5
Women's Training School, 34
Wyatt-Brown, Bertram, 45, 189n1, 192n34, 194n60